The VEGAN and AMAZII recipes of JACKFRUIT

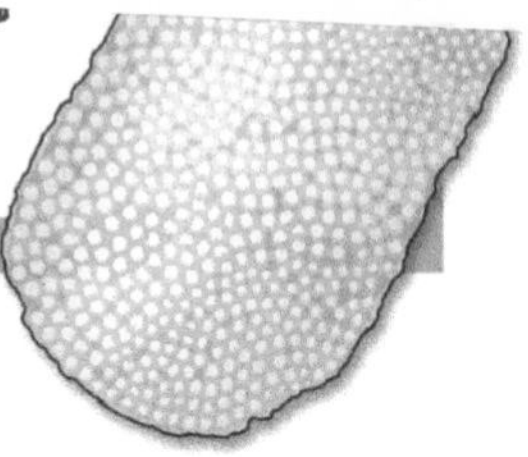

Gluten free · Soy free · Nut free

G000069854

Original title in French:
Les recettes véganes de jackfruit : l'extraordinaire fruit du jacquier:
sans gluten, sans soya, sans noix

Copyright © 2019, Nadine Primeau, Originally published by Éditions Un Monde Conscient:
www.unmondeconscient.org

THE VEGAN AND AMAZING RECIPES OF JACKFRUIT: GLUTEN-FREE, SOY-FREE, NUT-FREE

Author: Nadine Primeau
Photography and culinary design: Nadine Primeau
Images: p.9 Pixabay.com; p.15-17: unsplash.com; vegetables drawn in black: freepik.com

Translated from French to English by: Sarah Abiz-Strugala

© 2019, A Conscious World
All rights reserved for all countries
No part of this book may be reproduced in any
form without the written permission of the publisher.

Website: www.aconsciousworld.org

ISBN: 978-2-924371-49-7 (paper)
ISBN: 978-2-924371-50-3 (pdf)

Legal Deposit – Bibliothèque et Archives nationales du Québec 2019
Legal Deposit – Library and Archives of Canada 2019

LIMIT OF LIABILITY
Neither the author nor the publisher can be held responsible for errors that may have inadvertently
crept into the recipes and comments.

TABLE OF CONTENTS

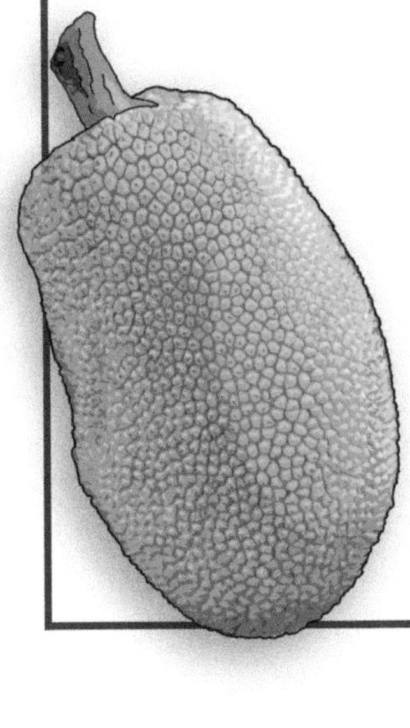

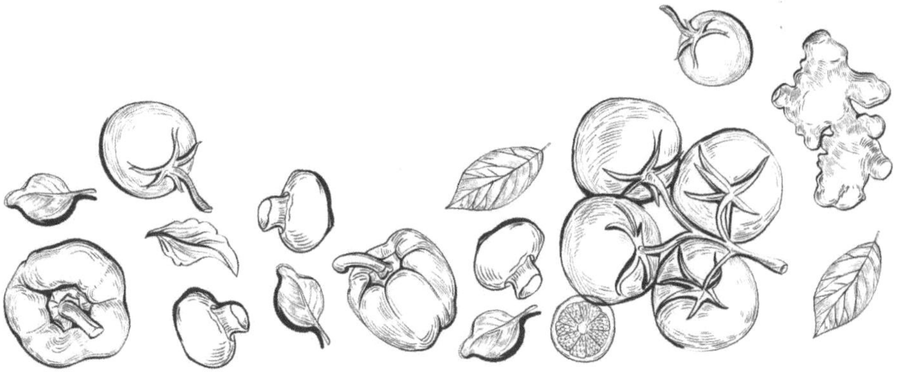

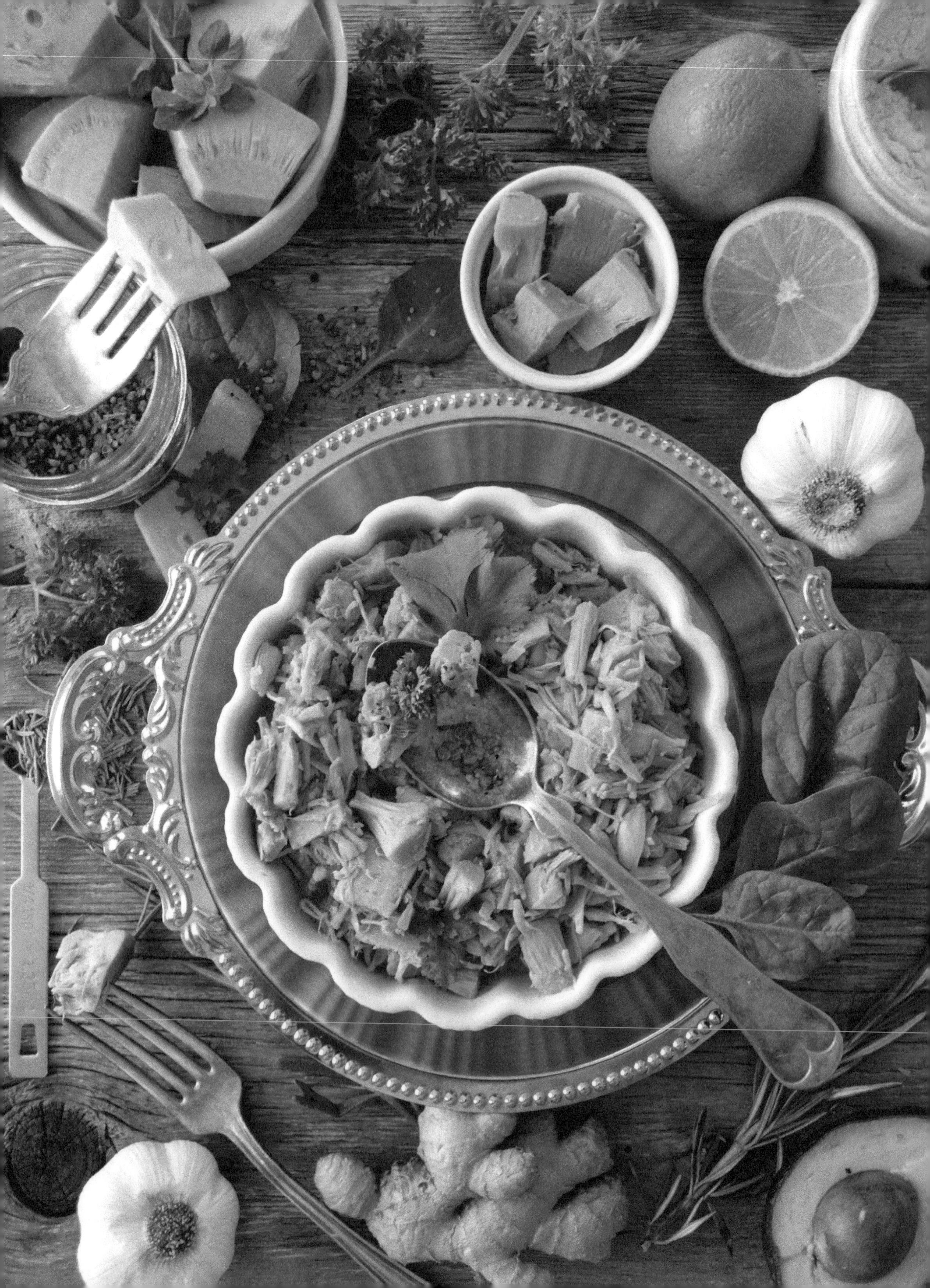

THE EXTRAORDINARY ON THE TABLE!

I am very happy to present you this new cookbook whose theme is the surprising and extraordinary jackfruit! Do you know it?

For my part, I discovered jackfruit a few years ago when I was vegetarian and I was looking for recipes on the Internet. At that time, it seemed very far-fetched to cook a fruit for meals, even more to imitate meat. But as curiosity had won out because the resemblance to the meat was so blatant and amazing, I went ahead with that idea.

Although the result was very surprising, because the jackfruit looked like meat in every way, I did not take this path at this time; I explain why a little further in the book. Added to that, the jackfruit was not very accessible in my area and I was not satisfied with the cooking of the recipe that I had found and cooked.

Still, over time, for many reasons, I became vegan while eating gluten-free foods. And quietly, the idea of returning to the jackfruit came to me. This idea made me go through a long questioning as to imitate meat or not because the jackfruit is the perfect imitation!

It was really when I made peace in myself with the principle of imitating meat that I fully embarked on the culinary discovery of this fruit! In this regard, you will find on page 15 the section "Let's philosophize a little", which is the "fruit" of my reflections on the famous question: "should we imitate meat to feed on it?". It was therefore after having gone through this inner journey that I went to cook the jackfruit with a lot of passion and love as you will discover in this book!

To cook the recipes that I present to you as a passionate for vegan cooking and because jackfruit is an extraordinary discovery that mimics meat wonderfully, I am literally immersed in my culinary memories, the ones I liked to savor before veganism! I thought of the many dishes that I loved to taste and also of those who remind me of my childhood.

I also remembered the dishes that I always ordered at the restaurant and that brought me a real happiness! Of course, I was also inspired by my current tastes, which are always my favorites!

In my opinion, the jackfruit is one of the most impressive and wonderful, because it amalgamates pretty well with all types of cuisines; in fact, I have not seen the limit yet! You will see it over the recipes, whatever the spices and the sauce, it takes the taste that we want to give it. That's why you'll find it in this book cooked in Greek, Indian, Asian and more to fully savor the infinite potential of this extraordinary fruit! That's why it's more than perfect! Long live the jackfruit!

I hope that just like me you will like the jackfruit for all the potential it has, because it has everything to please and create a new vegan culinary world!

Sincerely yours! With all my love,

Nadine Primeau
www.nadineprimeau.com
www.le-sarrasin-vegetalien.org

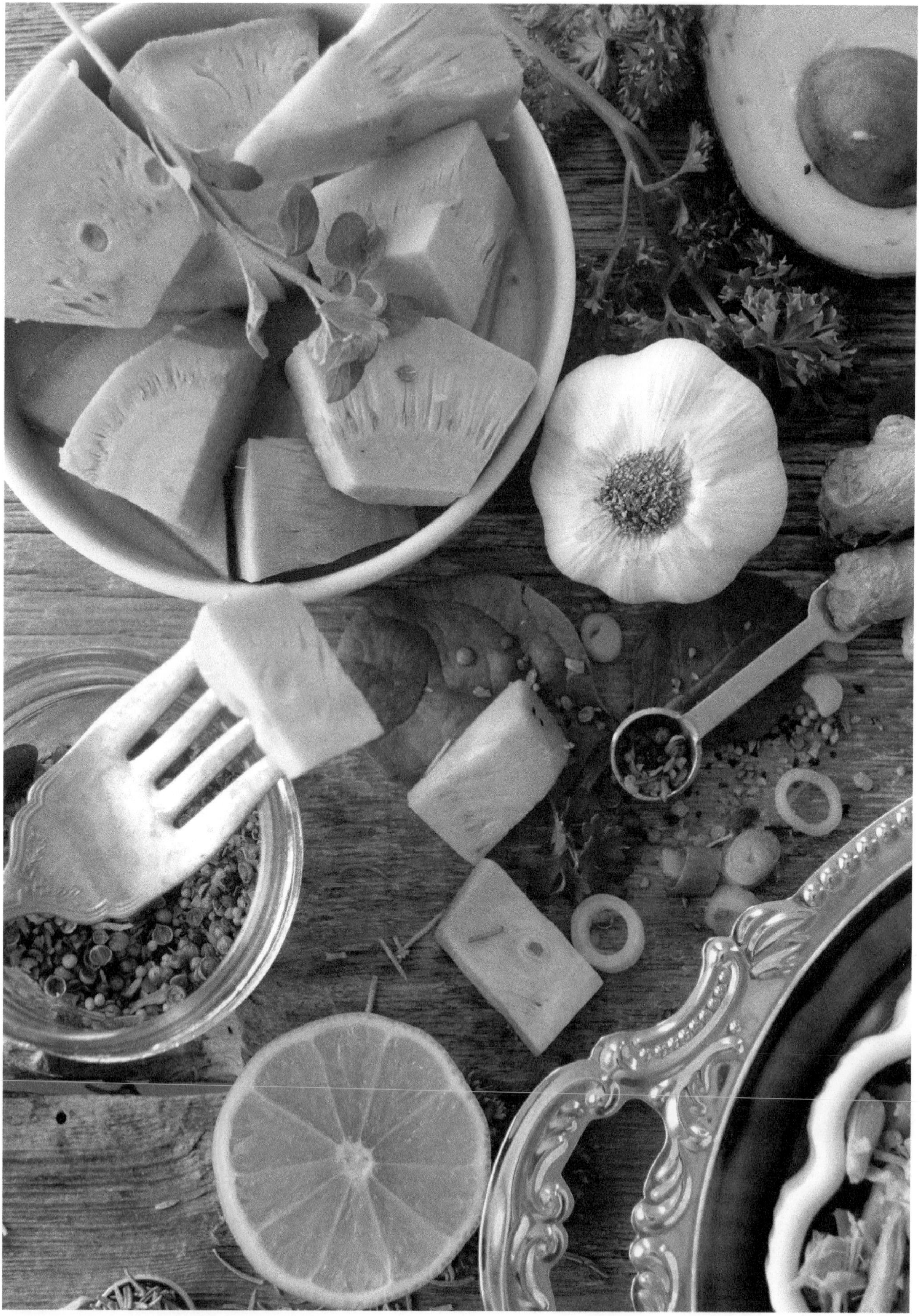

JACKFRUIT, WHO ARE YOU?

The origins of jackfruit

The jackfruit, whose botanical name is "Artocarpus heterophyllus", is a tree of the Moraceae family, including the fig tree and the white mulberry tree. It is from India, among others.

It is mainly in the warm and humid tropical regions that the tree and its fruit with many virtues are grown. They are found mainly in India, Thailand, Malaysia, Madagascar, Brazil, Reunion Island and recently began to be grown in the southern United States.

As for the jackfruit, the fruit itself that comes from the tree of the same name, it is one of the most surprising and extraordinary fruits! **Indeed, the jackfruit is THE biggest fruit in the world growing in trees.** At maturity, jackfruits can even weigh up to 100 pounds, and can reach thirty-six inches long by twenty inches in diameter... Really impressive!

Like the banana, the jackfruit continues to ripen after being picked, so its flavor is hardly affected if harvested a little earlier. Talking about taste, that of jackfruit when it is mature is between the taste of banana, apple, pineapple and mango. It is as if this fruit contained all these flavors at the same time; so every bite is a surprising experience.

Although the fruit of the jackfruit has long been regarded as the "fruit of the poor", now it is experiencing an unequaled revival and has been demanded everywhere since it is known as a perfect substitute for meat!

How to consume the jackfruit?

The way we eat jackfruit and cook it depends on how mature it is. Thus, a young jackfruit, that is to say, which has not yet reached maturity and whose skin is bright green, can be consumed as:

Substitute for meat
To the delight of everyone, but especially vegetarian and vegans, the jackfruit becomes the perfect substitute for meat! Whether grilled, boiled or fried, very versatile, it transforms itself with the spices and sauce with which it is cooked. It is also the young and green jackfruit that we cook throughout this book to transform it in an extraordinary and vegan way!

A vegetable
In some parts of the world, when not ripe, jackfruit can be prepared as a vegetable. It can be cooked alone or accompanied with other foods such as vegetables or rice.

If you have jackfruit fruits that are ripe (with dark or even brownish skin) or you let a jackfruit fruit ripen, you can literally use it as:

A fruit
When mature, the jackfruit will have a sweet taste. At choice, you can taste the raw or cooked fruit, a bit like an apple. Whether grated or cut into pieces, the jackfruit can be added to fruit salads and smoothies. It can also be eaten mashed or in jam, or even turned into juice. Whether for breakfast, for a snack or for dessert, you can add it everywhere, the only limit is the imagination!

Did you know that ... ?

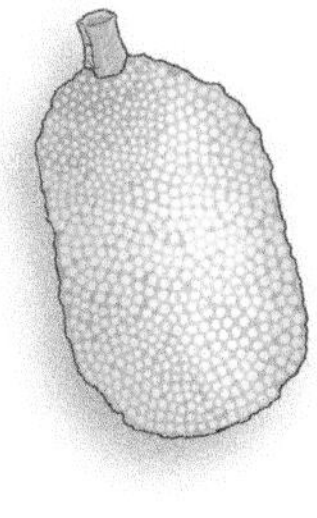

The jackfruit, the tree itself, provides high quality wood?
Indeed, the jackfruit is known to be resistant to rot and it is also used to make furniture and musical instruments.

We can also cook the seeds of jackfruit fruit?
When the jackfruit's fruit is ripe, the seeds inside get to their maximum size and you can make delicious Indian dishes, stir-fries, hummus and more!

The jackfruit is cooked all over the world?
Here are its different names according to the languages: jackfruit is called "jacquier" in French, "boluómì" in Chinese, "jaca" in Spanish, "katahal" in Hindi and "jaque" in Creole.

12 REASONS TO CONSUME JACKFRUIT

The jackfruit is gaining popularity around the world and is recognized for its many health benefits and advantages. Indeed, it contains almost all the vitamins and minerals we need! So it's no wonder they say that jackfruit:

1- Strengthens the immune system
Since jackfruit is high in vitamin C, it has the effect of protecting against many infections. It supports the functioning of blood cells, stimulating the immune system.

2- Maintains the health of the skin
Thanks to its rich vitamin A content, the jackfruit fruit can maintain healthy eyes and skin. It prevents problems with vision, including macular degeneration and night blindness.

3- Improves digestion
The jackfruit contains dietary fiber known as laxative. Thus, it improves digestion and prevents constipation.

4- Eliminates free radicals and toxins
Jackfruit provides the body with antioxidants, phytonutrients and flavonoids that destroy free radicals and expel toxins from the body.

5- Prevents anemia
The jackfruit fruit is filled with manganese, copper, magnesium, niacin, pantothenic acid, folate and vitamins A, C, E, K and B6, all of which are essential for blood formation. Also, the jackfruit increases your body's ability to absorb iron, which prevents anemia.

6- Maintains blood pressure
As this fruit contains potassium known for its ability to maintain the level of sodium in the body, this is beneficial for preventing strokes, heart attacks and high blood pressure.

7- Helps with weight loss
Since the jackfruit is low in calories and fat and has no cholesterol, this fruit promotes weight loss. Consuming it regularly is beneficial to enjoy its nutrients.

8- Promotes a healthy thyroid
This fruit is an excellent source of copper, a mineral essential for thyroid metabolism, hormone production and absorption.

9- Acts on bone health
The jackfruit is an excellent source of calcium, essential for strengthening and promoting bone health. It has the ability to prevent osteoporosis. In addition, this fruit is rich in potassium, which can increase bone density and reduce calcium loss through the kidneys
.

10- Prevents cancer
The jackfruit is known to contain lignans, isoflavones and saponins, which are themselves phytonutrients known for their powerful anti-aging and anti-cancer properties.

11- Reduces the risk of heart disease
The jackfruit is significantly beneficial for the heart. It is an excellent source of vitamin B6, known for its ability to reduce homocysteine levels in the blood.

12- Has anti-inflammatory properties
The jackfruit contains phenolic and phytochemical compounds, which have anti-inflammatory and antifungal properties. These properties also act to regulate inflammatory skin reactions such as acne.

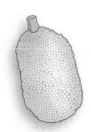

Nutrition facts of the green jackfruit

1/2 cup (125 ml) of green jackfruit contains around:

50 calories	6 grams of carbohydrates
2,4 grams of protein	3% of calcium
2 gram of fat	18% of vitamin C
3 grams of fiber	

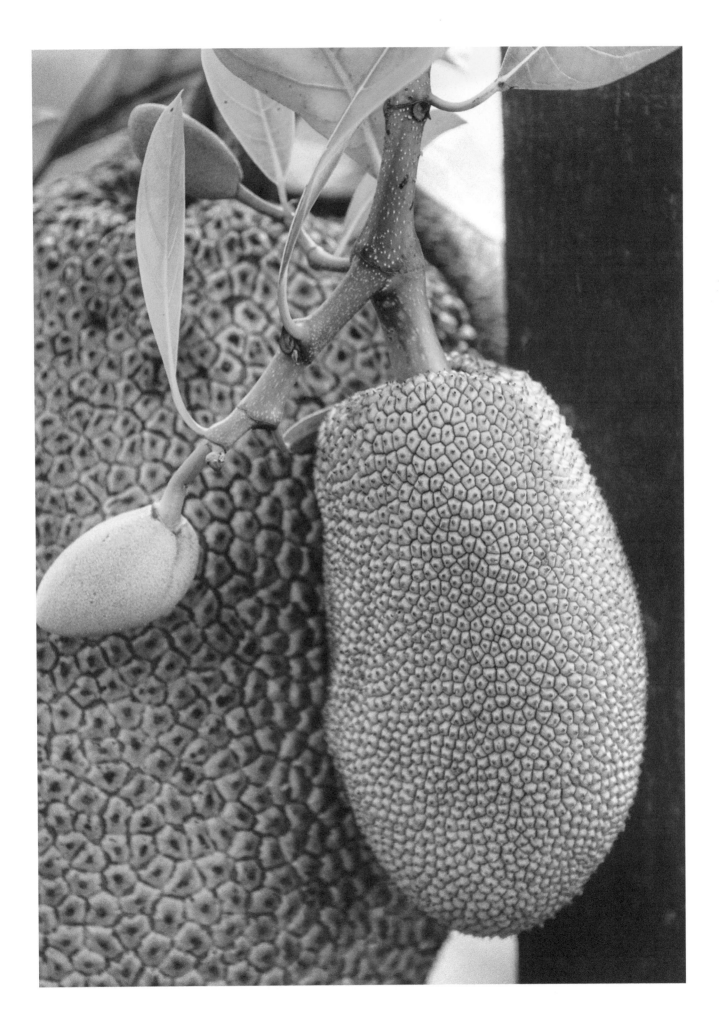

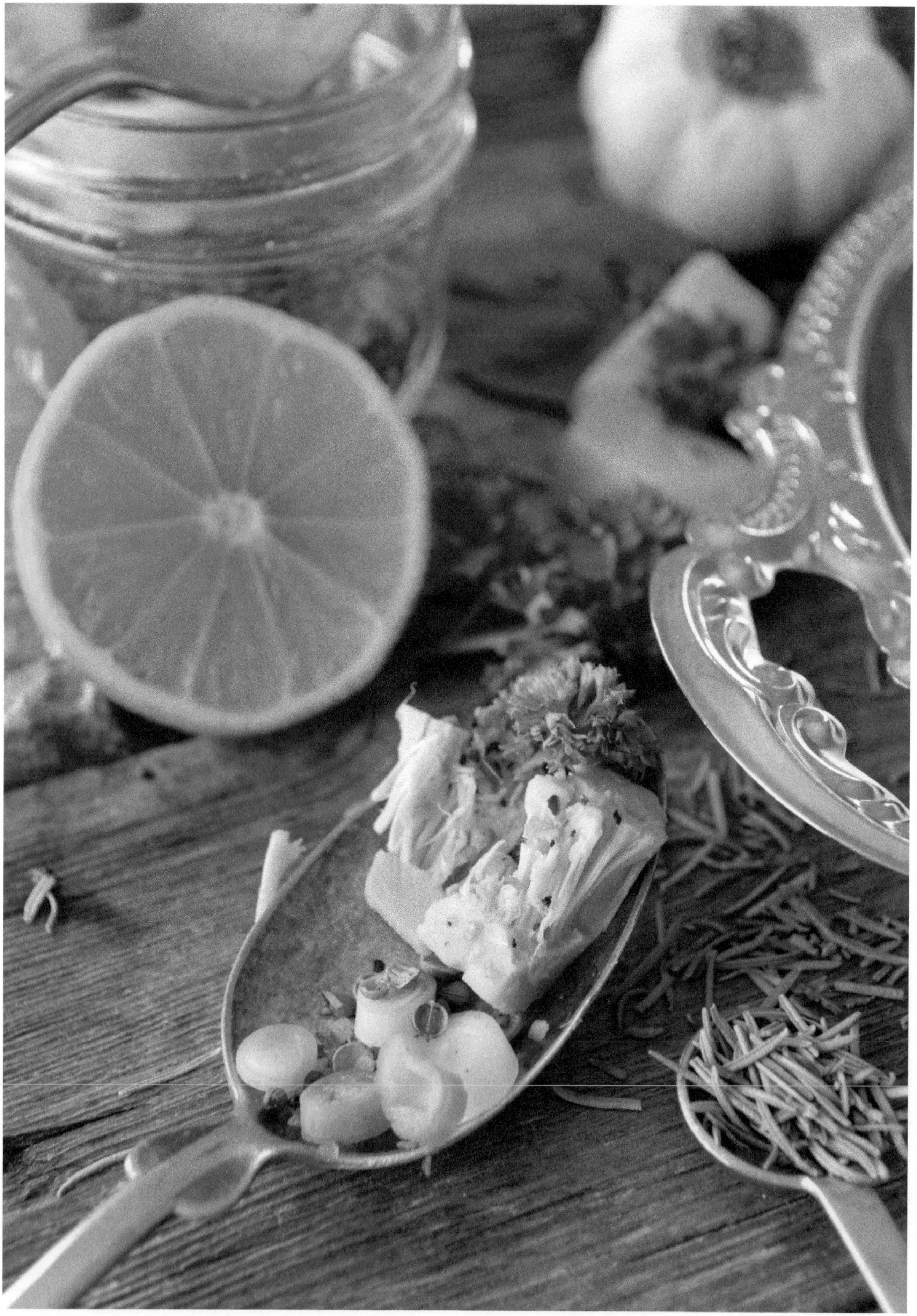

PRACTICAL INFORMATION ON THE JACKFRUIT

Where to find jackfruit?

One of the first questions we ask ourselves when we want to cook the jackfruit is: "where to find it?". Although it can sometimes be a challenge to get it, more and more, it becomes popular and therefore easier to find.

- **The Internet** is one of the first places that makes jackfruit accessible. You will find jackfruit in cans, which is used in the recipes of this book, organic or not, and all kinds of by-products that are gaining ground on the market as vegan products.
- Fortunately, more and more, we also find the jackfruit in cans in **bio/health stores.** All you have to do is request it and if it's not available, the staff will certainly be happy to order it for you.
- The jackfruit in cans is easy to find in **Asian grocery stores** and there is often more than one brand.

Asides, if you go to an Asian grocery store to get canned jackfruit, it's a safe bet that you will find **fresh jackfruit**. Take the opportunity to make a detour in the fruit and vegetable department to admire this fruit! In case you go only to buy fresh jackfruit, it is better to call before going to make sure there are some in stock as they are in high demand.

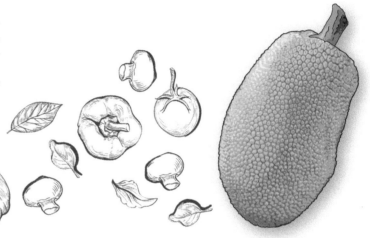

Which cans of jackfruit to choose?

As most of the recipes in this book are created for the purpose of reproducing tasty vegan dishes, here **we use young and green jackfruit in a can that is kept in water or in brine.** Be careful to read the labels especially if it is your first time because there is also jackfruit kept in sweet syrup. These are not the cans we are looking for.

For my part, since I cook with as few additives as possible in my everyday life and I want a better world in terms of ethics and Consciousness, I opted for the Cha's Organics brand for this book. (I have no remuneration for the mention.)

Just as the saying goes "eat is to vote", I chose this company which, in addition, is from Quebec (hello local purchase!) Because its values join mine. This brand, unlike many others, is organic, does not add any chemical additives and all this, in addition to being fair trade. In addition, I chose this company because the amount of jackfruit found in their cans is stable, there is almost always 250 grams per can of 14 oz (400 ml) of young jackfruit in brine. This is not the case for other brands

(i.e. 20 oz (560 ml) jackfruit cans in water or brine) where the amount of jackfruit can vary from about 50 to 70 grams in different cans. Of course, in the end, it can make a difference when cooking!

For your information here, even though the recipes in this book were cooked with 14 oz (400 ml) cans, be aware that it is still possible to cook recipes with 20 oz cans. All you have to do is use a scale and weigh the jackfruit that comes out of the can to get the contents in grams for each recipe.

So, in concrete terms, if for example the recipe you cook requires 1 can of 14 oz (400 ml) of jackfruit, you will have to use 250 grams of jackfruit of your 20 oz. If the recipe requires 2 cans, it will take 500 grams of jackfruit and so on. And what's more interesting here is that you can freeze the unused jackfruit that comes from the cans for later use or cook the jackfruit in large quantities, as mentioned on page 87 in the section "Tips and tricks with the jackfruit".

HOW TO COOK THE JACKFRUIT?

To make it perfect!

In this section, I introduce you to the basic method for cooking jackfruit found in virtually every recipe in this book. This method that I recommend is simple and easy and has many reasons to be.

Indeed, as you will see by cooking recipes (except for a few exceptions), most of the time the jackfruit is boiled before starting. The reason for this procedure is very simple, this way it is easier to obtain the desired texture and tenderness that one wishes in order to perfectly imitate meat in vegan dishes.

Also, it allows to have a recipe that is cooked more quickly. Indeed, when the jackfruit is boiled beforehand, the jackfruit takes much less time to cook later in the recipe to achieve the desired result. If it is not boiled, it can take a long time to get the desired effect.

On my side, at the very beginning when I cooked the jackfruit a few years ago, even though I had followed the procedure as well as the suggested cooking time, the jackfruit still had some "undesirable" crunch that persisted. It is, among others, for this reason that I recommend boiling the jackfruit, so that it is perfect!

Also, when you open cans of jackfruit, it can differ in terms of tenderness. Depending on the different brands or companies that sell this fruit, the jackfruit can be "harder" or "firmer". Boiling the jackfruit beforehand becomes necessary so that the recipes are more uniform and "work", especially with regard to the cooking times afterwards.

Here is the basic method to cook the jackfruit. It will also allow you to do it in large quantities, you will find all the details on this subject on page 87.

BASIC METHOD FOR COOKING JACKFRUIT

As simple as 1-2-3!

Prerequisite:
For all recipes in this book, use young and green canned jackfruit that is kept in water or in brine. Although there is jackfruit in sweet syrup, it is not used to make these recipes.

Culinary creation:

1. To start, rinse and drain the jackfruit.

2. Then cut each piece of jackfruit into 3 or 4 pieces depending on their size. Here, we cut the jackfruit keeping the hardest part for each piece.

It is at this stage, that is, before it is cooked, that the jackfruit should be weighed if 20 oz (560 ml) cans are used, to find the equivalent of 14 oz (400 ml) cans. To find this equivalent, the jackfruit can be weighed out of the can or after being cut. For more details on this, see previous page.

While cutting the jackfruit, bring water to a boil. Then cook the jackfruit for 30 minutes over medium high heat, counting the cooking time when the water boils again.

3. When the jackfruit is ready, strain it and put it back in the cauldron where it's cooked. Use a potato masher or fork to loosen and pull almost all the jackfruit. Then continue with the desired recipe.

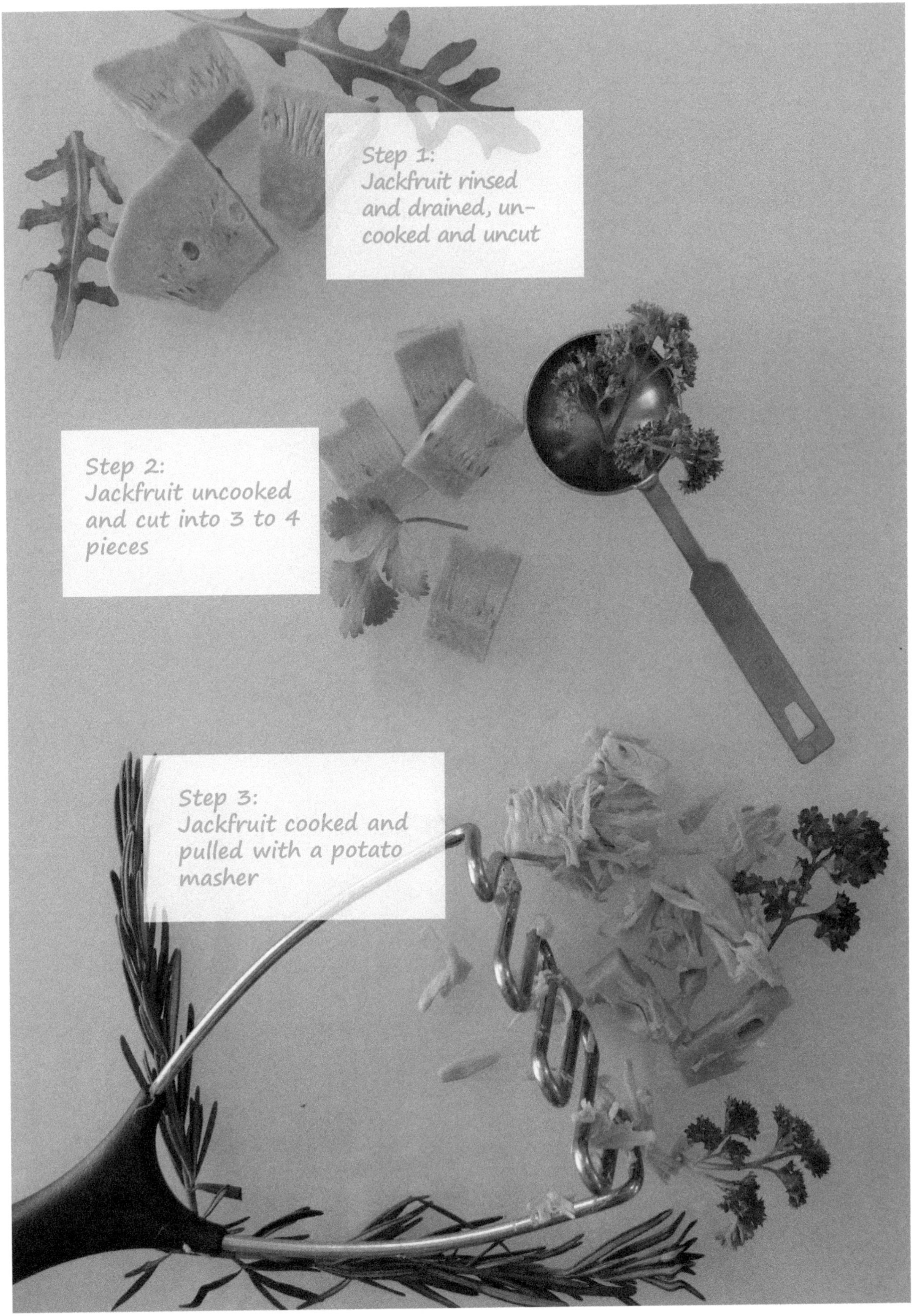
Step 1:
Jackfruit rinsed and drained, uncooked and uncut
Step 2:
Jackfruit uncooked and cut into 3 to 4 pieces
Step 3:
Jackfruit cooked and pulled with a potato masher

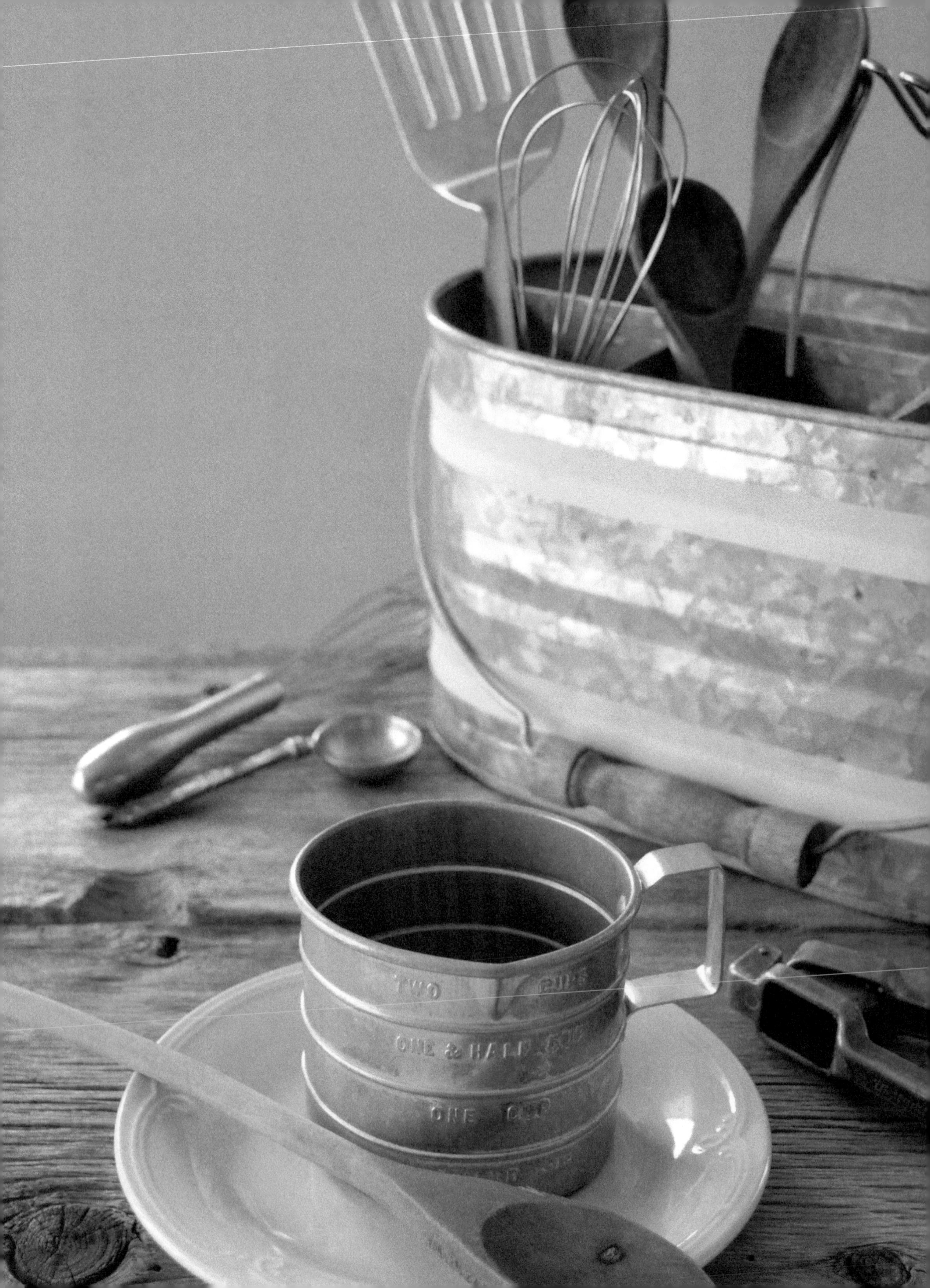
TWO
ONE & HALF
ONE

LET'S PHILOSOPHIZE A LITTLE …

Imitate meat or not? There is the question!

In this section, I wanted to share with you the "fruit" of my reflections on imitating meat and eating it because I myself had resistance to do it at the very beginning when I turned to veganism. As I explain, I had to go through some interior barriers to cook and replicate vegan dishes that mimic meat. I wanted to share with you these reflections that will probably be useful to some people in their journey and their questions.

On my side, at the time of writing, I have not eaten meat for more than six years and it's been more than four years since I became vegan. During my process, I went around in my own way looking for legitimate reasons - and there are so many! - to give up meat. Over time too, I saw and understood that consuming animal flesh was not necessary at the individual, humanitarian, societal or global level. My conclusion on many levels is that killing sentient beings to feed on them is not ethical and doesn't belong anymore at the time we live now. Of course, I'm not the only one to have realized all this, more and more people walk or have walked this path of consciousness.

However, even if it is proven that veganism is the solution to many ailments for animals, humans and the planet, before I went to imitate meat, I saw that, in my opinion, a gray area remained on which many people still argue today: should we imitate meat to feed on it?

Personally, to see several people debate on this point with opinions that are for and others who are against, and this, both for vegans and those in the making, I have long wondered. I have more than reflected and sought to clear up this gray area.

Even during this questioning that lasted several months, I myself stopped eating any imitation meat or any dish that referred to it. I also have to do my "mea culpa" here, the first time I cooked jackfruit about six years ago, I thought my meal was so much like meat I had a lot of trouble eating it. Also, in front of certain other imitations that were too similar to real animal flesh, commonly called meat, disgust and disdain arose. At that time, it was obvious that I was never going to eat it again.

In reality, it was not because I refused the imitations as such, I rather refused the meat that I still associated. But as I headed for veganism, I did not go further to raise awareness of this reality. I believed that at this point, by becoming a vegan, feeding on imitation meat was not "part of being vegan". So, I gave up all imitation to achieve this goal. For my part, I must say that I had this impression because here, without knowing it somehow, I answered a negative connotation widespread enough that insinuated that imitations, it was wrong! Why? Because quite often, what we hear when we reproduce a "false meat" in particular or a traditional dish, are derogatory or negative comments, and this, both from vegans and those in the making.

These comments, mostly based on the notion of good and bad, are often questions such as "why imitate meat? What is this obsession with reproducing meals with meat?". These questions can sometimes even be ridiculing to the point where one feels stuck and that one does not know what to answer.

On social networks, for example, I have often seen vegan people slip away and say that these "fake meat" recipes were for people who wanted to make the transition or that it was a "trick" to get people to veganism. Nothing more. Faced with these somewhat evasive answers, I often felt that those people who had been asked the question probably had the same uneasiness as me with these questions and comments saying that it was wrong. Also, it was probably the only "politically correct" answer that these people knew to "slip away" in order not to argue …

Honestly, I think it's here, when everyone's commenting on it, that we go through and find ourselves in the gray zone. At first glance, I know very well that some people may see some form of contradiction between stopping meat and imitating it and then eating it. At first glance, I also see this contradiction. But in my opinion, these people have not taken the time to clear up this area in them. Unfortunately, they hastily conclude on the subject, when in reality, there are so many benefits to veganism, whether with imitations - vegan dishes - or not.

Still, luckily, over time, this whole gray area has lit up for me. Despite the choice to cut all references to meat in my debut as a vegan (which restricted me in a certain way especially since in everyday life, I have to manage many food allergies in my family), I well realized that there was no harm in imitating and feeding on it! I would say rather that it's even the opposite! Foods that mimic meat do not hurt anyone, let alone animals! On the contrary, they help and contribute positively to the vegan cause: in the end, it means that the more people eat or cook it, the less animals are exploited and killed. And that is, of course, not to mention all the positive impact that these imitations have on the planet.

I have to say that to be able myself to imitate meat with the jackfruit and make a book out of it, one of the obstacles I have often encountered in my previous reflection is literally the sentence "if you like the imitations of meat, that means that you like meat!". Really, this association that many do and who nails the beak is the one that has long prevented me from turning to the jackfruit. But every time I heard that phrase, I searched inwardly for an answer to that conclusion that I felt was fast and wrong, in my opinion.

And one day, as I thought about it, I understood that what people generally liked about meat was basically the taste of spices, sauce and marinades. I had the proof with my two children who literally devoured everything I cooked and reproduced with the jackfruit because it had such a resemblance and the same taste with which we season traditional meals. This finding really made sense to me, it's as if it unlocked me from a point of view where I was

limited and allowed me to go further in my thinking: because most of the time what makes a dish what it is, is the spices, the sauce, the marinades; in short, the taste.

Obviously, I know that some like the texture. But honestly, who, of your entourage, have you ever seen eating their meat or only love it for the texture without any spice, salt, pepper, sauce, marinade, ketchup, or even without cooking it with nothing on it? For my part, I have not seen anyone around me either eating meat alone with nothing to "enhance", "soften" it, make it "better" or "spice it up".

And it is here that all this becomes interesting, in my opinion, and that we can clear up the gray area for everyone. Why? Because with the imitations of meat and especially with the jackfruit, we can reproduce the taste. So here when we eat meals where we mimic the meat, it is precisely the taste that comes out that we like. This is the indicator that animal flesh does not need to be there because it is all the seasonings that have a great impact on what we love. And it's so much better that we can reproduce the taste because people who "love meat" certainly like the taste! And here with the jackfruit, what is even more impressive is that we can also reproduce the texture;

there is really something to feast on! So when we eat vegan, why should we deprive ourselves of the taste and the texture if we can reproduce them and that besides, it does not cause animal suffering nor damage for the planet?

For my part, I would say that cooking to feed on imitation meat is a personal choice, even a preference, and in addition, it is a choice that does not cause harm to others (which is not the case of animal flesh that causes animal suffering). In my opinion, it's personal a bit like someone who likes to wear blue or green or who prefers to walk or to run. I know it is normal that some people do not like dishes or meals where the meat is imitated, some vegans do not want to eat anything that reminds them of meat. And I respect this preference because we are all different and have different paths.

But little anecdote here that goes in this direction, it was the case of my spouse at the beginning when I cooked the jackfruit, he refused categorically to eat it. He said that the resemblance to meat was too great. Honestly, he refused to eat it until the day we went to an Asian grocery store and he took a real jackfruit in his hands. It was really by seeing and touching the fruit that he was able to make new associations with the dishes I veganized because what he ate was not meat but fruit. It was truly in this way that he made peace with the jackfruit and stopped seeing and associating animal meat with it. Now, every time he eats jackfruit, he remembers that big fruit, he is now one of the most fervent!

In summary, I would say that whether or not we eat imitations of meat and that it is temporary or permanent for those who eat it, it should be seen positively since one of the common points we all have when we turn to veganism is that we want the good of animals and the planet. So, whether or not to eat dishes or references to meat, in both cases, it should all rally us to the same cause to advance to the best of animals, humans and the planet.

In my opinion, what explains the reason for these imitations is that we must consider that, at the time we are living in, the consciousness of people is changing. Right now, we are at a point in humanity where we have to bridge the old and the new, between what was and what will be. It is therefore normal to use references, precise landmarks to move forward. And it is here that imitations have their utility.

These act as landmarks in different ways. Whether these landmarks are "psychological" or "affective", it is therefore normal also in this sense to cook in a renewed version (imitations or vegan meat), and to use the known or the old, that is to say the taste because it is also a reference of the most important.

Maybe one day, in two hundred years (if the planet survives), there will be no more reference to meat, but, I honestly think that these are part of evolution, steps to travel to a better world. We should all be happy that the world is changing and that it is bringing renewal; Let's celebrate every time we can cook differently, because if we can imitate meat with vegetables, all the better! This is proof that we do not need to eat the one from animals!

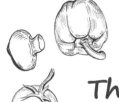

The VEGAN and AMAZING recipes of JACKFRUIT

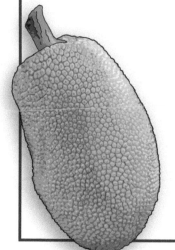
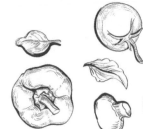

The VEGAN and AMAZING recipes of JACKFRUIT

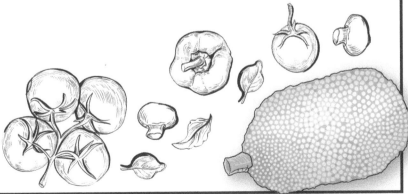

The jackfruit shish taouk is one of the most delicious! Join the useful to the pleasant by tasting it in a well-stocked plate or in a pita exactly like at the restaurant, yum!

SHISH TAOUK JACKFRUIT PLATE

- 2 x 14 oz (400 ml) cans of green jackfruit in water or brine, rinsed and drained (for a total of 500 g of jackfruit)
- 3 tbsp (45 ml) avocado oil
- 2 tbsp (30 ml) freshly squeezed lemon juice
- 2 tsp (10 ml) ground cumin

- 2 tsp (10 ml) granulated or powdered garlic
- 1 tsp (5 ml) paprika
- 1/2 tsp (2.5 ml) ground cilantro
- 1/2 tsp (2.5 ml) salt
- 1/2 tsp (2.5 ml) pepper

Culinary creation:

1. Preheat oven to 425 °F. If desired, first make the garlic sauce, recipe below.

2. Cut each piece of jackfruit into 3 or 4 pieces depending on their size. In a cauldron, bring water to a boil and cook the jackfruit for 30 minutes over medium high heat. Meanwhile, gather all the spices in a small dish, reserve.

3. When the jackfruit is ready, strain it and put it in an ovenproof 9 x 13-inch dish. Use a potato masher or fork to loosen and pull almost all the jackfruit. Then add the oil, the lemon juice and the spices by sprinkling and mixing well to evenly distribute them all over the jackfruit.

4. Bake for 30 minutes, stirring occasionally. For an even more "shish taouk" effect, then grill for 5 to 10 minutes, checking and mixing often. Serve with the fattoush salad, garlic potatoes, pickled turnips, pepperoncini and rice. Makes 2 to 3 servings for plate or 3-4 pitas.

FATTOUSH GREEN SALAD

- 4 cups (1000 ml) Romaine lettuce, finely chopped
- 1 cup (250 ml) finely chopped parsley
- 2 Lebanese cucumbers sliced into half slices
- 2 tomatoes cut into cubes
- Some sliced radishes
- 1/4 cup (60 ml) avocado oil

- 1 tbsp (15 ml) lemon juice
- 2 tsp (10 ml) minced garlic (2 cloves)
- 2 tsp (10 ml) sumac
- 1 tsp (5 ml) dried mint
- Salt and pepper to taste

Culinary creation:

1. In a bowl, add the salad, parsley and all the vegetables. Pour all over the avocado oil, lemon juice and sprinkle the rest of the spices. Mix well and serve immediately. Makes 2 to 3 large portions or 4 to 6 small ones.

GARLIC SAUCE

- 1 cup (250 ml) of water
- 1/4 cup (60 ml) avocado oil
- 1/4 cup (60 ml) olive oil
- 5 to 6 large garlic cloves cut in 2 without the germ

- 3 tbsp (45 ml) apple cider vinegar
- 1 tsp (5 ml) xanthan gum
- 1/2 tsp (2.5 ml) salt

Culinary creation:

1. In a blender, pulse all ingredients until thickened. Refrigerate 1 hour before serving.

GARLIC CUBES

Recipe on page 63 in the section "Potatoes & Co"

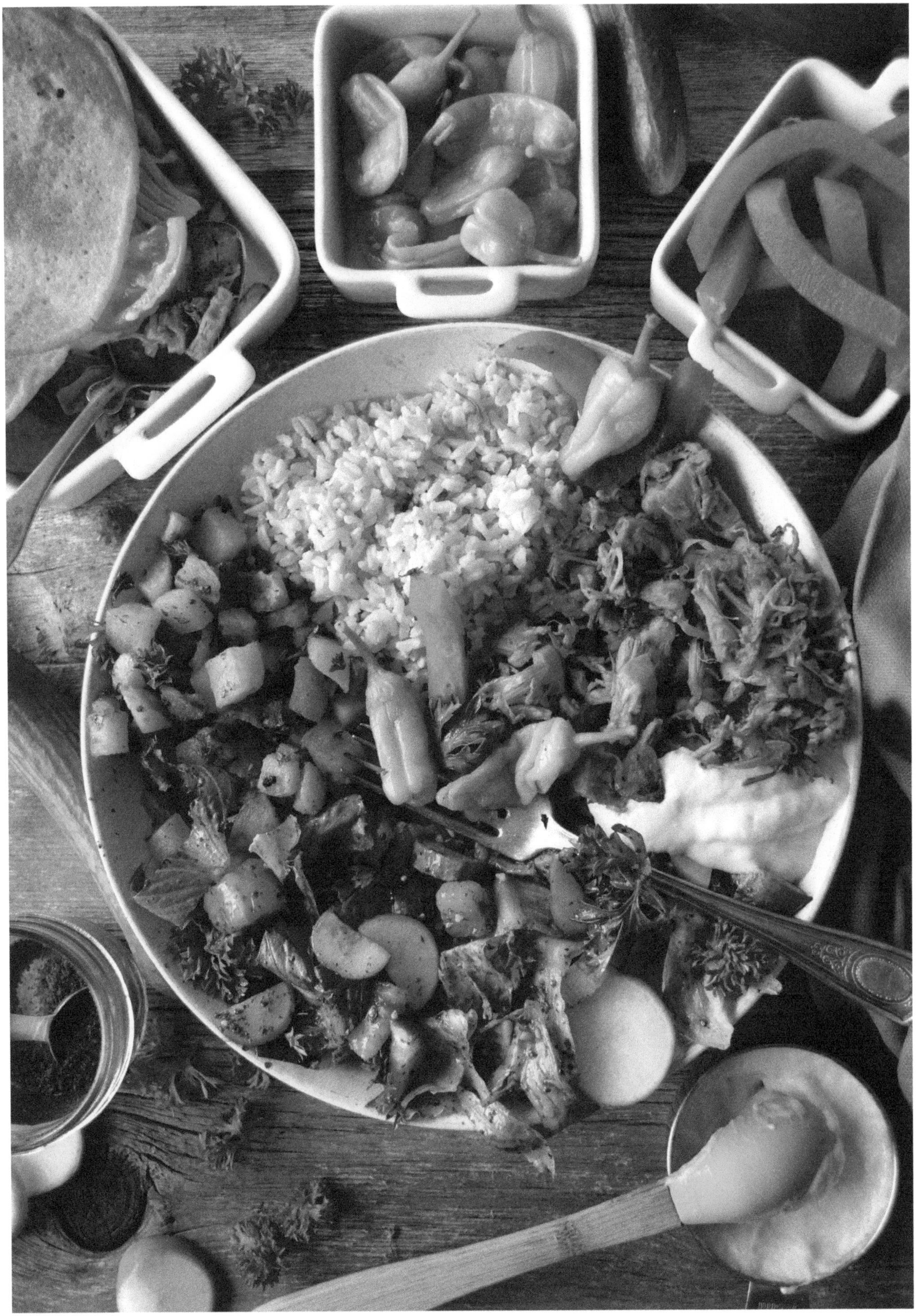

This simple recipe of bacon-flavored jackfruit, oh so delicious, will charm your taste buds forever! An assured success that will delight the young and the elderly, because the bacon-flavored jackfruit will follow you as much in different sandwiches or dishes as in different salads; it is the most exquisite in Caesar salad!

BLT WITH JACKFRUIT BACON

Bacon-flavored jackfruit

- 2 x 14 oz (400 ml) cans of green jackfruit in water or brine, rinsed and drained (for a total of 500 g of jackfruit)
- 3 tbsp (45 ml) soy-like sauce, recipe on page 44
- 3 tbsp (45 ml) avocado oil
- 2 tsp (10 ml) liquid smoke
- 2 tsp (10 ml) granulated or powdered garlic
- 2 tsp (10 ml) smoked paprika
- 1 tsp (5 ml) maple syrup
- 1/4 tsp (1.25 ml) salt

For the BLT sandwich

- Slices of bread at choice, roasted or not
- 1 to 2 sliced tomatoes
- Mixed salads or spinach
- Vegan mayo, recipe below

Culinary creation:

1. Preheat oven to 425°F.

2. Cut each piece of jackfruit into 3 or 4 pieces depending on their size. In a cauldron, bring water to a boil and cook the jackfruit for 30 minutes over medium high heat. When the jackfruit is ready, strain it and pour it into an 8.5 x 11-inch dish. Use a potato masher or fork to loosen and pull almost all the jackfruit.

3. Add the remaining ingredients of the bacon-flavored jackfruit and mix well. Bake for 15 minutes, stirring occasionally. Grill for about 15 minutes, stirring a few times as well. Serve as hot or cold in sandwich with sliced tomatoes, vegan mayo and lettuce at choice to get a very tasty BLT. Makes about 4 sandwiches.

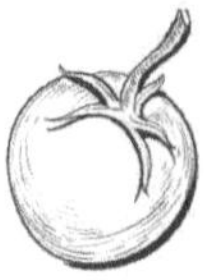

Variation: Use the bacon-flavored jackfruit with vegan cheese to spread or grill, recipe on page 54, to create and enjoy a great "grilled cheese" or create a traditional "club sandwich" by adding an extra slice of bread with chicken style jackfruit, recipe on page 70, yum!

VEGAN MAYO WITH COCONUT MILK

- 1/2 cup (125 ml) canned reduced fat coconut milk
- 1/2 cup (125 ml) avocado oil
- 1 tbsp (15 ml) freshly squeezed lemon juice
- 1 tsp (5 ml) yellow mustard
- 1 tsp (5 ml) shredded garlic in jar
- 1/4 tsp (1.25 ml) salt
- 1/4 tsp (1.25 ml) xanthan gum

Culinary creation:

1. In a cylindrical container (designed in height to accommodate a blender stand or Mason jar with wide opening), add all the ingredients of the vegan mayo except avocado oil and xanthan gum.

2. Pulse the ingredients for at least 30 seconds to aerate the mixture. Then add the oil in a thin stream while continuing to pulse without stopping. The mayo should begin to form on its own. After adding all the oil, add the xanthan gum to thicken and make the mayonnaise firmer. Pulse a few more seconds until thickening. Refrigerate. Can be kept 7 to 10 days in the refrigerator.

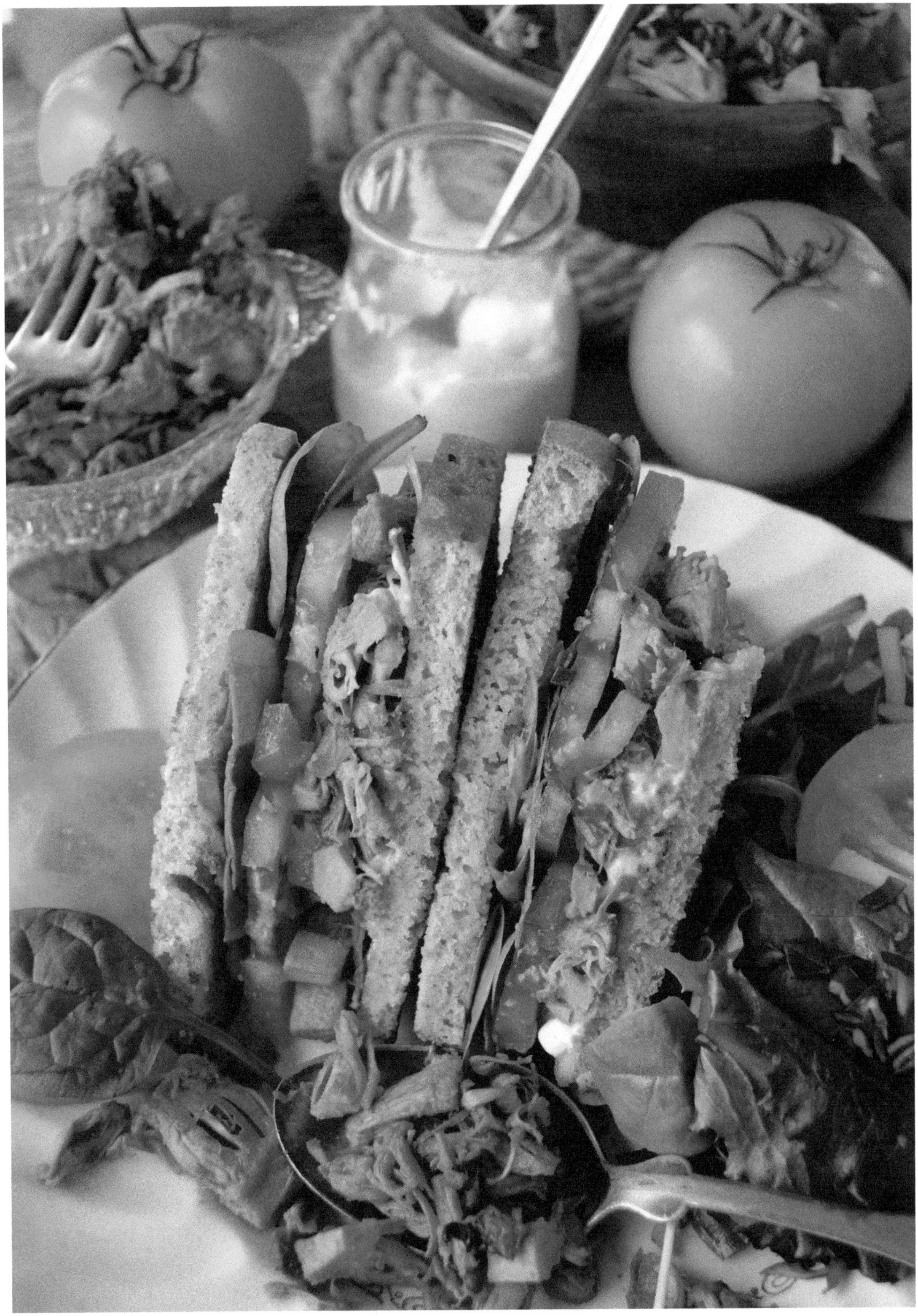

The possibilities are endless with the jackfruit that can be transformed with the flavors you want. Here, we appreciate the taste of Vietnam in this recipe of jackfruit meatballs, you will ask for more!

VIETNAMESE JACKFRUIT MEATBALLS

- 1 x 14 oz (400 ml) can of green jackfruit in water or brine, rinsed and drained (for a total of 250 g of jackfruit)
- 1 very finely chopped green onion
- 10 chopped mint leaves
- 1/4 cup (60 ml) already cooked brown rice
- 3 tbsp (45 ml) potato starch
- 1 tbsp (15 ml) nutritional yeast
- 1 tbsp (15 ml) soy-like sauce, recipe on page 44

- 1 tbsp (15 ml) ground flaxseed
- 1 tbsp (15 ml) chia seeds
- 1 tbsp (15 ml) coconut sugar
- 1 tbsp (15 ml) minced cilantro
- 1 tbsp (15 ml) maple syrup
- 2 tsp (10 ml) minced garlic (2 cloves)
- 1/2 tsp (2.5 ml) salt (more to taste)
- 1/2 tsp (2.5 ml) lemongrass powder

Culinary creation:

1. Preheat oven to 400°F. Precook and prepare the jackfruit according to the basic method explained on page 12, then reserve to let cool. Meanwhile, in a blender or coffee grinder, reduce chia seeds to powder and assemble with dry ingredients in a bowl, set aside.

2. When the jackfruit is cool a little, cut it finely on a cutting board with a large knife. Add the jackfruit and the remaining ingredients, except the maple syrup, with the already prepared dry ingredients. Mix well. By hand, compact the entire mixture until a large ball is formed. Then form the meatballs with the equivalent of one tablespoon (15 ml) of preparation.

3. In a skillet with a little oil, cook the meatballs over medium heat for about 5 minutes, turning occasionally. Before the next step, salt and pepper to taste, drizzle with the maple syrup and stir the pan to coat the meatballs.

4. Transfer to an 8.5 x 11-inch parchment-covered dish. Bake for about 15 minutes, turning the meatballs 2 or 3 times during this time. Makes 20 balls. Serve on rice of your choice or rice noodles or konjac as illustrated.

VIETNAMESE SWEET SALTY SAUCE

- 1/2 cup (125 ml) water
- 1/3 cup (80 ml) soy-like sauce, recipe on page 44
- 1/4 cup (60 ml) maple syrup
- 2 tbsp (30 ml) lime juice

- 2 tbsp (30 ml) cornstarch or arrowroot
- 2 tsp (10 ml) minced garlic (2 cloves)
- 1/2 tsp (2.5 ml) hot pepper flakes (optional)

Culinary creation:

1. In a medium saucepan, combine all ingredients, bring to boil and whisk constantly to dissolve starch and until the sauce has thickened, set aside. Serve over rice and/or meatballs.

VEGETABLE SALAD, TASTE OF VIETNAM

Salad, taste of Vietnam
- 2 Lebanese cucumbers cut into quarters
- 2 sliced green onions
- 2 diced avocados
- 3 cups (750 ml) broccoli cut into small bunches
- 3 cups (750 ml) cauliflower florets
- 1/3 cup (80 ml) sliced green olives
- 2 tbsp (30 ml) chopped cilantro
- Salt and pepper to taste

Sweet and salty vinaigrette
- 1/2 cup (125 ml) avocado oil
- 1/4 cup (60 ml) soy-like sauce, recipe on page 44
- 2 tbsp (30 ml) nutritional yeast
- 1 tbsp (15 ml) minced garlic in jar 4 tsp (20 ml) maple syrup
- 4 tsp (20 ml) apple cider vinegar

Culinary creation:

1. Make the vinaigrette by putting all the ingredients in a dish or jar with a lid, shake and set aside.

2. In a large bowl, combine all salad ingredients except the avocados and add vinaigrette to taste, mix. Cut and add the avocados at the very last minute before serving to prevent them from changing color. Makes 4 to 6 servings.

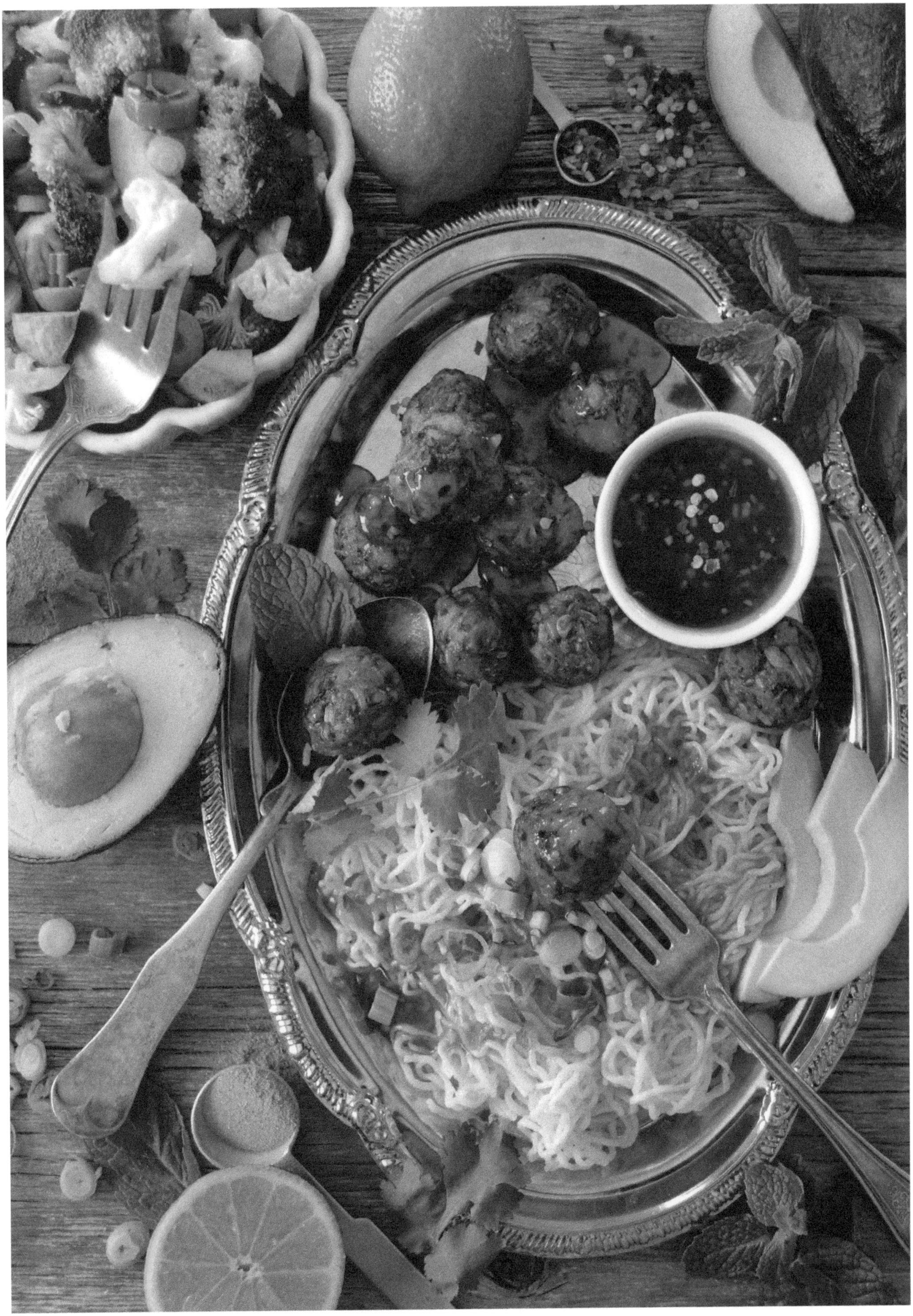

The burritos are so comforting and friendly! There is now something to celebrate with this jackfruit burritos recipe because you can now enjoy this vegan delight all year long!

BURRITOS DELIGHT OF LIME-CHIPOTLE JACKFRUIT

Jackfruit and preparation for Burritos

- 2 x 14 oz (400 ml) cans of green jackfruit in water or brine, rinsed and drained (for a total of 500 g jackfruit)
- 2 tsp (10 ml) minced garlic (2 cloves)
- 1 tbsp (15 ml) smoked paprika
- 1 tsp (5 ml) granulated or powdered garlic
- 1 tsp (5 ml) onion powder
- 1 tsp (5 ml) oregano
- 1 tsp (5 ml) salt
- 1/2 tsp (2.5 ml) pepper
- 1/2 tsp (2.5 ml) ground chipotle

- 2 cups (500 ml) cooked brown rice
- 1 cup (250 ml) canned black beans
- 1 sliced onion
- 1 green pepper cut in small strips
- 1 red pepper cut in small strips
- 1 tomato cut into small cubes

Others

- 6 to 8 tortillas, recipe on page 48
- Avocado slices to taste (optional)
- Chipotle lime sauce, recipe below and/or lime juice

Culinary creation:

1. Cut each piece of jackfruit into 3 or 4 pieces depending on their size. In a cauldron, bring water to a boil and cook the jackfruit for 30 minutes over medium high heat. Meanwhile, gather all the spices in a small dish, reserve.

2. When the jackfruit is ready, strain it and put it back in the cauldron. Use a potato masher or fork to loosen and pull almost all the jackfruit, reserve.

3. In a skillet with a little oil, sauté onion and chilies until tender. Add the minced garlic and mix. Then add the jackfruit, brown rice, black beans, diced tomato. While mixing to heat up the ingredients, sprinkle the spices everywhere.

4. Meanwhile, heat the tortillas and garnish each with the mixture. Add the southwest style chipotle lime sauce, recipe below and/or a drizzle of lime juice. Makes about 6 to 8 burritos.

CHIPOTLE LIME SAUCE

- 1 cup (250 ml) water
- 1/4 cup (60 ml) avocado oil
- 1/4 cup (60 ml) olive oil
- 2 tbsp (30 ml) lime juice
- 2 tbsp (30 ml) nutritional yeast
- 2 tbsp (30 ml) minced garlic in jar
- 2 tsp (10 ml) smoked paprika
- 1 tsp (5 ml) salt
- 1/2 tsp (2.5 ml) xanthan gum
- 1/4 tsp (1.25 ml) ground chipotle (or more to taste)

Culinary creation:

1. In a blender, pulse all ingredients for a few seconds until the mixture thickens and is homogeneous. Refrigerate 1 hour before serving.

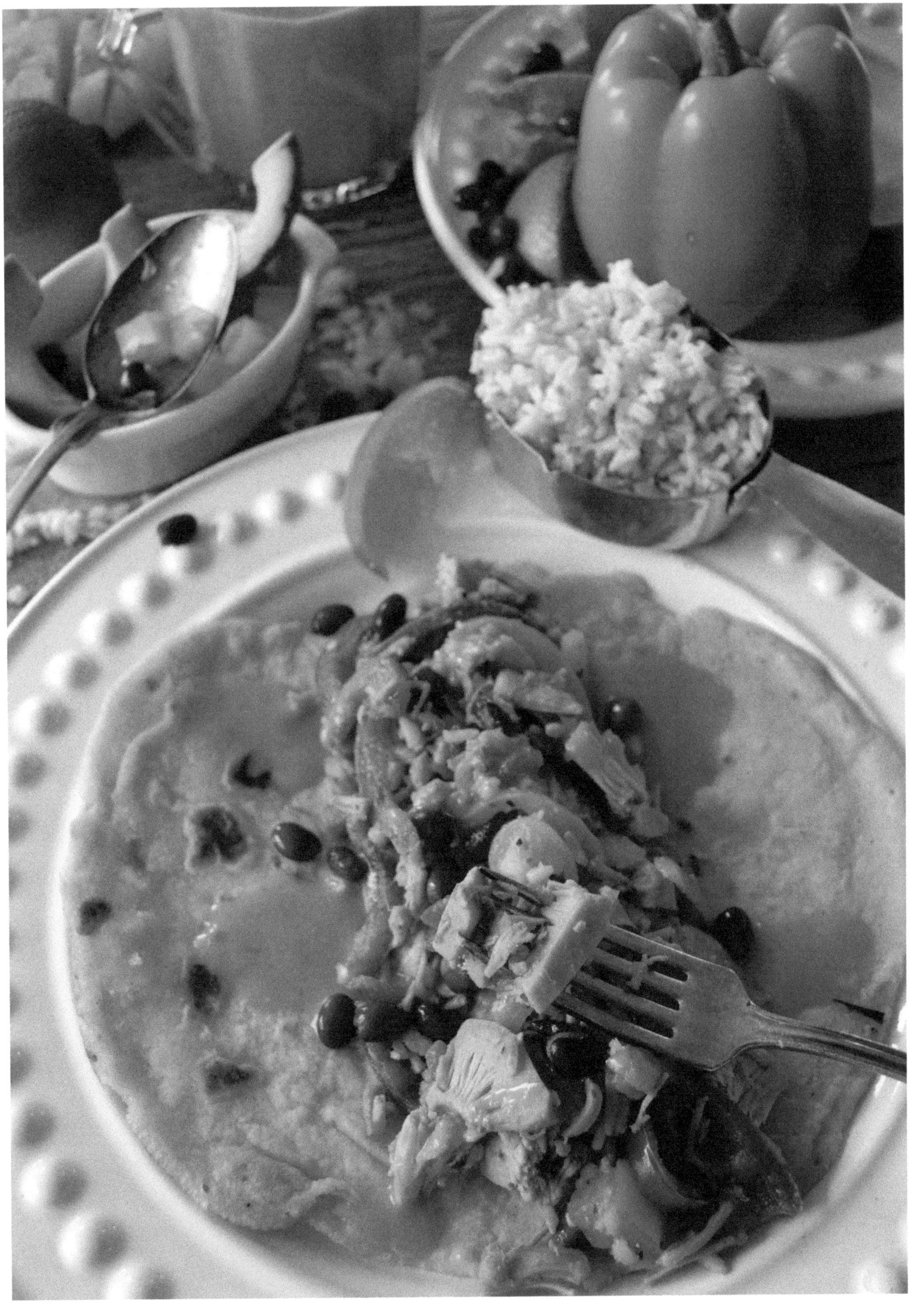

What's more enjoyable than a curry that is succulent and just as easy and quick to cook? Versatile and tasty to perfection, this recipe is a base to create to infinity because one can even add 1 or 2 vegetables from the fridge to prolong the pleasure!

FAST JACKFRUIT CURRY

- 2 x 14 oz (400 ml) cans of green jackfruit in water or brine, rinsed and drained (for a total of 500 g jackfruit)
- 2 large onions diced
- 1 cup (250 ml) vegetable broth
- 1 x 28 oz (796 ml) can of diced tomatoes
- 1 x 14 oz (400 ml) can of reduced fat coconut milk (or regular)
- 2 tbsp (30 ml) curry
- 1 tbsp 1/2 (22.5 ml) brown rice flour
- 1 tbsp (15 ml) chopped fresh ginger
- 1 tbsp (15 ml) minced garlic (3 cloves)
- Salt and pepper to taste

Culinary creation:

1. Cut each piece of jackfruit into 3 or 4 pieces depending on their size. In a cauldron, bring water to a boil and cook the jackfruit for 30 minutes over medium high heat.

2. When the jackfruit is ready, strain it and put it back in the cauldron. Use a potato masher or fork to loosen and pull almost all the jackfruit, reserve.

3. In a large skillet or large cauldron, heat oil over medium heat. Add the onion and cook until tender. Add oil as needed. Then add garlic and ginger and cook for 1 minute, mixing to bring out the flavor. Sprinkle the curry and the flour, coat the onions well and cook another 1 minute.

4. Deglaze with the vegetable broth. Add the coconut milk and tomatoes and bring to a boil. Add jackfruit, salt and pepper to taste. Cover and cook for 15 to 20 minutes, reducing the intensity. Serve with basmati rice and/or naan express bread, recipe on page 48.

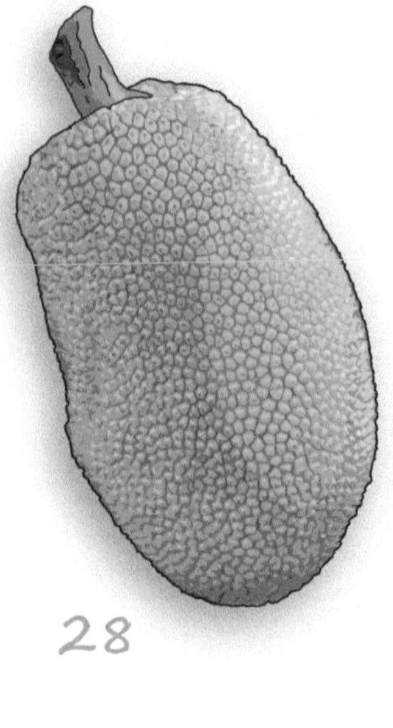

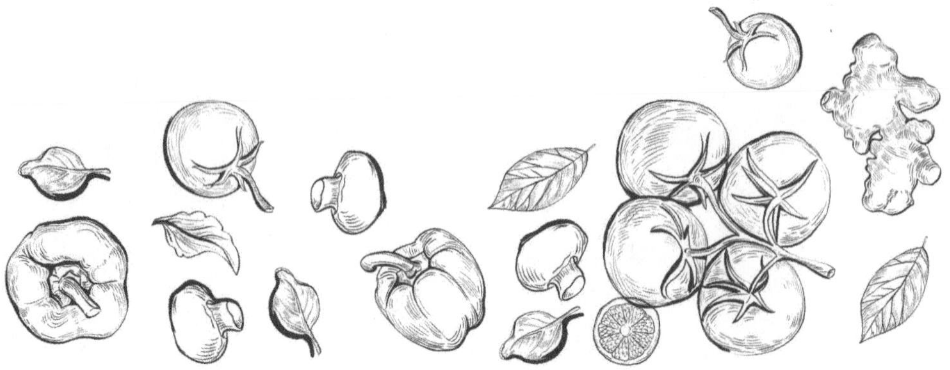

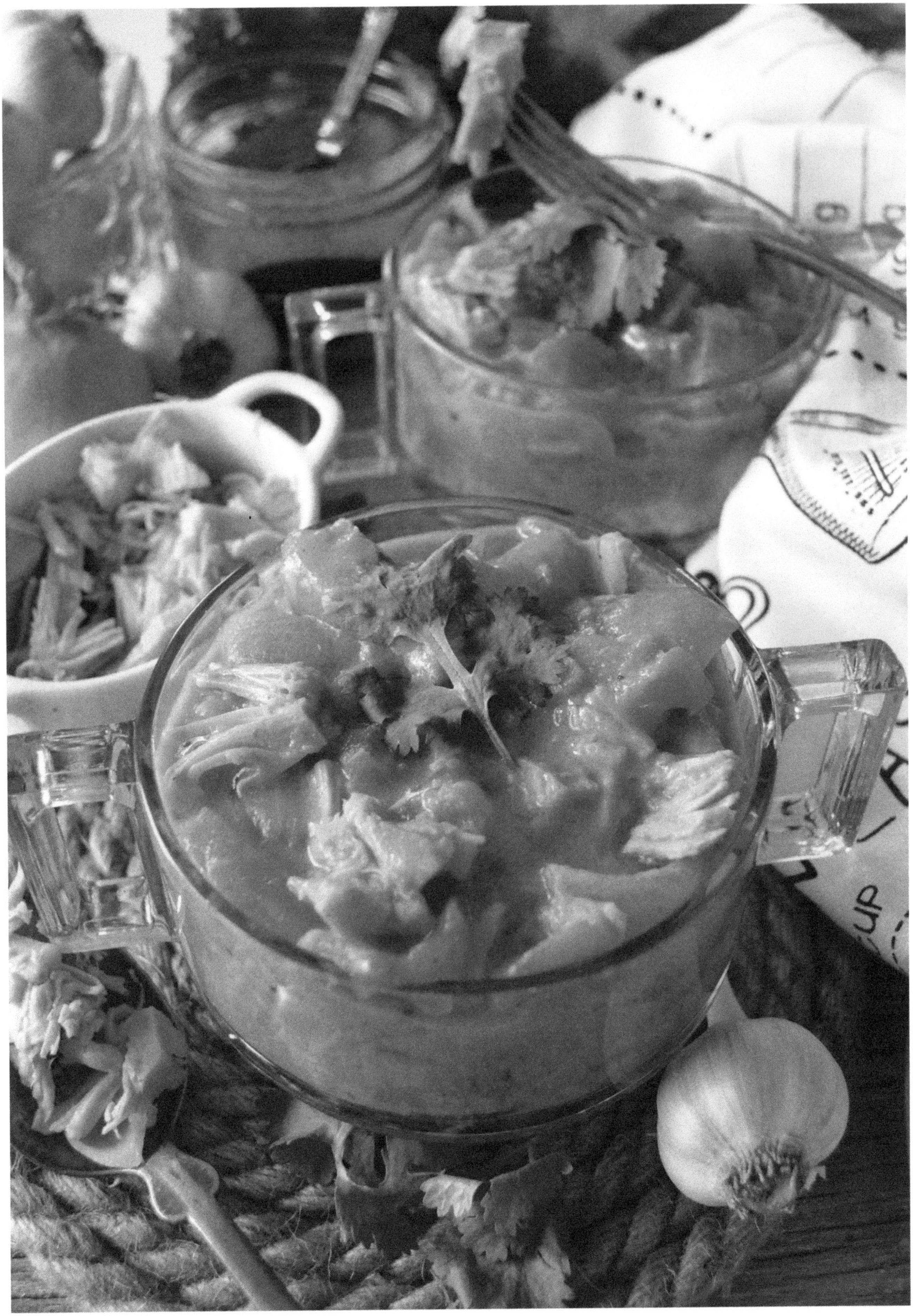

Whether it's cooking for your everyday meals or for more festive occasions, with this pulled jackfruit turkey-style, you will turn your dish into a memorable day!

PULLED JACKFRUIT TURKEY-STYLE

- 4 x 14 oz (400 ml) cans of green jackfruit in water or brine, rinsed and drained (for a total of 1000 g of jackfruit)
- 1/3 cup (80 ml) avocado oil
- 4 tsp (20 ml) minced garlic (4 cloves)
- 4 tsp (20 ml) onion powder
- 2 tsp (10 ml) granulated or powdered garlic
- 1 tsp (5 ml) thyme
- 1 tsp (5 ml) salt
- 1 tsp (5 ml) marjoram
- 1 tsp (5 ml) of savory
- 1/2 tsp (2.5 ml) pepper
- 1/2 tsp (2.5 ml) coconut sugar

Culinary creation:

1. Preheat oven to 425°F.
2. Cut each piece of jackfruit into 3 or 4 pieces depending on their size. In a cauldron, bring water to a boil and cook the jackfruit for 30 minutes over medium high heat. Meanwhile, to make the jackfruit, gather all the spices and coconut sugar in a small dish, mix and reserve.
3. When the jackfruit is ready, drain and put in a 9 x 13-inch baking dish. Use a potato masher or fork to loosen and pull almost all the jackfruit. Then add the oil, minced garlic and spices by sprinkling and mix well to distribute evenly.
4. Bake for 20 minutes, stirring occasionally. Then grill for 5 to 10 minutes or a little more to taste, checking and stirring often the jackfruit for an even more "pulled-dried turkey" effect. While the jackfruit is baking, if desired, prepare the sauce below to serve with the pulled jackfruit-style turkey. Makes 4 servings.

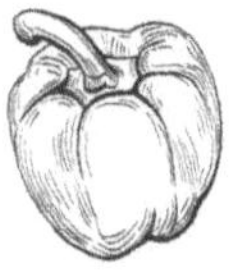

Variation: Add a few drops of liquid smoke to the remaining of the pulled jackfruit turkey-style and make a sandwich with the vegan mayo, recipe on page 22, to get a great smoked turkey sandwich, yum!

VEGAN WHITE SAUCE

- 2 cups (500 ml) water
- 1/4 cup (60 ml) brown rice flour
- 2 tbsp (30 ml) avocado oil
- 4 tsp (20 ml) onion powder
- 1 tsp (5 ml) salt
- 1/4 tsp (1.25 ml) coconut sugar
- 1/4 tsp (1.25 ml) thyme
- 2 pinches of sage (not ground)
- Pepper to taste

Culinary creation:

1. In a saucepan over low heat, whisk the brown rice flour in the oil. When the flour begins to bubble, add thyme and sage, whisk again to incorporate and cook a few more seconds. Add the water and remaining ingredients, pepper if desired. Bring to a boil while whisking constantly until the sauce thickens. Boil for a few seconds, remove from heat and serve. For a slightly lighter sauce, add 2 tablespoons (30 ml) of water.

CHEESE FLAVORED CRUSHED POTATOES

Recipe on page 64 in the section "Potatoes & Co"

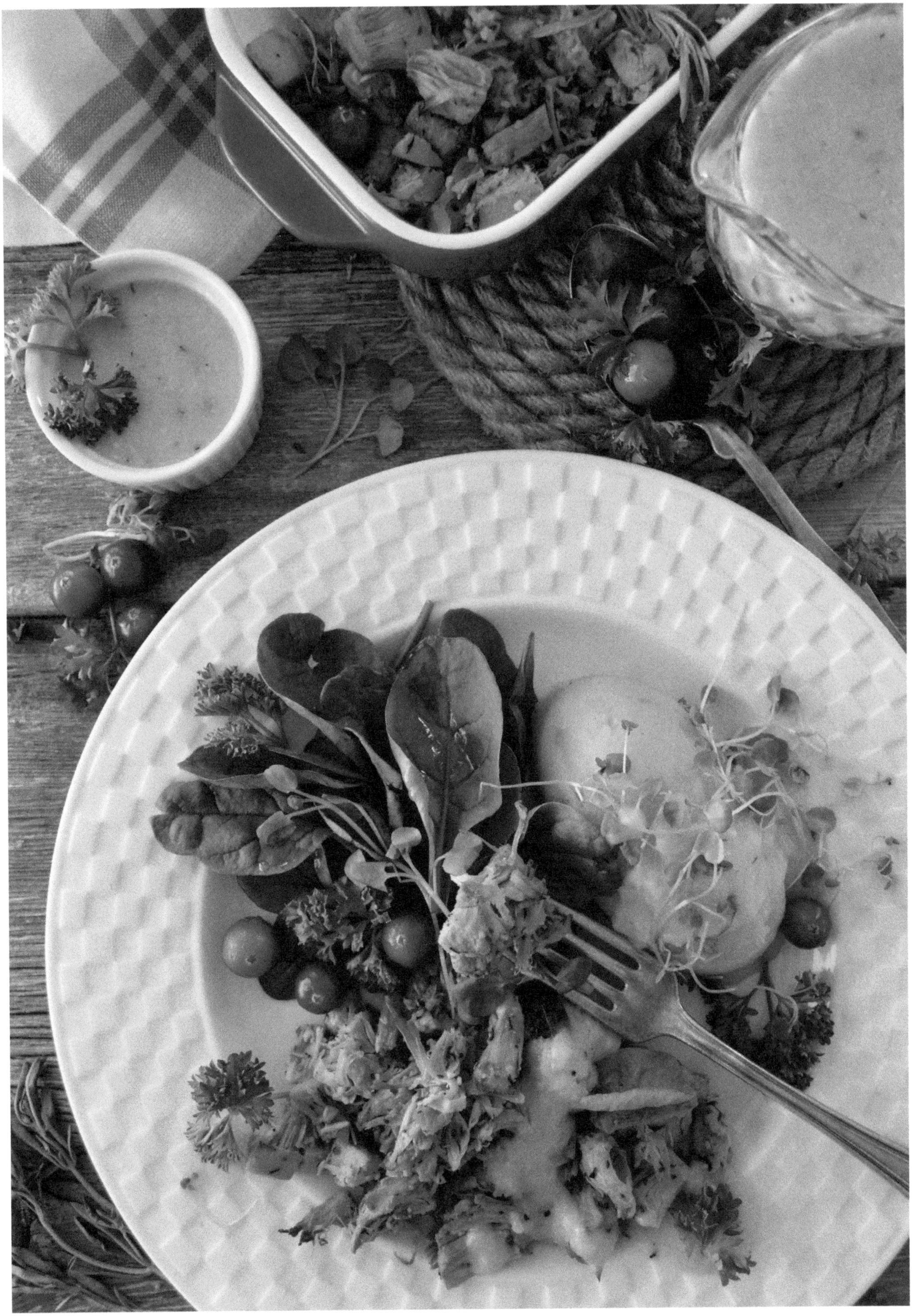

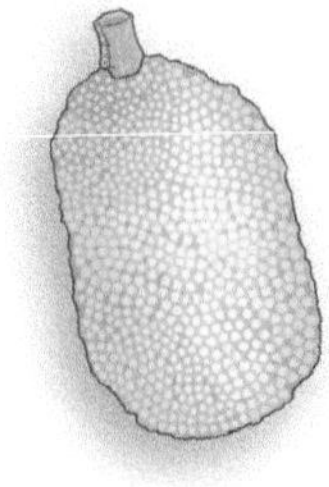

The jackfruit is truly a perfect ally to reproduce chicken! It works so well here in this recipe that will bring together in joy all your family and the good taste of this essential!

FAMOUS JACKFRUIT PIE CHICKEN-PIE-STYLE

Jackfruit garnish

- 2 x 14 oz (400 ml) cans of green jackfruit in water or brine, rinsed and drained (for a total of 500 g jackfruit)
- 1 onion cut into cubes
- 1 carrot finely chopped
- 1 chopped celery stalks
- 1/2 cup (125 ml) fresh green peas (frozen or not)
- 2 tbsp (30 ml) onion powder
- 1 tbsp (15 ml) granulated or powdered garlic
- 1/2 tsp (2.5 ml) salt
- 1/4 tsp (1.25 ml) pepper

Other

- 2 pie crusts, recipe on page 48

Bechamel

- 1/2 cup (125 ml) brown rice flour
- 1/4 cup (60 ml) avocado oil
- 1 cup 1/3 (330 ml) unsweetened vegetable milk
- 1 cup 1/3 (330 ml) water
- 1/3 cup (80 ml) nutritional yeast
- 2 tsp (10 ml) minced garlic (2 cloves)
- 1 tsp (5 ml) salt
- 1/4 tsp (1.25 ml) rosemary grains
- 1/4 tsp (1.25 ml) sage (not ground)
- 1/4 tsp (1.25 ml) thyme

Culinary creation:

1. Preheat oven to 350°F. Spray with vegetable coating a 9-inch pie plate.
2. Prepare 2 pie crusts, recipe on page 48, or any other pie crust. Precook and prepare the jackfruit according to the basic method explained on page 12 and reserve.
3. Make the jackfruit filling. In a skillet with a little oil, sauté the onions for a few minutes. Then add celery, carrots and peas, cook a few more minutes to soften them. Then add the jackfruit on the vegetables as well as the onion powder, the garlic powder, the salt and the pepper. Mix well to coat and add oil as needed to prevent sticking. Remove from heat and reserve.
4. Then make the bechamel. In a small bowl, combine the nutritional yeast, salt, rosemary, sage and thyme and set aside. In a large cauldron over medium heat, whisk the brown rice flour in oil and cook for about 30 seconds after the flour has begun to bubble. Then add the water, milk and minced garlic by whisking constantly and bringing the mixture to a boil. Add the reserved dry ingredients while the bechamel boils, boil for 1 minute and remove from heat. Then add the cooked vegetables and jackfruit to the bechamel, mix and set aside.
5. When the pie crust is ready, take the dough out of the wrap and place it directly on a new plastic wrap about 12 x 20 inches (30 x 50 cm). Place parchment paper over the dough and roll with a rolling pin until you have a pie shell about 12 inches in diameter (30 cm). Carefully remove the parchment and place the pie plate upside down on the dough. Use the corners of the plastic wrap by pasting them under the pie plate to turn the dough and pie plate at the same time. Turn the plate over and before removing it, remove the plastic film "glued" below it. Place the plate, push the dough into the plate, slide it into the interior and carefully remove the plastic wrap from the top of the dough. With your fingers and the remaining dough, repair any imperfections.
6. Pour the famous jackfruit pie into the pie shell. Repeat the same procedure to roll the other dough crust. Here, to turn the dough on the pie, place the pie plate on one side of the plastic wrap to prevent it from moving and lift the other side of the plastic wrap vertically back and forth on the pie. Remove the plastic wrap gently. Cut the excess dough, repair any imperfections and seal the doughs together with your fingers. With the tip of a knife, make a few inserts to get the steam out. Bake for 1 hour. Makes 6-8 servings.

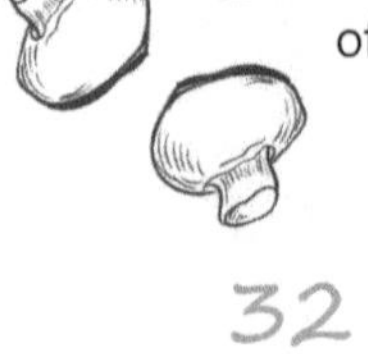

Variation: Replace the celery, carrot and peas with 1 tray of 227 grams of sliced mushrooms and 1/2 cup (125 ml) of broccoli in small bunches (pan-fried with onion) to vary the flavors, yum!

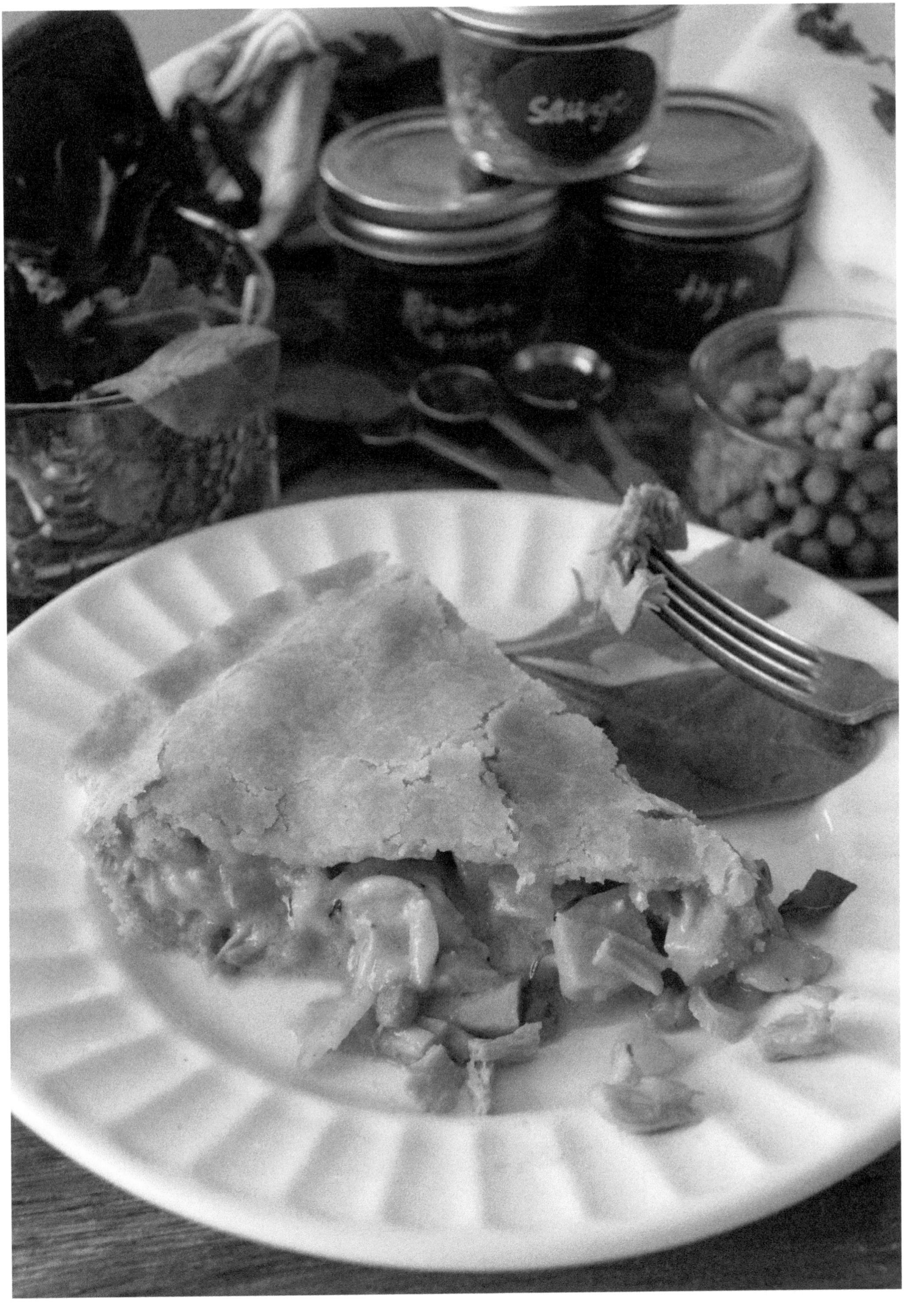

Because jackfruit can also be combined with the flavors of the sea, here we use seaweed to find the taste so appreciated by those who love fish. Delicious and appetizing with lemon or mayo, of course everything is to eat the vegan way, that is to say without fish!

JACKFRUIT FISHLESS FILLETS

- 2 x 14 oz (400 ml) cans of green jackfruit in water or brine, rinsed and drained (for a total of 500 g jackfruit)
- 1 cup (250 ml) brown rice already cooked
- 1/3 cup (80 ml) potato starch
- 1/3 cup (80 ml) nutritional yeast
- 2 tbsp (30 ml) ground flaxseed
- 2 tbsp (30 ml) chia seeds
- 4 tsp (20 ml) onion powder
- 2 tsp (10 ml) maple syrup
- 2 tsp (10 ml) minced garlic (2 cloves)
- 1 tsp (5 ml) salt
- 1/2 tsp (2.5 ml) dry mustard
- 1/2 tsp (2.5 ml) paprika
- 1/4 tsp (1.25 ml) tarragon
- 1/4 tsp (1.25 ml) dill
- 2 vegan omega 3 capsules made from seaweed
- 2 sheets of nori (optional)

Culinary creation:

1. Preheat oven to 400°F. Place parchment paper on a baking sheet.

2. Cut each piece of jackfruit into 3 or 4 depending on size. In a cauldron, bring water to a boil and cook the jackfruit for 30 minutes over medium high heat.

3. Meanwhile, chop the nori sheets into thin strips, rolling them over to cut more finely and quickly. Then, in a blender or coffee grinder, add the nori strips and the chia seeds and reduce them to powder. Combine them with all the other ingredients in a large bowl, mix well and set aside.

4. When the jackfruit is ready, strain it and put it back in the cauldron. Use a potato masher or fork to loosen and pull the whole jackfruit, cool a little. Then cut the jackfruit thinly on a cutting board with a large knife.

5. In the bowl with the remaining ingredients, add the jackfruit. Mix well. By hand, knead and compact the entire mixture until a large ball is formed. Always by hand, then form the triangular shaped fillets with the equivalent of 1/4 cup (60 ml) of preparation or weigh the obtained weight of the mixture and divide into 12 equal parts. If desired, brown the fillets on each side before putting in the oven or place each fillet directly on the baking sheet and bake for 25 to 30 minutes, turning halfway through cooking. Give 10 to 12 fillets of jackfruit.

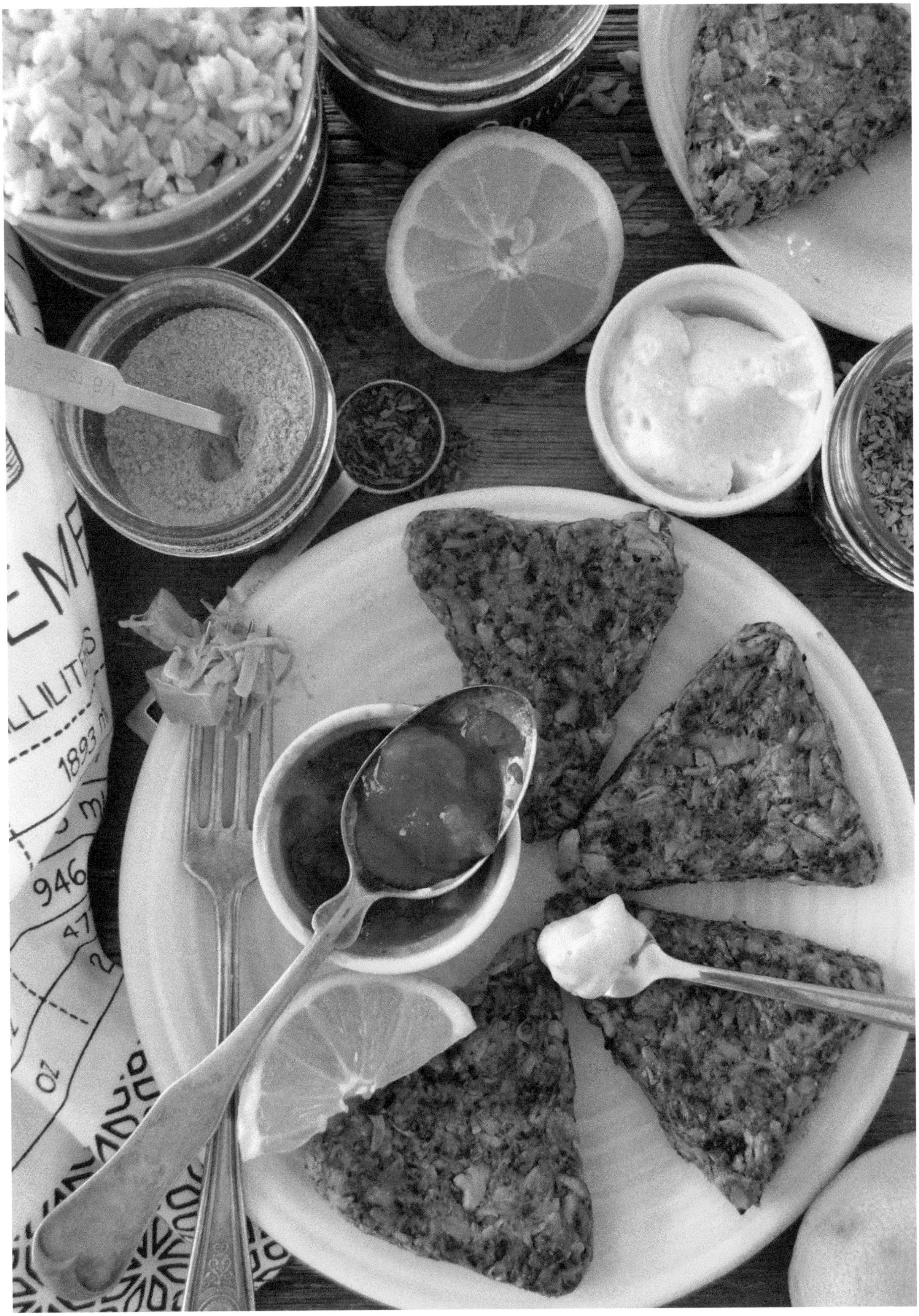
1893 ml
946

Here's a successful culinary challenge with this totally new recipe where the jackfruit turns wonderfully into hamburgers exactly the way we like them: firm, tasty and vegan! Everything to create the perfect jackfruit hamburger!

PERFECT JACKFRUIT HAMBURGER

Jackfruit hamburger
- 1 x 14 oz (400 ml) can of green jackfruit in water or brine, rinsed and drained (for a total of 250 g jackfruit)
- 1/2 cup (125 ml) cooked brown rice
- 2 tbsp (30 ml) potato starch
- 2 tbsp (30 ml) nutritional yeast
- 1 tbsp (15 ml) ground flaxseed
- 1 tbsp (15 ml) chia seeds
- 1 tsp (5 ml) onion powder
- 1/2 tsp (2.5 ml) ground chipotle
- 1/2 tsp (2.5 ml) salt
- 1/2 tsp (2.5 ml) liquid smoke

Garnish
- 4 to 5 hamburger buns
- Vegan cheddar to spread or to toast, recipe on page 54
- Leaves of curly lettuce
- Garlic cabbage salad (use grated cabbage and mix to taste with garlic sauce, recipe on page 20)
- Sliced tomatoes
- Sliced dill pickled pickles
- Condiments to choose from: ketchup, mustard, relish, vegan mayo, recipe on page 22

Culinary creation:

1. Precook and prepare the jackfruit according to the basic method explained on page 12. Meanwhile, in a blender or coffee grinder, grind the chia seeds into powder and gather with the ingredients of the hamburger patties in a bowl, set aside.

2. When the jackfruit is pulled according to the basic method, let it cool a little and then cut it finely on a cutting board with a large knife.

3. Add the jackfruit with the remaining ingredients. Mix well. By hand, compact the entire mixture until a large ball is formed. By hand, then form the hamburger patties with the equivalent of 1/4 cup (60 ml) of preparation.

4. In a skillet over medium heat and in a little oil, cook the patties for about 5 minutes to grill while turning occasionally. Assemble with the ingredients of your choice. Makes 4 to 5 hamburger patties.

BAKED ONION RINGS

- 1 large onion
- 1 cup (250 ml) corn flour, to flour
- 1 cup (250 ml) corn flour, for coating
- 1 cup (250 ml) unsweetened plant-based milk

- 1 tsp 1/2 (7.5 ml) salt
- 1 tsp (5 ml) onion powder
- 1 tsp (5 ml) granulated or powdered garlic

Culinary creation:

1. Preheat oven to 400°F. Place a parchment paper on a baking sheet. Omit this step if cooking in a deep fryer or cauldron where you will put about 2 1/2 inches of oil (7 cm).

2. Cut the onion 1/4 inch (0.7 cm) thick and loosen into rings, set aside. In a first bowl, add a cup (250 ml) of corn flour which will initially serve to flour the rings, reserve.

3. In another bowl, add the other cup of corn flour, onion powder, garlic powder and salt. Mix well. Add to this mixture the plant-based milk and whisk until smooth, reserve. (If this preparation becomes a little too thick in the process, it becomes more difficult to coat the rings, in this case, add 1 tsp (5 ml) of plant-based milk at a time to liquefy the mixture so it looks like a crepe preparation).

4. In the first bowl, add the onion rings and flour each of them by mixing with a wooden spoon. Here, it is possible to flour all of them at the same time. Then remove the rings by placing them on a plate. With a pair of pliers or with your fingers, then dip each ring into the preparation of the second bowl and roll it immediately afterwards into the remaining flour of the first bowl. Place on the parchment paper the time to make the rest of the rings.

5. Before putting in the oven, use an oil spray with avocado oil (you can also gently brush or omit this step for deep-frying) and spray the rings on each side. Bake for 20 minutes, turning rings halfway through cooking. It is also possible to spray oil again during cooking. Serve immediately.

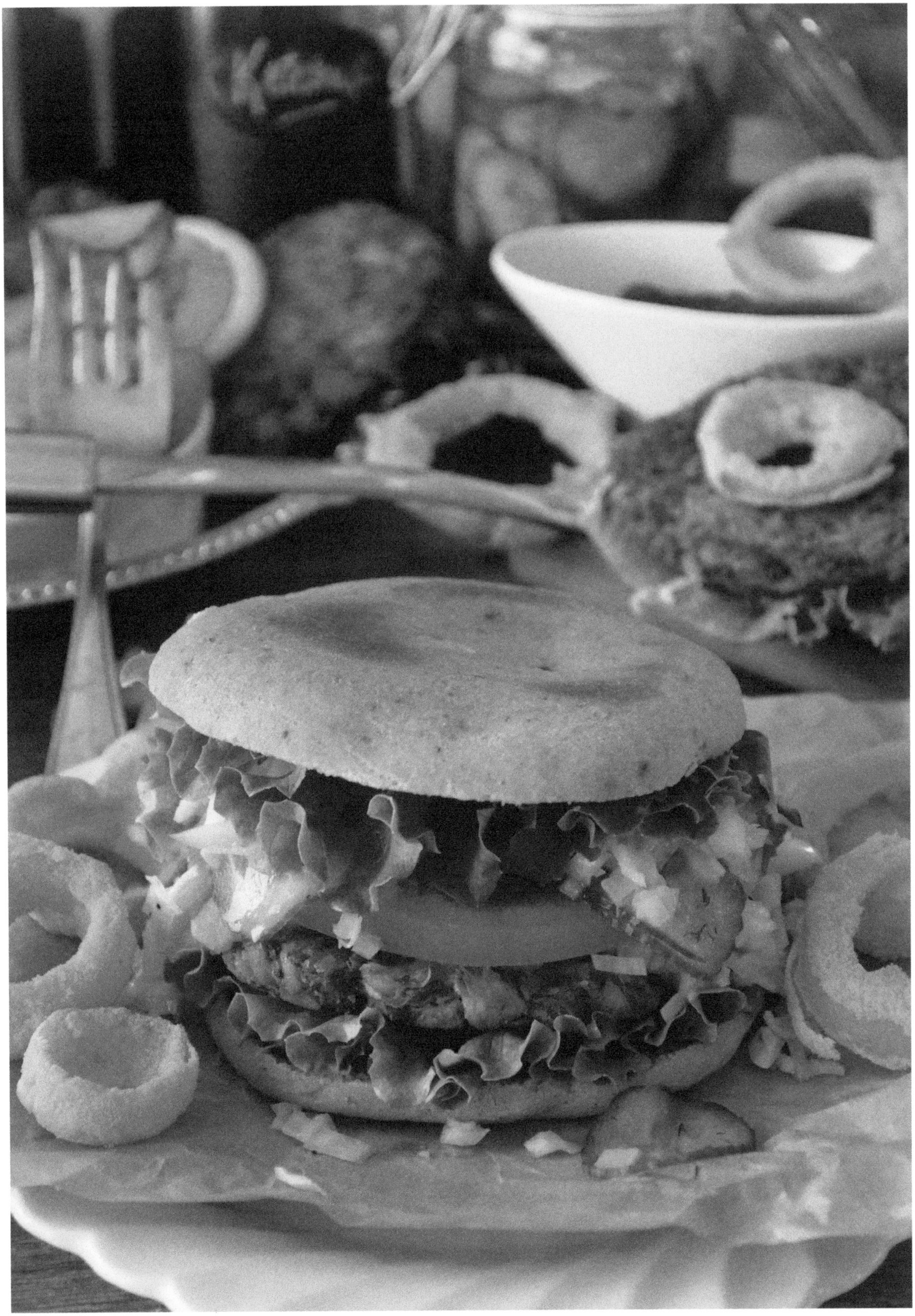

When the taste is at the rendezvous exactly like at the restaurant, there is something to celebrate! This is the case here with this recipe which is perfectly reminiscent of gyros in Greek restaurants ... What happiness to enjoy!

GREEK-STYLE JACKFRUIT ON GYROS

- 3 x 14 oz (400 ml) cans of green jackfruit in water or brine, rinsed and drained (for a total of 750 g of jackfruit)
- 1/4 cup (60 ml) avocado oil
- 1/4 cup (60 ml) freshly squeezed lemon juice
- 2 tbsp (30 ml) oregano
- 2 tbsp (30 ml) granulated or powdered garlic
- 2 tsp (10 ml) onion powder

- 1 tsp (5 ml) salt
- 1 tsp (5 ml) thyme
- 1/2 tsp (2.5 ml) dried dill
- 1/2 tsp (2.5 ml) marjoram
- 1/2 tsp (2.5 ml) dry mustard
- 1/16 tsp (0.3125 ml) chili powder

Others
- 6 gyros, recipe on page 48
- Leaves of Romaine lettuce
- 1 to 2 sliced tomatoes
- 1 small red onion cut into slices
- Tzatziki sauce, recipe below

Culinary creation:

1. Preheat oven to 425°F. First make the tzatziki sauce if desired.

2. Cut each piece of jackfruit into 3 or 4 pieces depending on their size. In a cauldron, bring water to a boil and cook the jackfruit for 30 minutes over medium high heat. Meanwhile, gather all the spices in a small dish, reserve.

3. When the jackfruit is ready, strain it and put it in an ovenproof 8.5 x 11-inch dish. Use a potato masher or fork to loosen and pull almost all the jackfruit. Then add the oil, lemon juice and spices by sprinkling and mixing well to distribute them all over the jackfruit.

4. Bake for 30 minutes, stirring occasionally. For an even more dried effect, grill the last 5 to 10 minutes, checking and stirring often. Meanwhile, make the gyros and prepare the vegetables. To serve, garnish each gyros with Romaine lettuce, jackfruit, sliced tomatoes, red onions and tzatziki sauce. Makes 6 servings.

TZATZIKI SAUCE

- 1 Lebanese cucumber finely cut into cubes
- 1/2 cup (125 ml) of reduced fat coconut milk
- 1/2 cup (125 ml) water
- 2 tbsp (30 ml) avocado oil
- 2 tbsp (30 ml) freshly squeezed lemon juice
- 1 tbsp (15 ml) minced garlic (3 cloves)

- 3/4 tsp (3.75 ml) xanthan gum
- 1/2 tsp (2.5 ml) dried dill
- 1/2 tsp (2.5 ml) dried mint
- 1/2 tsp (2.5 ml) salt
- Pepper to taste

Culinary creation:

1. In a blender, pulse until thickened all ingredients except the cucumber. Add in an airtight container with the cucumbers and mix. Refrigerate about 1 hour before serving. Can be kept about 1 week.

GREMOLATA, *parsley salad*

- 3 cups (750 ml) well compacted finely chopped parsley
- 3 garlic cloves, finely chopped, germ removed
- 3 tbsp (45 ml) avocado oil

- 1 tbsp (15 ml) freshly squeezed lemon juice
- 1/4 tsp (1.25 ml) dried mint
- Salt and pepper to taste

Culinary creation:

1. In a dish, combine all the ingredients and mix well. Refrigerate 1 hour before serving.

SEASONED QUARTERS

Recipe on page 65 in the section "Potatoes & Co"

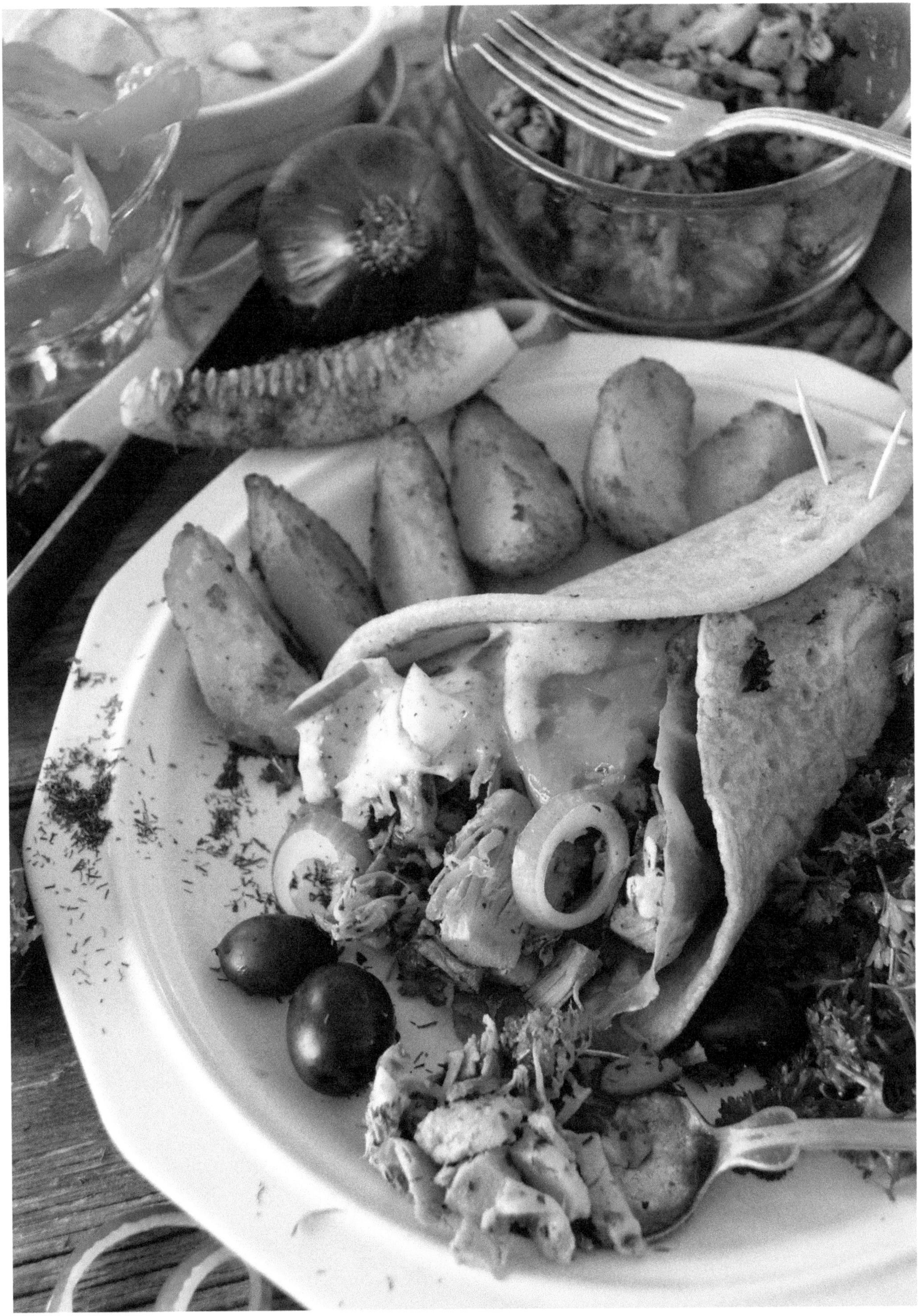

A classic in Indian cuisine! Who will know that in this wonderful taste of "butter chicken" spices the main ingredient is jackfruit? Skeptics will be confused and be convinced!

INDIAN JACKFRUIT "BUTTER CHICKEN" STYLE

- 2 x 14 oz (400 ml) cans of green jackfruit in water or brine, rinsed and drained (for a total of 500 g jackfruit)
- 2 large sliced onions
- 1 x 28 oz (796 ml) can of diced tomatoes
- 1 x 400 ml can of coconut milk (reduced in fat or not)
- 2 tbsp (30 ml) chopped fresh ginger
- 2 tbsp (30 ml) minced garlic or (4 to 6 pods)
- 2 tbsp (30 ml) Garam Masala
- 2 tsp 1/2 (12.5 ml) ground cilantro
- 2 tsp (10 ml) ground cumin
- 1 tsp 1/2 (7.5 ml) salt
- 1/2 tsp (2.5 ml) chili powder
- 1/16 tsp (0.3125 ml) ground cinnamon

Culinary creation:

1. Cut each piece of jackfruit into 3 or 4 pieces depending on their size. In a cauldron, bring water to a boil and cook the jackfruit for 30 minutes over medium high heat. Meanwhile, gather all the spices in a small dish, reserve. In a bowl, mash the diced tomatoes with a blender stand and set aside.

2. After the cooking time, drain the jackfruit and put it back in the cauldron. Use a potato masher or fork to loosen and pull almost all the jackfruit, reserve.

3. In a large skillet or cauldron, sauté the onions in a little oil and cook over low heat until tender, adding oil as needed. Then add garlic and ginger and cook for 1 minute. Sprinkle the spices on the onions and mix to coat, cook 1 minute to bring out the flavor. Finally, add the tomatoes, coconut milk and jackfruit and cook covered for about 20 minutes over medium heat, stirring occasionally. Serve with rice of your choice, Aloo Gobi style cauliflower, lime and cilantro cabbage salad and naan breads, recipe on page 48. Makes about 6 servings.

.

INDIAN STYLE ALOO GOBI CAULIFLOWER

- 1 whole medium cauliflower cut into florets
- 1 sliced onion
- 2 cups (500 ml) diced tomatoes
- 2 medium potatoes cut into cubes (peeled or not)
- 1 tbsp (15 ml) chopped fresh ginger
- 1 tbsp (15 ml) minced garlic (3 cloves)
- 1 tsp (5 ml) cumin grains
- 1 tsp (5 ml) mustard seeds
- 2 tsp (10 ml) ground turmeric
- 1 tsp 1/2 (7.5 ml) Garam Masala
- 1 tsp (5 ml) paprika
- 1 tsp (5 ml) ground cumin
- 1 tsp (5 ml) salt (more to taste)
- 1/4 tsp (1.25 ml) chili powder

Culinary creation:

1. In a cauldron, precook the diced potatoes in water for 5 to 7 minutes; when ready, drain and reserve. Meanwhile, in a small dish, combine turmeric, Garam Masala, paprika, ground cumin, salt and chili powder, set aside.

2. Heat a little oil in a skillet over medium heat and add the onion. Cook for 2 to 3 minutes and then add ginger, minced garlic, cumin and mustard seeds. Cook for about 1 minute to bring out the flavor. Add the remaining spices by sprinkling and coating the onions, add oil as needed and cook for a few seconds.

3. Add the diced tomatoes, crushing them a little. Finally add the potatoes and cauliflower, coat well. Reduce heat and cover, simmering for about 15 minutes or until potatoes and cauliflower are tender. Makes 6 servings.

CABBAGE SALAD WITH LIME AND CILANTRO

- 4 cups (1000 ml) grated green cabbage
- 3 tbsp (45 ml) avocado oil
- 3 tbsp (45 ml) chopped fresh cilantro
- 1 tbsp (15 ml) lime juice
- Salt and pepper to taste

Culinary creation:

1. In a bowl, add the cabbage and spread the rest of the ingredients on it, mix well, adjust to taste and savor!

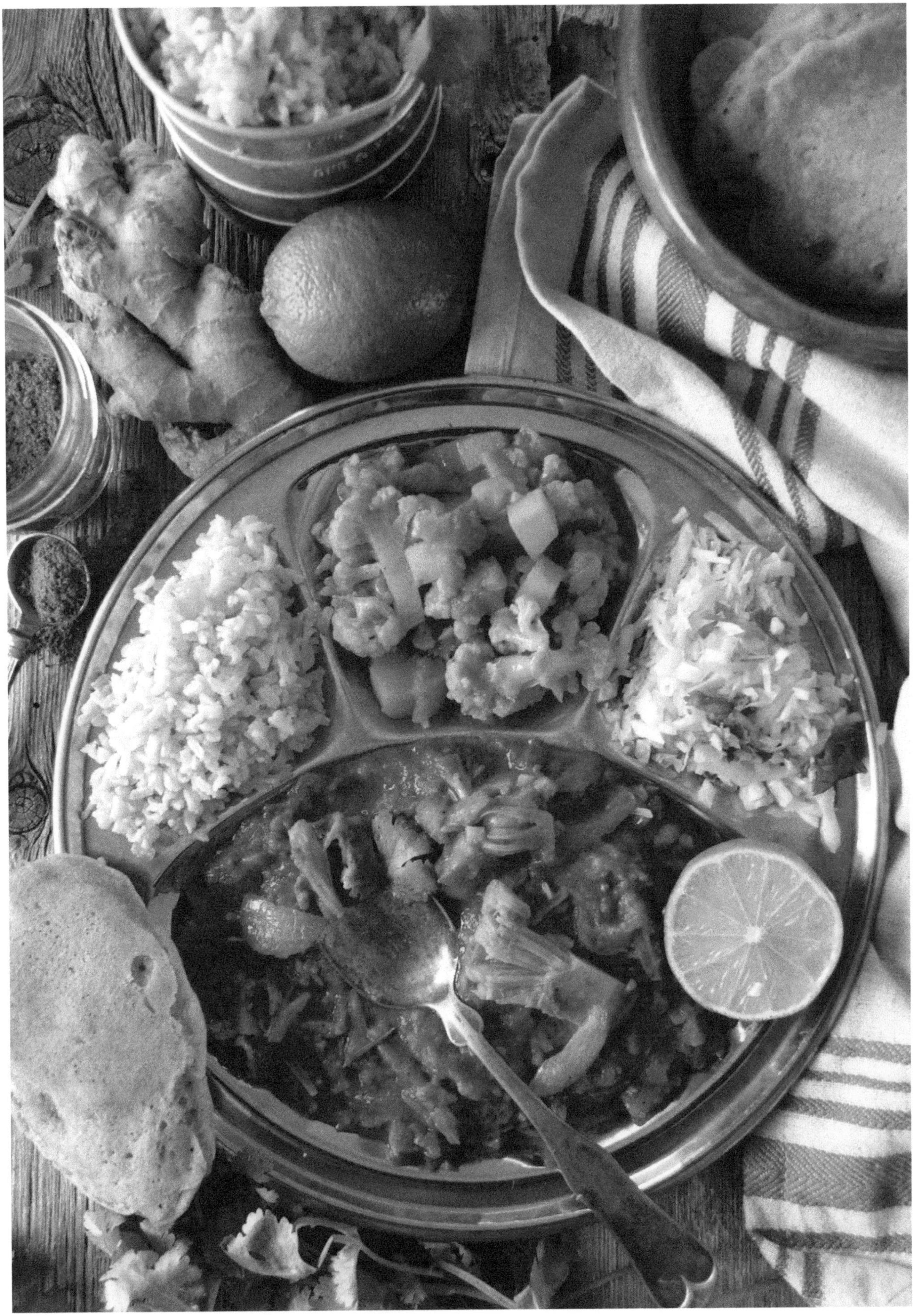

In this recipe, enjoy the Asian jackfruit which is used in two ways: sushi or chop suey! You will enjoy twice this delicious taste for the happiness of all!

DOUBLE SUCCULENT ASIAN JACKFRUIT

- 2 x 14 oz (400 ml) cans of green jackfruit in water or brine, rinsed and drained (for a total of 500 g of jackfruit)
- 1/4 cup (60 ml) avocado oil
- 2 tbsp (30 ml) soy-like sauce, recipe on page 44
- 2 tsp (10 ml) minced garlic (2 cloves)

- 2 tsp (10 ml) chopped fresh ginger
- 2 tsp (10 ml) rice vinegar
- 2 tsp (10 ml) maple syrup
- 1 tsp (5 ml) sesame oil
- Salt to taste

Culinary creation:

1. Precook and prepare the jackfruit according to the basic method explained on page 12. Let cool a little and refrigerate the jackfruit in a dish with all the ingredients to marinate at least 1 hour up to 24 hours in advance. (Continue according to the chosen recipe.)

SUSHI with Asian jackfruit

- 2 x 14 oz (400 ml) green jackfruit cans prepared according to the previous recipe, Asian jackfruit
- 2 cups (500 ml) "calrose" rice (sushi rice)
- 2 tbsp (30 ml) rice vinegar
- 2 tbsp (30 ml) maple syrup
- 1 tsp (5 ml) salt
- 1/2 cup (125 ml) soy-like sauce for dipping sushi, recipe on page 44

- 3-4 avocados cut into thin strips
- 3 Lebanese cucumbers cut in 6 to 8 strips
- 1 red pepper sliced into thin strips
- 1/2 cup (125 ml) baby spinach
- 1/2 cup (125 ml) alfalfa
- 8 sheets of nori

Culinary creation:

1. While the jackfruit marinates in the refrigerator, cook the rice by rinsing it first several times with warm water. In cauldron, bring 7 cups (1750 ml) of water to a boil and cook in low heat for 15 to 20 minutes, stirring occasionally. When the rice is cooked, drain it and rinse it a little. Refrigerate at least 2 hours to cool. When the rice is cold, add the rice vinegar, maple syrup and salt. Mix well.

2. On the counter, place a nori sheet on a sushi mat and spread about 2/3 cup (160 ml) of rice on the sheet, leaving a width of ¾ inch (2 cm) at the top of the sheet. For convenience, place a plastic wrap over the rice and spread it gently by hand or with a small rolling pin. Remove the film to garnish.

3. In center, place in order: 1 row of spinach leaves, about 1/4 cup (60 ml) **cooled and already marinated jackfruit**, 2 cucumber strips, 2 chili strips, 2-3 strips of avocados and alfalfa. Starting from the bottom of the sushi mat (the part closest to you), roll up, taking care to squeeze the sushi with the mat so that it stays well and the sushi sticks enough. Refrigerate each sushi roll while you repeat this step for the remaining ingredients.

4. With a well-oiled knife, cut each roll into 8 equal parts. Makes about 8 rolls of 8 sushi.

CHOP SUEY with Asian jackfruit

- 2 x 14 oz (400 ml) green jackfruit cans prepared according to the above jackfruit Asian recipe
- 3 to 4 cups (750 to 1000 ml) sprouted beans
- 1 tray of 227g mushrooms cut in 4
- 4 to 5 minis bok choy undone leaves
- 2 cups (500 ml) broccoli in florets
- 1 onion chopped in strips
- 1 carrot cut into julienne
- 1 green zucchini sliced into quarters

Sauce
- 1 cup 3/4 (430 ml) water
- 1/4 cup (60 ml) soy-like sauce, recipe on page 44
- 3 tbsp (45 ml) brown rice flour
- 1 tbsp (15 ml) minced garlic (3 cloves)
- 1 tbsp (15 ml) chopped fresh ginger
- 1/2 tsp (2.5 ml) sesame oil
- Salt and pepper to taste

Culinary creation:

1. Preheat oven to 425°F. Transfer the Asian jackfruit, already marinated, to an ovenproof 8.5 x 11-inch dish and bake for about 30 minutes, stirring occasionally. Meanwhile, in a skillet with a little oil, sauté the onions with the mushrooms for 5 minutes. Add the carrot julienne, broccoli, zucchini and cook for another 2 to 3 minutes.

2. Then sprinkle the flour over the vegetables, add the ginger and garlic and mix to distribute well. Add the sauce remaining ingredients. Bring to a boil and cook over low heat for 5 to 10 minutes. At the very end, add the bok choy and sprouted beans, cook for an additional minute or to taste. To serve, add the jackfruit to the chop suey. Makes 4 servings.

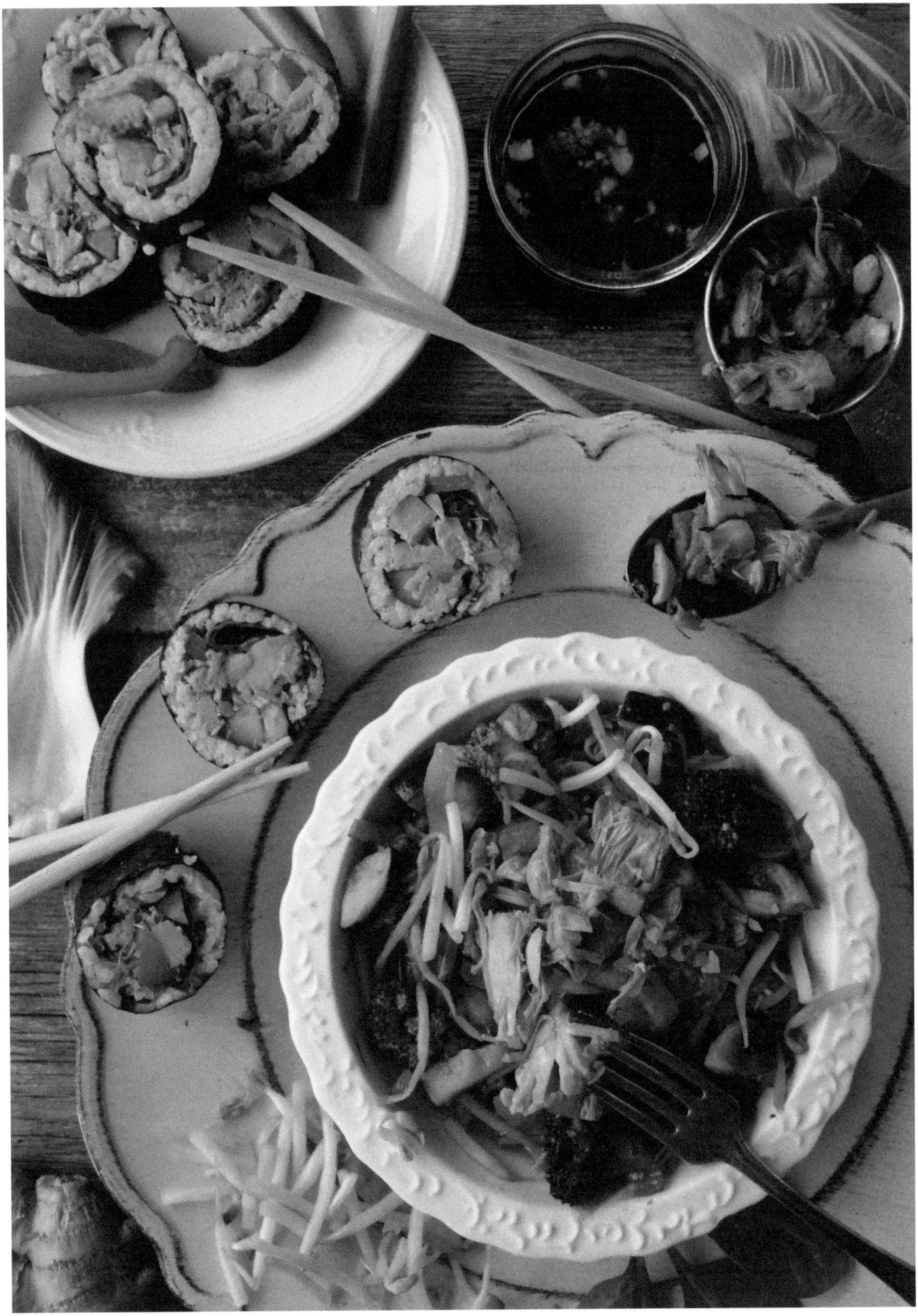

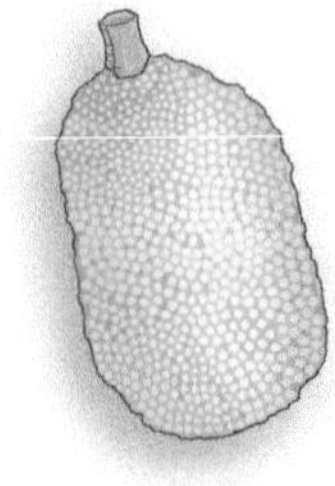

Inspired by traditional Teriyaki style dishes, the teriyaki jackfruit will transport you to a new world flavor's with its perfectly sweet taste. Another appetizing recipe with the jackfruit that is so versatile!

TERIYAKI JACKFRUIT

- 2 x 14 oz (400 ml) cans of green jackfruit in water or brine, rinsed and drained (for a total of 500 g jackfruit)
- 1 onion chopped in strips
- 1 broccoli cut into florets
- 1 red pepper cut into strips
- 1 tray of 227 g sliced mushrooms
- Chopped green onions and sesame seeds to decorate
- Salt and pepper to taste

Teriyaki sauce

- 1 cup 1/3 (330 ml) water
- 1 cup (250 ml) maple syrup
- 1 cup (250 ml) soy-like sauce, recipe below
- 1/2 cup (125 ml) tomato paste
- 3 tbsp (45 ml) arrowroot or cornstarch
- 2 tbsp (30 ml) minced garlic (3 to 6 pods)
- 2 tbsp (30 ml) chopped fresh ginger

Culinary creation:

1. Cut each piece of jackfruit into 3 or 4 pieces depending on their size. In a cauldron, bring water to a boil and cook the jackfruit for 30 minutes over medium high heat. Meanwhile, gather all the ingredients of the sauce in a cauldron, reserve.
2. When the jackfruit is ready, strain it and put it back in the cauldron. Use a potato masher or fork to loosen and pull virtually all the jackfruit or as you like, reserve.
3. Add the ingredients of the sauce to the boil and add the jackfruit. Reduce the heat to simmer a little, enough time to cook the vegetables.
4. In a large skillet, fry the vegetables in a little oil until desired. Serve with rice of your choice, rice noodles or sobas (100% buckwheat noodles) as shown in the picture. Makes 4 large portions.

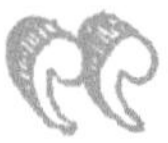

Here is one of my recipes created some time ago and that follows me everywhere! This recipe that mimics soy sauce is a must for anyone who cannot tolerate soy ... The perfect substitute!

SOY-LIKE SAUCE

- 1 cup (250 ml) water
- 1/3 cup (80 ml) coconut sugar
- 3 tbsp 1/2 (52.5 ml) balsamic vinegar
- 3 tbsp (45 ml) salt

Culinary creation:

1. In a bowl or glass jar, dissolve the coconut sugar and salt with the water and balsamic vinegar, mix well. Pour into a glass container to refrigerate. Shake before using exactly like soy sauce, but without soy. Can be kept about 2 months in the refrigerator.

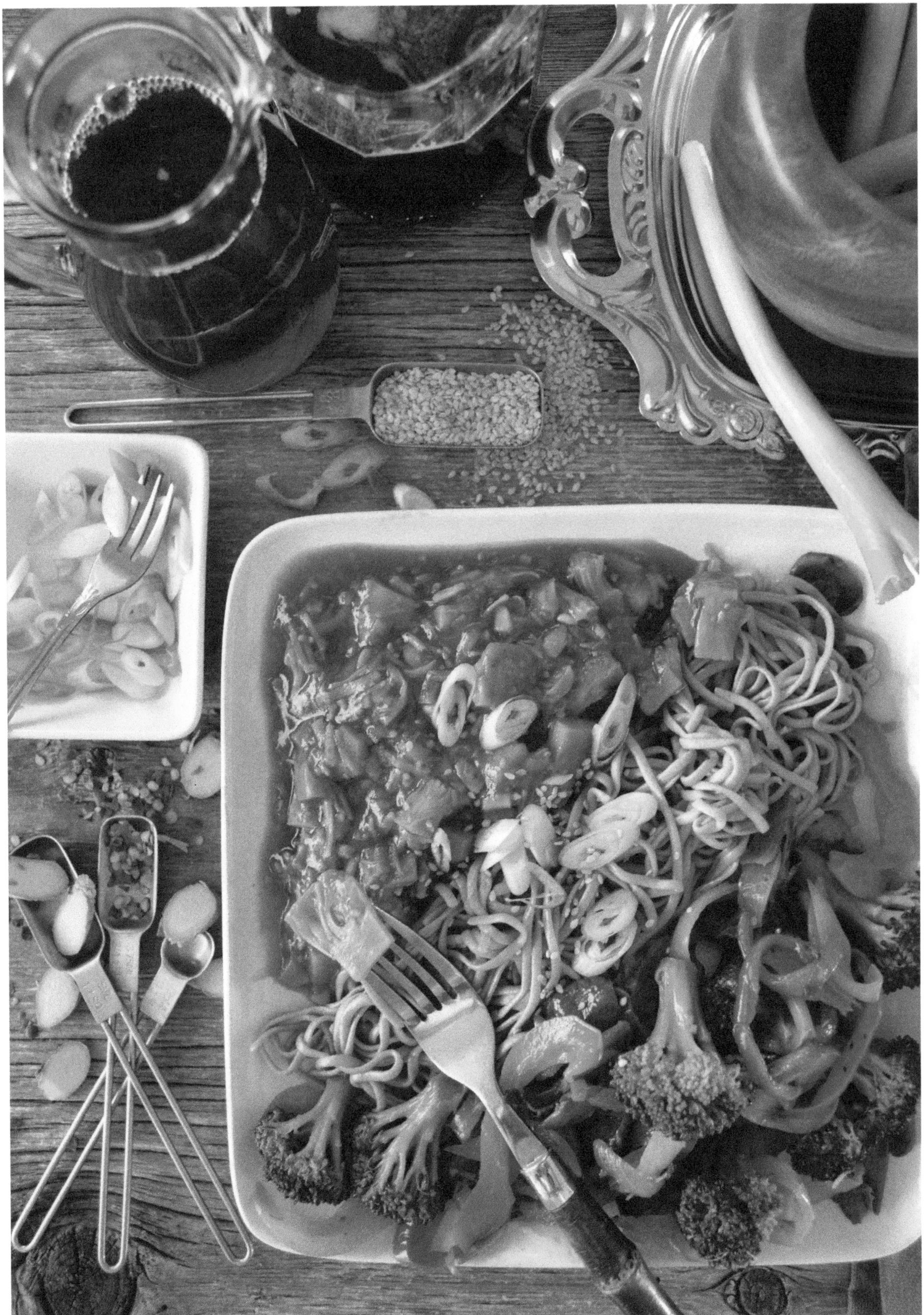

This tasty recipe with a delicate semi-sweet and semi-sour taste comes from my former culinary repertoire where I cooked "African beef". No need for "meat" because the proof is made here that everything is in the taste of sauce and spices!

THE AFRICAN

- 2 x 14 oz (400 ml) cans of green jackfruit in water or brine, rinsed and drained (for a total of 500 g jackfruit)
- 2 onions cut into cubes
- 2 chopped celery stalks
- 1 minced green pepper
- 2 trays of 227 g mushrooms cut into strips
- 1 x 28 oz (796 ml) diced tomatoes
- 1 cup 1/2 (375 ml) tomato sauce

- 1/2 cup (125 ml) water
- 1/3 cup (80 ml) maple syrup
- 3 tbsp (45 ml) apple cider vinegar
- 3 tbsp (45 ml) vegan Worcestershire sauce, recipe below
- 1 tbsp (15 ml) minced garlic (3 cloves)
- 1 tsp 1/2 (7.5 ml) salt
- 1 tsp (5 ml) granulated or powdered garlic
- 1/4 tsp (1.25 ml) pepper

Culinary creation:

1. Preheat oven to 415°F.

2. Cut each piece of jackfruit into 3 or 4 pieces depending on their size. In a cauldron, bring water to a boil and cook the jackfruit for 15 minutes over medium high heat. Meanwhile, prepare the vegetables. When the cooking time is over, drain and put the jackfruit back in the pot. Use a potato masher to loosen and pull almost all the jackfruit. Pour the vegan Worcestershire sauce all over it, mix well and set aside.

3. In a large pan or casserole, fry the chopped vegetables for 5 to 8 minutes. After this time, add the minced garlic and cook for another minute. Add remaining ingredients including the jackfruit and bring to a boil.

4. Pour into a 9 x 13-inch baking dish if a pan is used (or leave in the casserole), cover and cook for about 1 hour and 15 minutes, stirring occasionally. Serve with rice, quinoa, pasta, or on bread. Makes 6-8 servings

VEGAN WORCESTERSHIRE SAUCE

- 1 cup (250 ml) apple cider vinegar
- 1/4 cup (60 ml) coconut sugar
- 1/4 cup (60 ml) soy-like sauce, recipe on page 44
- 1/4 cup (60 ml) water
- 2 tbsp (30 ml) lemon juice
- 1 tsp 1/2 (7.5 ml) salt
- 1 tsp (5 ml) mustard powder

- 1 tsp (5 ml) onion powder
- 1/2 tsp (2.5 ml) ground ginger
- 1/2 tsp (2.5 ml) black pepper
- 1/4 tsp (1.25 ml) granulated or powdered garlic
- 1/8 tsp (0.625 ml) ground pepper
- 1/8 tsp (0.625 ml) cinnamon

Culinary creation:

1. In a blender, pulse all the ingredients. Pour into a saucepan and bring to a boil. Simmer on low heat for 15 minutes. Cool completely. Filter if desired before bottling. Refrigerate, can be kept for about 3 months in the refrigerator.

RICE WITH CHIVES

- 2 cups (500 ml) brown rice (uncooked)
- 1/3 cup (80 ml) chopped fresh chives
- 1/3 cup (80 ml) avocado oil
- 1 tbsp 1/2 (22.5 ml) onion powder
- 3/4 tsp (3.75 ml) salt
- 6 to 8 sliced green onions

Culinary creation:

1. In a large cauldron of boiling water, cook about 2 cups (500 ml) of brown rice (to obtain an equivalent of 7 cups 1/2 (1875 ml) of cooked rice). When the rice is ready, drain it and add the remaining ingredients, mix and serve with the African jackfruit.

SALAD WITH ARUGULA AND CARAWAY

- 5 cups (1250 ml) well packed arugula
- 1/4 cup (60 ml) avocado oil
- 1 tsp 1/2 (7.5 ml) caraway seeds
- 1 tsp (5 ml) maple syrup
- 1/2 tsp (2.5 ml) apple cider vinegar
- Salt and pepper to taste
- Shoots to taste

Culinary creation:

1. In a bowl, add the arugula and pour the remaining ingredients onto it. Mix well and adjust to taste.

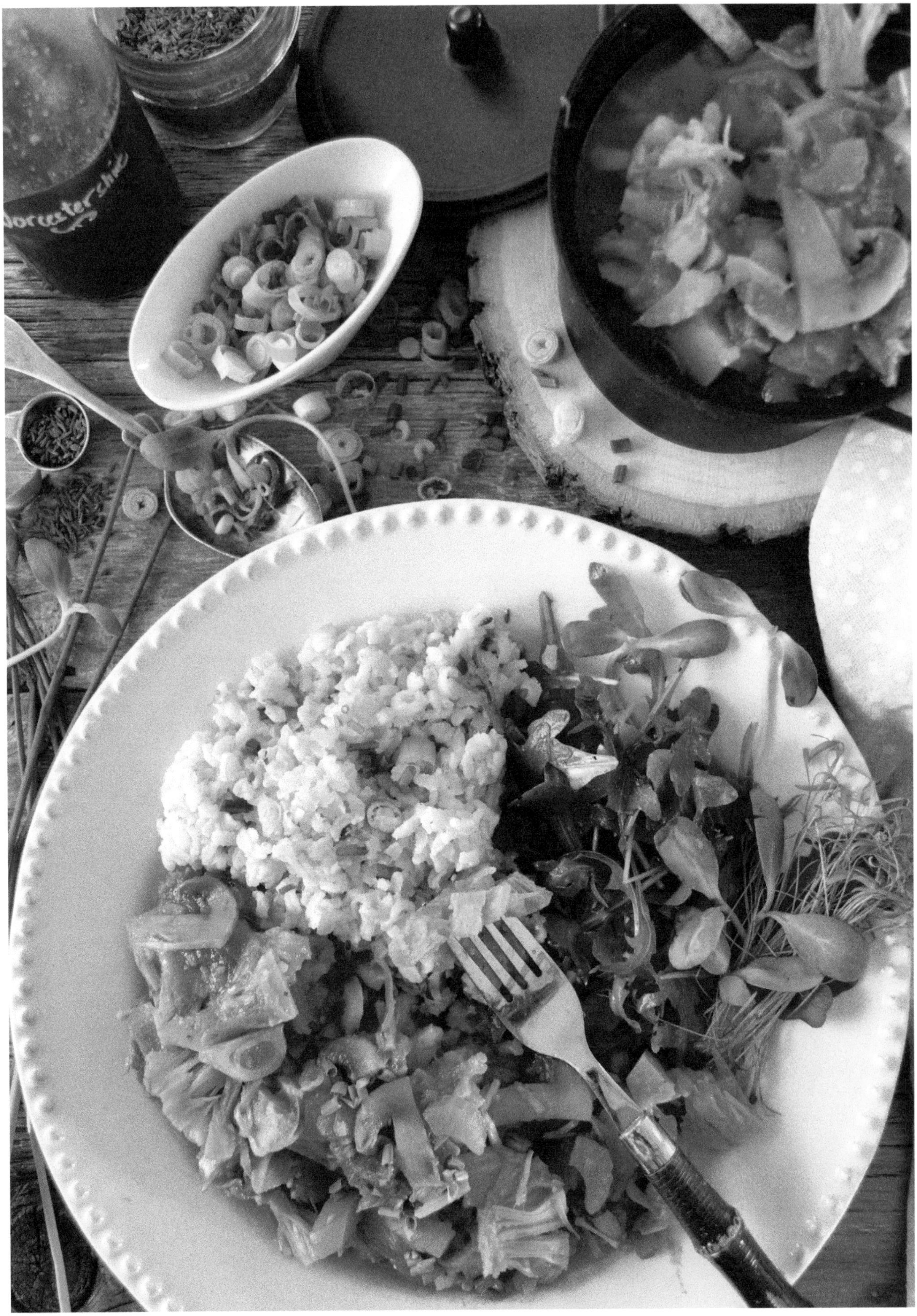

THE GLUTEN-FREE CORNER

GYROS

- 2 cups (500 ml) brown rice flour
- 1 cup (250 ml) water
- 1 cup (250 ml) unsweetened plant-based milk
- 1/3 cup (80 ml) tapioca flour
- 2 tsp (10 ml) onion powder
- 2 tsp (10 ml) granulated or powdered garlic
- 1 tsp (5 ml) salt
- 1/2 tsp (2.5 ml) xanthan gum

Culinary creation:

1. In a bowl, mix all dry ingredients, make a well and add milk and water. With a whisk or hand mixer, mix again to obtain a homogeneous paste and let rest about 5 minutes.

2. Pour a little less than 1/2 cup (125 ml) of the mixture into a frying pan preheated over medium heat with oil. Using a spatula to lift, spread the dough with the tip of the spatula starting from the inside and bringing the dough to the outside. Spread a few times with the spatula to obtain a uniform thickness and to obtain a gyros of about 7 inches (17 cm). Cook 1 to 2 minutes per side and serve with the desired ingredients. Makes 6 servings. Can be kept 7 days in the refrigerator.

GYROS is used in the following recipe:
- Greek-style jackfruit on gyros on page 38

TORTILLAS

- 2 cups 1/3 (580 ml) water
- 2 cups (500 ml) brown rice flour
- 1/3 cup (80 ml) tapioca flour
- 1 tbsp (15 ml) onion powder
- 1 tbsp (15 ml) granulated or powdered garlic
- 1 tsp (5 ml) salt
- 1/2 tsp (2.5 ml) xanthan gum

Culinary creation:

1. In a bowl, mix all dry ingredients, make a well and add water. Whisk, mix again to obtain a homogeneous paste and let stand about 5 minutes.

2. Pour about 1/2 cup (125 ml) of the mixture into a preheated frying pan over medium heat with a little oil. Using a spatula to lift, spread the dough with the tip of the spatula starting from the inside and bringing the dough to the out-side. Spread a few times with the spatula to obtain a uniform thickness and a tortilla about 8 inches (20 cm). Bake 1 to 2 minutes per side and serve with the desired ingredients. Makes 8 servings. Can be kept 7 days in the refrigerator.

TORTILLAS are used in the following recipes:
- Burritos delight of lime-chipotle jackfruit on page 26
- Quesadillas treat of jackfruit on page 70
- Jackfruit rolls 3 ways on page 76

EXPRESS NAAN BREADS

- 2 cups (500 ml) brown rice flour
- 1 cup (250 ml) unsweetened plant-based milk
- 1/2 cup (125 ml) water
- 1/3 cup (80 ml) tapioca flour
- 1 tbsp (15 ml) baking powder
- 1/2 tsp (2.5 ml) salt

Culinary creation:

1. In a bowl, mix all dry ingredients, make a well and add milk and water. Whisk, mix to obtain a homogeneous paste. Let the mixture rest for 5 minutes.

2. Pour about 1/4 cup (60 ml) of the mixture into a preheated pan with oil and spread the dough to obtain a bread of the size of your hand. Cook 1 minute per side over medium low heat.

3. Before serving, grill in the oven or toaster for crispy texture. Can be frozen. Makes about 8 naan breads.

NAAN BREADS are used in the following recipes:
- Fast jackfruit curry on page 28
- Indian jackfruit "butter chicken" style on page 40

PIE CRUST (2 CRUSTS)

- 1 cup 1/3 (330 ml) brown rice flour
- 1/2 cup (125 ml) potato starch
- 1/2 cup (125 ml) tapioca flour
- 2 tsp (10 ml) guar gum
- 2 tsp (10 ml) xanthan gum
- 1 tsp (5 ml) salt
- 4/5 cup (200 ml) vegan margarine
- 1/4 cup (60 ml) very cold water

Culinary creation:

1. In a bowl, whisk all the dry ingredients of the pie crust and make a well. Add the water and whisk with the flour until the water is soaked with flour. Place the margarine in the center over the water already soaked with flour and using a dough cutter, break up into pieces by incorporating all the flour mixture.

2. When the margarine is cut into small pieces, gather the mixture by hand and knead. If the dough crumbles again after 30 seconds of kneading, add 1 tsp (5 ml) of margarine at a time, kneading again each time to absorb.

3. Divide the resulting dough into two equal discs and wrap each one in plastic wrap. Refrigerate at least 30 minutes to 1 hour before using. If the dough has cooled for more than 3 hours, allow to stand for 10 minutes at room temperature before using.

4. To use the pie dough, continue with recipe instructions.

PIE CRUST is used in the following recipes:
- Famous jackfruit pie chicken-pie-style on page 32
- Pie of yesteryear with jackfruit meat on page 56

Your taste buds and those of your guests will be filled with this classic recipe of General Tao, jackfruit version! With its generous sauce, this dish is a true delight that will be unanimous and that will always make you want to start cooking again!

THE GENERAL TAO JACKFRUIT

General Tao Jackfruit

- 3 x 14 oz (400 ml) cans of green jackfruit in water or brine, rinsed and drained (for a total of 750 g of jackfruit)
- 3/4 cup (180 ml) cornstarch
- 1 tbsp (15 ml) avocado oil
- 1 tbsp (15 ml) soy-like sauce, recipe on page 44
- 1 tbsp (15 ml) rice vinegar
- 1 tbsp (15 ml) maple syrup
- 1 tsp 1/2 (7.5 ml) granulated or powdered garlic
- 3/4 tsp (3.75 ml) salt
- 1/2 tsp (2.5 ml) ground ginger

Sauce

- 2 cups 1/4 (560 ml) vegetable broth
- 1/3 cup (80 ml) maple syrup
- 1/3 cup (80 ml) soy-like sauce, recipe on page 44
- 1/3 cup (80 ml) tomato paste
- 1/4 cup (60 ml) cornstarch
- 3 tbsp (45 ml) minced garlic (6-9 cloves)
- 3 tbsp (45 ml) finely chopped ginger
- 1 to 2 tsp (5 to 10 ml) red spicy pepper paste

Culinary creation:

1. Cut each piece of jackfruit into 3 or 4 pieces depending on their size. In a cauldron, bring water to a boil and cook the jackfruit for 30 minutes over medium high heat.
2. Meanwhile, in a medium saucepan, combine all the sauce ingredients and set aside. Preheat oven to 300°F.
3. When the jackfruit is ready, drain it. By hand or with a fork, delicately pull each piece of jackfruit taking care not to undo the base that holds them, the goal being to keep them whole. Add to a bowl or dish with a lid as the pieces are prepared. Then add the remaining ingredients except the cornstarch, mixing well to distribute them all over the jackfruit.
4. Then transfer the jackfruit into a freezer bag with cornstarch and shake the bag to coat each piece. Or, if a dish with a lid is used, add the cornstarch, close the dish and shake to coat the cornstarch. Add 1 to 2 tablespoons (15 to 30 ml) cornstarch if some of the pieces are not covered with cornstarch.
5. In a large skillet, brown the third of the jackfruit pieces in the oil over medium heat for about 5 to 10 minutes, or until golden and crisp on each side. Add oil as needed. When a quantity of jackfruit is cooked, transfer it to a baking dish and set aside in the oven while the rest of the jackfruit cooks. When the pieces are all cooked, keep them in the oven while preparing the rest of the ingredients.
6. Bring the sauce to a boil, whisking constantly until thick. Serve the General Tao jackfruit drizzled with the sauce. Serve with basmati rice, broccoli, bean sprouts, sautéed onions in a pan or any other Asian vegetable. Makes 4 servings.

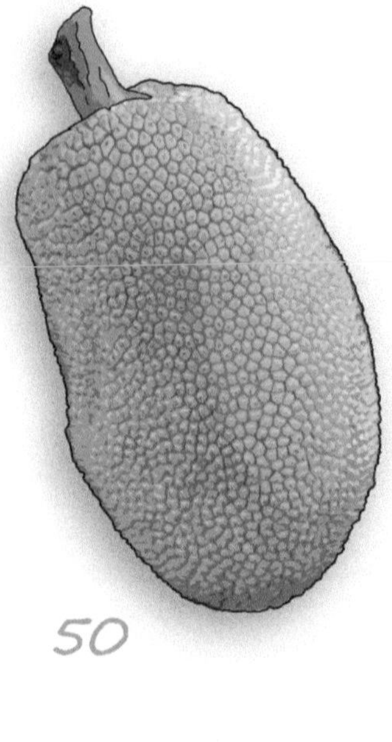

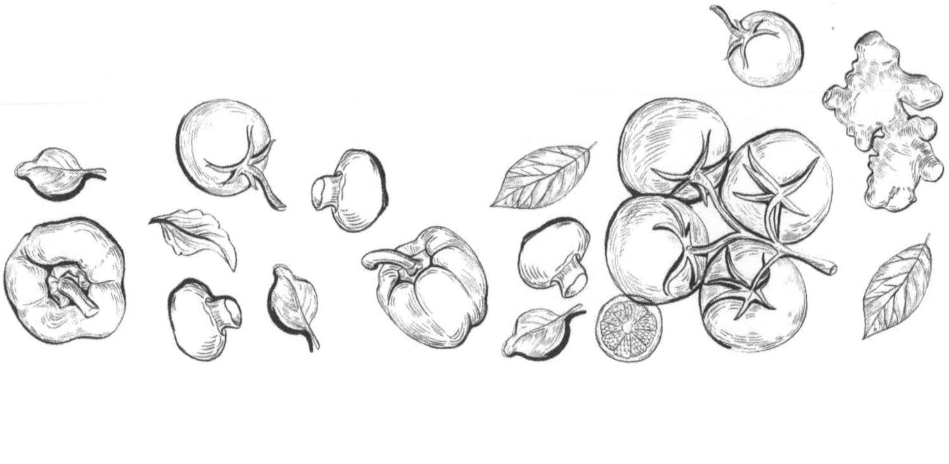

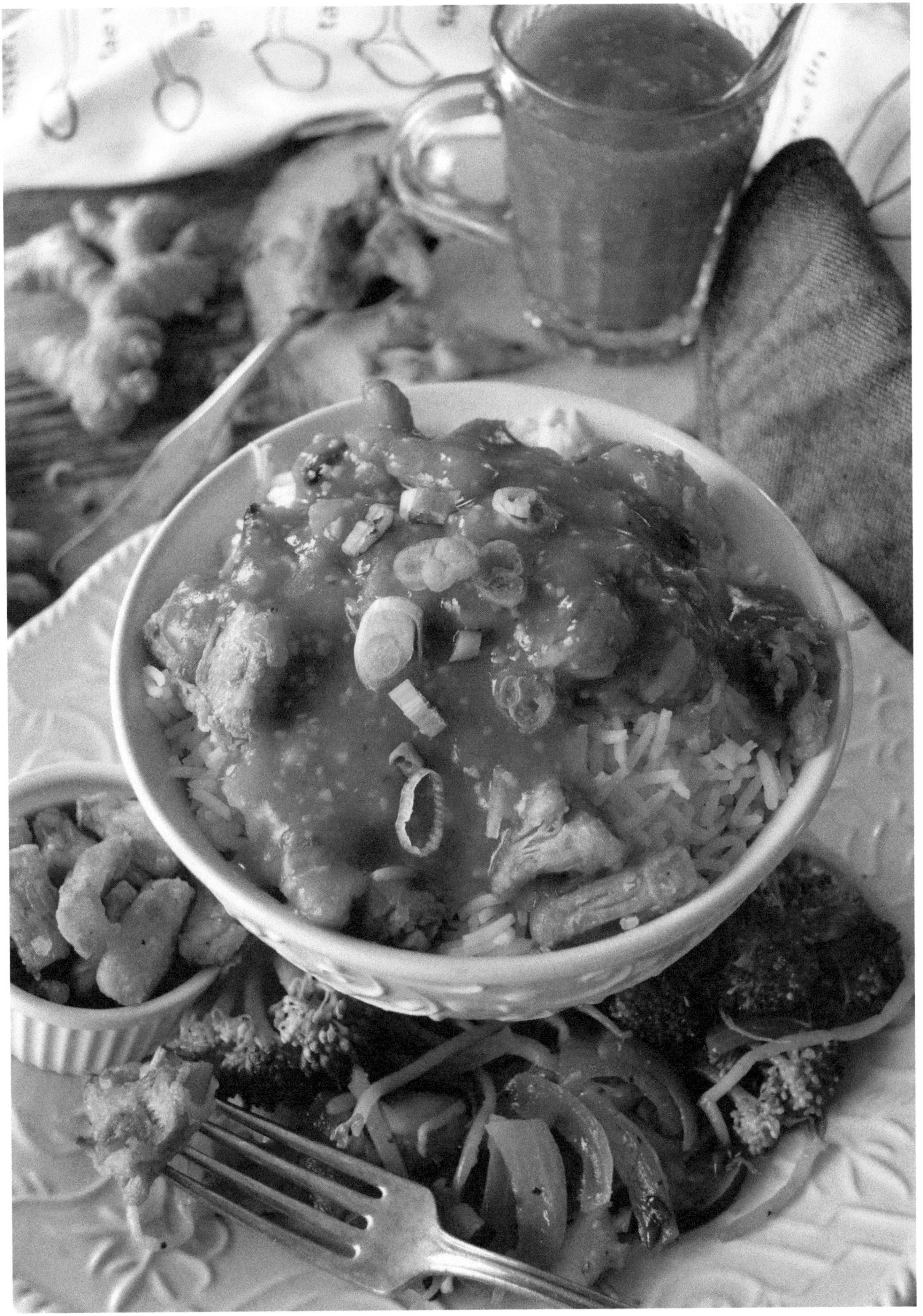

This jackfruit parmigiana recipe is a dream come true! Worthy of the best parmigiana ever, you will succumb to happiness by tasting this classic tasty and exquisite Italian, all made, of course, without animal cruelty!

THE JACKFRUIT PARMIGIANA

Italian jackfruit cutlets

- 1 x 14 oz (400 ml) can of green jackfruit in water or brine, rinsed and drained (for a total of 250 g jackfruit)
- 1/2 cup (125 ml) brown rice already cooked
- 2 tbsp (30 ml) nutritional yeast
- 2 tbsp (30 ml) potato starch
- 1 tbsp (15 ml) ground flaxseed
- 1 tbsp (15 ml) chia seeds
- 2 tsp (10 ml) Italian seasonings, recipe below
- 1 tsp (5 ml) granulated or powdered garlic
- 1 tsp (5 ml) onion powder
- 1/2 tsp (2.5 ml) salt

For the coating

- 1/3 cup (80 ml) brown rice flour (to flour)
- 1 cup (250 ml) brown rice flour
- 1 cup (250 ml) unsweetened plant-based milk
- 1 tbsp (15 ml) tapioca flour
- 1 tbsp (15 ml) potato starch
- 1/2 tsp (2.5 ml) salt
- 1 cup (250 ml) gluten-free breadcrumbs

For baking

- 2 cups (500 ml) tomato sauce to taste (more to taste)
- Vegan cheese grated to choice

Culinary creation:

1. Precook and prepare the jackfruit according to the basic method explained on page 12. Meanwhile, in a blender or coffee grinder, grind the chia seeds into powder and place them in a bowl with the remaining ingredients of the cutlets, reserve.

2. Preheat oven to 400°F. Prepare 3 plates for coating the cutlets. The first with a third of a cup of brown rice flour to flour; the second with plant-based milk, brown rice flour cup, tapioca flour, potato starch and salt for soaking (here mix until smooth); the third with breadcrumbs to coat, reserve.

3. When the jackfruit is prepared according to the basic method and is cool enough, cut it finely on a cutting board with a large knife. In the bowl, add the jackfruit with the already gathered ingredients, mix well. By hand, compact the entire mixture until a large ball is formed.

4. Make each jackfruit cutlet with the equivalent of 1/3 cup (80 ml) of preparation and flatten it between 2 plastic wraps to obtain a cutlet about 5 x 4 inches (13 x 10 cm). Then coat each cutlet by passing them one at a time in the 3 plates according to the order presented in the 2nd step. Use a spatula to transfer cutlets from one plate to another and place in a 9 x 13-inch baking dish. Bake for 20 minutes, turning halfway through cooking. Preheat the tomato sauce.

5. After the cooking time, pour the tomato sauce (about 1/2 cup (125 ml) of sauce on each cutlet) and add the vegan cheese. Bake for another 10 minutes and then toast to taste. Give 4 cutlets.

 Variation: Make meatballs using 1 tbsp (15 ml) of preparation for each ball. Brown them in the pan for 3 minutes and cook for 20 minutes at 400°F in the oven, turning occasionally. The most delicious on spaghetti with tomato sauce, yum!

ITALIAN SEASONINGS

- 1 tbsp (15 ml) oregano
- 1 tbsp (15 ml) basil
- 1 tbsp (15 ml) rosemary grains
- 1 tbsp (15 ml) thyme

- 1 tbsp (15 ml) marjoram
- 2 tsp (10 ml) granulated or powdered garlic
- 1 tsp (5 ml) sage (not ground)

Culinary creation:

1. In an airtight jar, mix all the spices and add to your favorite recipe.

SPAGHETTI WITH PARSLEY AND LEMON GARLIC

- 1 pack of 340 g gluten-free spaghetti*
- The zest of 1 lemon
- 1/4 cup (60 ml) chopped parsley
- 2 tbsp (30 ml) lemon juice
- 2 tbsp (30 ml) avocado oil

- 2 tbsp (30 ml) nutritional yeast
- 1 tbsp (15 ml) minced garlic (3 cloves)
- 1 tsp (5 ml) granulated or powdered garlic
- 1/2 tsp (2.5 ml) salt

Culinary creation:

1. Cook the pasta according to the manufacturer's instructions, drain when ready and return to the cauldron. Add the remaining ingredients by stirring with a pair of tongs. Serve immediately.   * Adjust the ingredients accordingly for a pasta pack of another size.

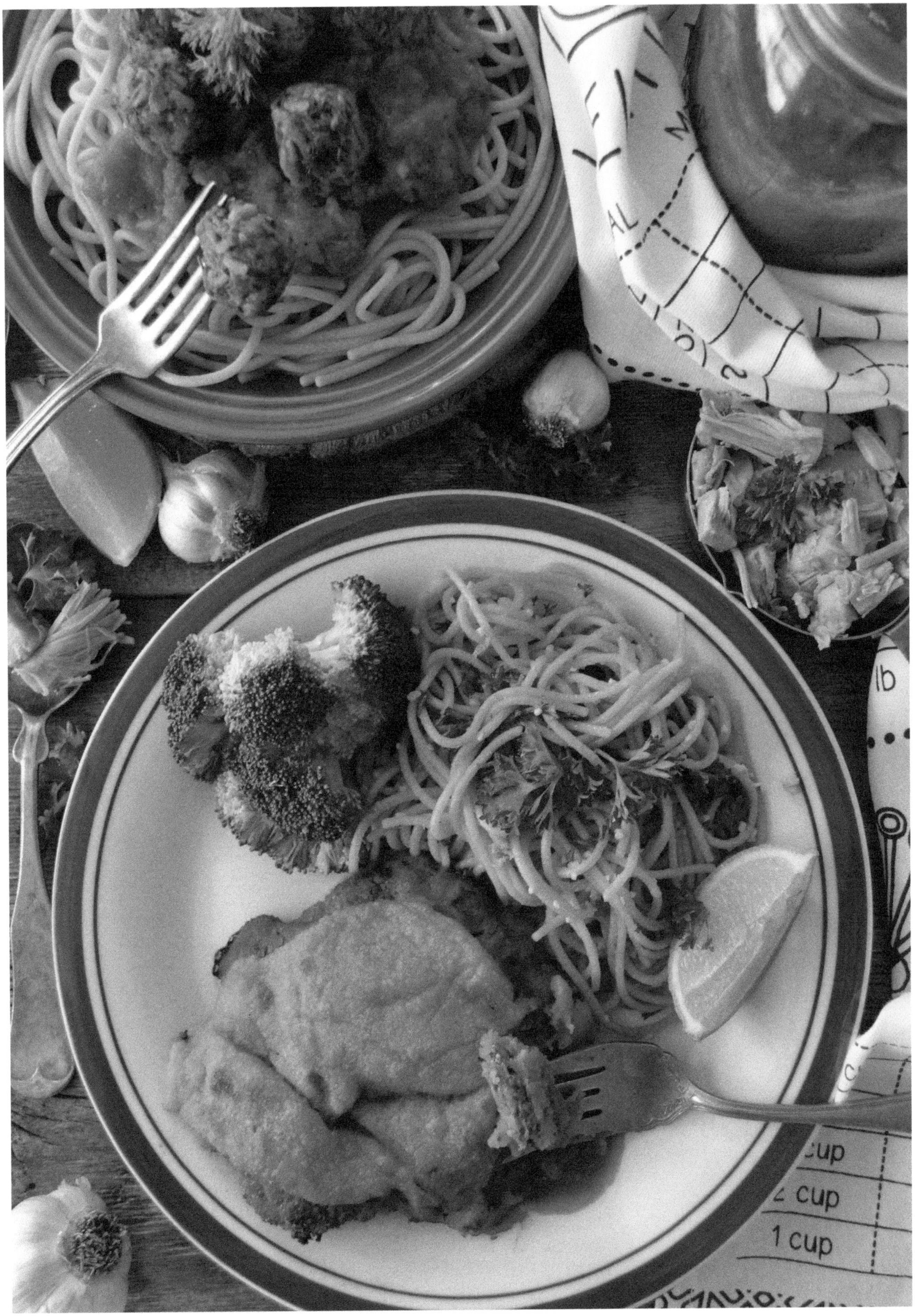
lb
cup
1 cup

These buns remind me so much of my childhood and especially family reunions where there was always a recipe of garnished breads! To enjoy alone, with family or friends, these breads garnished with jackfruit will transport you in a perfect atmosphere where the pleasure of taste is at the rendezvous!

BREAD GARNISHED WITH CHEESE & STEAK STYLE JACKFRUIT

- 2 x 14 oz (400 ml) cans of green jackfruit in water or brine, rinsed and drained (for a total of 500 g jackfruit)
- 1 large onion cut into cubes
- 1 tray of 227 g sliced mushrooms
- 2/3 cup (160 ml) water
- 3 tbsp (45 ml) Worcestershire sauce, recipe on page 46
- 1 tbsp (15 ml) minced garlic (3 cloves)

- 1 tbsp (15 ml) brown rice flour
- 1 tsp 1/2 (7.5 ml) of steak spices
- 1 tsp (5 ml) granulated or powdered garlic
- 1 tsp (5 ml) onion powder
- 1 tsp (5 ml) smoked paprika
- Salt and pepper to taste

Others
- 4 to 8 breads depending on size (4 GF hot dog breads or 8 GF breads)
- Mustard and/or vegan mayo, recipe on page 22, for spreading inside the breads
- 1 cup (250 ml) of vegan cheddar to spread or to toast, recipe hereinafter

Culinary creation:

1. Preheat oven to 350°F. Cut each piece of jackfruit into 3 or 4 pieces depending on their size. In a cauldron, bring water to a boil and cook the jackfruit for 30 minutes over medium high heat. Meanwhile, gather the spices and brown rice flour in a small dish, reserve.

2. When the jackfruit is ready, strain it and put it back in the cauldron. Use a potato masher or fork to loosen and pull almost all the jackfruit. Pour the vegan Worcestershire sauce over the jackfruit, mix and set aside.

3. In a skillet, heat a little oil and cook the onions and mushrooms until tender. Add oil as needed. When the vegetables are cooked, add the minced garlic and the prepared spices and cook another minute to bring out the flavor of the spices. Add water and the jackfruit, mix.

4. Heating up the jackfruit, spread some breads with vegan mayo and/or mustard and garnish each bread with jackfruit. Add 1 to 2 tablespoons (15 to 30 ml) of vegan cheddar on top of each bread. Place in a baking dish. Bake for 15 minutes and then grill to taste.

VEGAN CHEDDAR TO SPREAD OR TO TOAST

- 2 cups (500 ml) cubed potatoes
- 1 cup (250 ml) carrots cut into slices
- 2/3 cup (160 ml) nutritional yeast
- 1/2 cup (125 ml) avocado oil
- 2 tbsp (30 ml) tapioca flour
- 1 tsp (5 ml) salt
- 1/2 tsp (2.5 ml) onion powder
- 1/2 tsp (2.5 ml) granulated or powdered garlic
- 1/2 tsp (2.5 ml) smoked paprika

Culinary creation:

1. In a cauldron, bring water to a boil and cook the potatoes with the carrots until tender.

2. When the vegetables are cooked, drain and then add in a blender with the oil. Pulse until smooth, add remaining ingredients and pulse again. Refrigerate vegan cheddar when chilled. Can be stored about 7 to 10 days in the refrigerator.

FRIES "NOT TOO SPICY"

Recipe on page 63 in the section "Potatoes & Co"

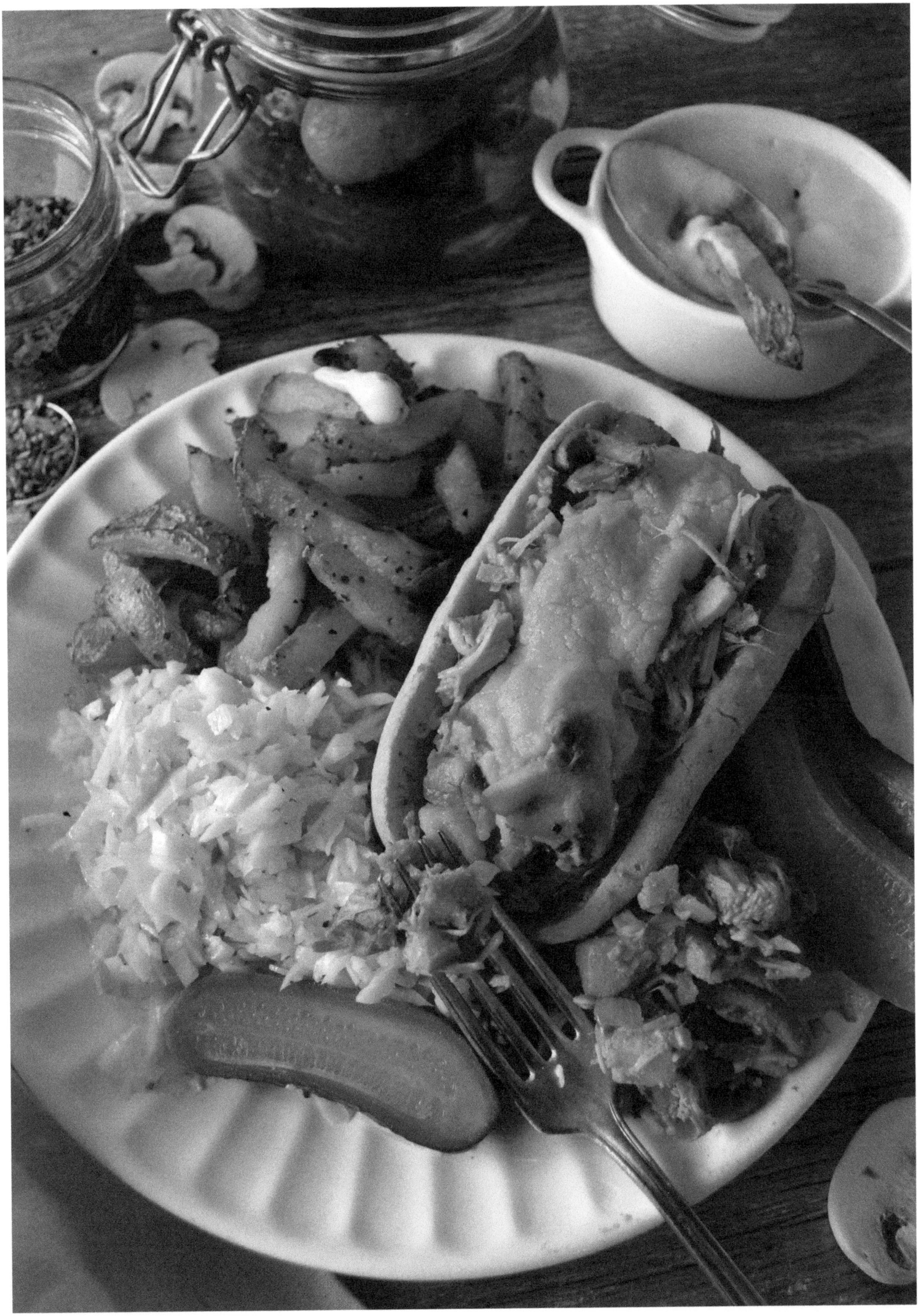

Here is a typical Quebec dish, one of the most traditional, that I had the great joy of "veganize" thanks to the jackfruit. This festive meal often cooked during Thanksgiving and Christmas celebrations can now go through the years to accompany you in small or big parties!

PIE OF YESTERYEAR WITH JACKFRUIT MEAT

- 2 pie crusts, recipe on page 48
- 2 x 14 oz (400 ml) cans of green jackfruit in water or brine, rinsed and drained (for a total of 500 g jackfruit)
- 2 chopped onions diced
- 2 medium potatoes cut into small cubes
- 1 cup 3/4 (430 ml) water
- 1/4 cup (60 ml) nutritional yeast
- 2 tbsp (30 ml) minced garlic (6 cloves)
- 2 tsp (10 ml) brown rice flour
- 2 tsp (10 ml) onion powder
- 1 tsp (5 ml) salt
- 1 tsp (5 ml) granulated or powdered garlic
- 1/2 tsp (2.5 ml) mustard powder
- 1/2 tsp (2.5 ml) oregano
- 1/2 tsp (2.5 ml) savory
- 1/2 tsp (2.5 ml) thyme
- 1/4 tsp (1.25 ml) nutmeg
- 1/4 tsp (1.25 ml) pepper
- 1/4 tsp (1.25 ml) sage (not ground)
- 1/8 tsp (0.625 ml) cinnamon
- 1/8 tsp (0.625 ml) ground clove

Culinary creation:

1. Prepare 2 pie crusts, recipe on page 48. Precook and prepare the jackfruit according to the basic method explained on page 12 and reserve. Meanwhile, in a small dish, combine all dry spices with salt, brown rice flour and nutritional yeast, mix to obtain a uniform spice mixture and set aside.

2. In a skillet with a little oil, sauté the onions for a few minutes. Then add the minced garlic and cook for another minute. Add a little oil to the onions and sprinkle half of the spices together, coat the onions well and cook a few more seconds to bring out the flavor of the spices.

3. Pour the water, bring to a boil and then decrease the intensity. Add the potatoes and the remaining spice mixture and simmer for a few minutes to reduce the liquid by half and precook the potatoes. Add the jackfruit and mix again. Let simmer 5 to 10 minutes more or until you see almost no liquid at the bottom of the pan.

4. Meanwhile, preheat oven to 350°F, spray avocado oil over a 9-inch pie plate and prepare the pie crust. For a pie crust made with the recipe on page 48, place a disc directly on a new plastic film about 12 x 20 inches (30 x 50 cm), well spread over the countertop. Place a parchment paper over the dough and roll with a rolling pin until you have a 12-inch diameter (30 cm) crust.

5. Gently remove the parchment and place the pie plate upside down on the dough. Use the corners of the plastic wrap by pasting them under the pie plate to turn the dough and pie plate at the same time. Turn the plate over and before removing it, remove the plastic film glued below it. Place the plate, push the dough into the plate, slide it inside and carefully remove the plastic wrap from the top of the dough. With your fingers and the remaining dough, repair any imperfections. Then pour the pie filling into the pie crust.

6. For the other crust, repeat the same procedure to roll the dough. But here, to turn the dough on the pie, place the pie plate on one side of the plastic wrap to prevent it from moving and lift the other side of the plastic wrap vertically back and forth fall on the pie. Remove the plastic wrap gently. Cut the excess dough, repair any imperfections and seal the crusts together with your fingers. Make small insertions with a knife to bring out the steam. Bake for 1 hour. Makes 6-8 servings. Serve with crushed potatoes, brown sauce and vegetables.

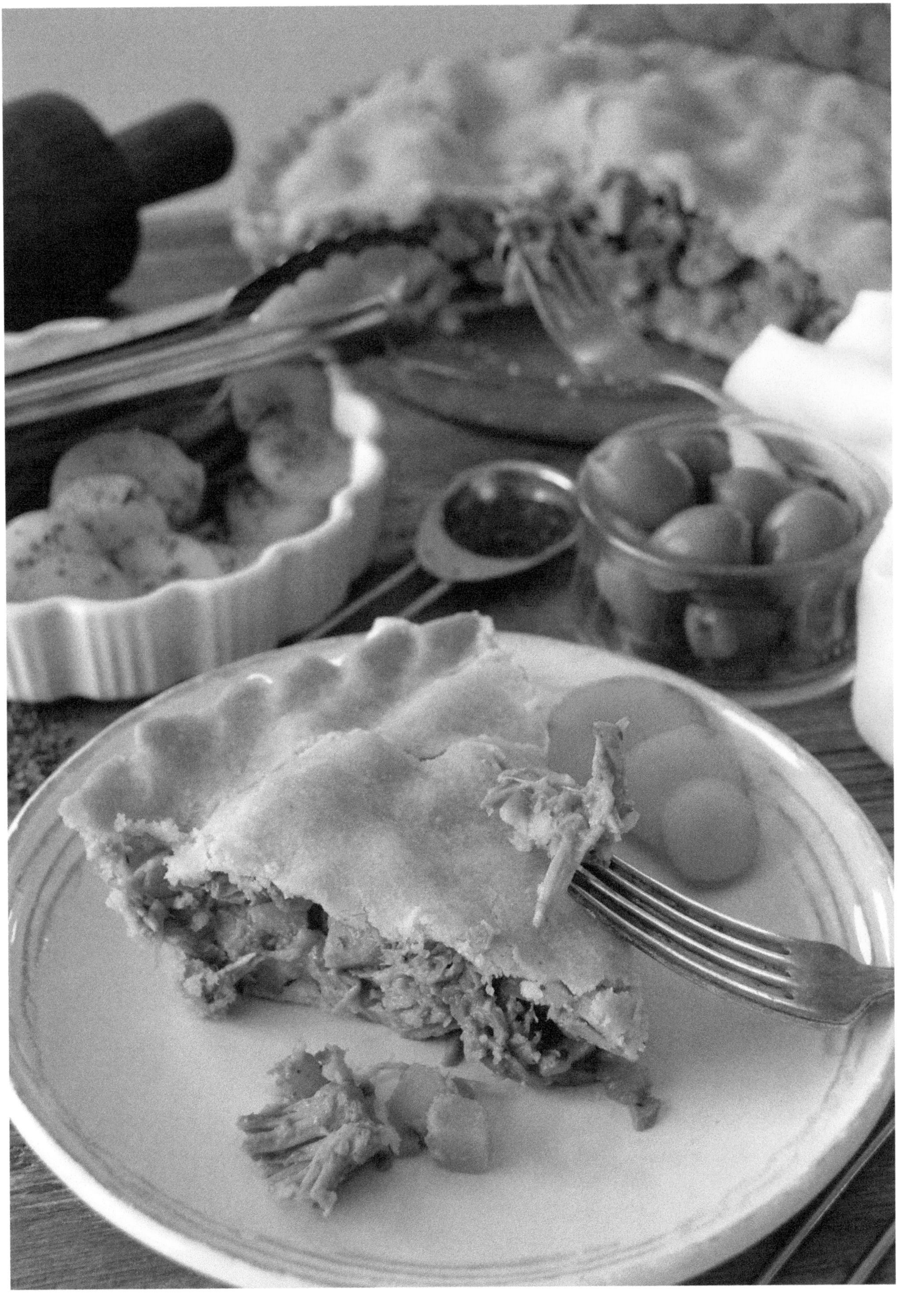

Because jackfruit is also perfect with pasta, why not give it a Mediterranean feel to enjoy it? Here is a delicious recipe with jackfruit, to put on the menu every week!

MEDITERRANEAN STYLE PASTA WITH JACKFRUIT

- 1 x 14 oz (400 ml) can of green jackfruit in water or brine, rinsed and drained (for a total of 250 g jackfruit)
- 1 x 28 oz (796 ml) diced tomatoes
- 2 chopped red onions
- 1 tray of 227 g mushrooms cut into wedges
- 1 red pepper cut into strips
- 1 x 14 oz (400 ml) drained and sliced artichokes
- 1/3 cup (80 ml) sun-dried tomatoes in oil cut into pieces
- 1/3 cup (80 ml) sliced Kalamata olives
- 2 cups (500 ml) coarsely chopped fresh spinach
- 1 tbsp (15 ml) minced garlic (3 cloves)
- 1 tbsp (15 ml) onion powder
- 1/2 tsp (2.5 ml) salt (more to taste)
- 1/2 tsp (2.5 ml) chili powder (more to the taste)
- 1/4 tsp (1.25 ml) Provence herbs
- 1 gluten free pasta box for 3-4 servings

Culinary creation:

1. Cut each piece of jackfruit into 3 or 4 pieces depending on their size. In a cauldron, bring water to a boil and cook the jackfruit for 30 minutes over medium high heat. Meanwhile, cut and prepare the vegetables and make the tomato sauce. To do this, in a blender or with a blender stand, reduce the diced tomatoes in a bowl with the onion powder, chili powder and salt, set aside.

2. When the jackfruit is ready, strain it and put it back in the cauldron. Use a potato masher or fork to loosen and pull almost all the jackfruit, set aside.

3. In a frying pan, sauté the onions, mushrooms and pepper until tender. Add minced garlic and Provence herbs, mix well.

4. Add the jackfruit, artichokes, sun-dried tomatoes, olives and tomato sauce, mix again. Simmer covered for about 10 minutes to let the flavors blend. Meanwhile, cook pasta. Before serving, finally incorporate the spinach in the preparation, salt and pepper to taste. Makes 3 to 4 servings.

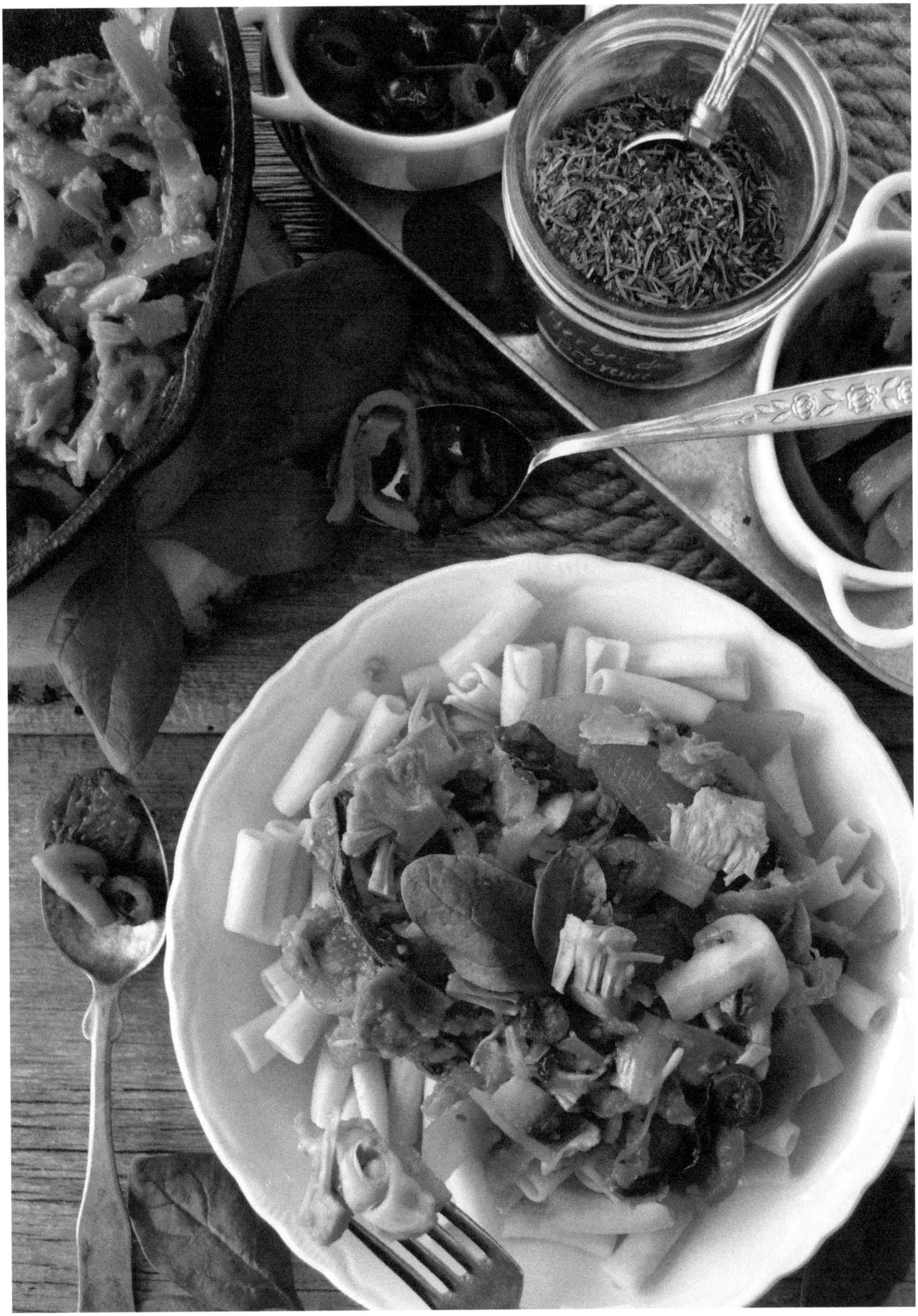

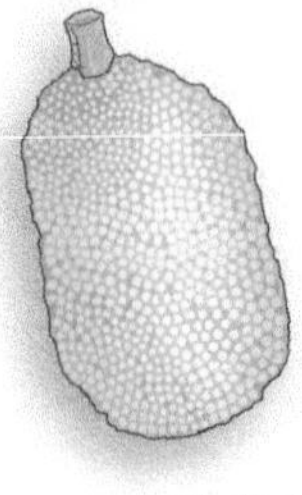

Whether served with rice, quinoa, buckwheat or lettuce to taste as in this recipe, the jackfruit poke bowl will quickly become a great ally to create perfect recipes to your taste!

POKE BOWL WITH JACKFRUIT SHAWARMA

Jackfruit shawarma

- 1 x 14 oz (400 ml) can of green jackfruit in water or brine, rinsed and drained (for a total of 250 g jackfruit)
- 2 tbsp (30 ml) avocado oil
- 2 tsp (10 ml) ground cumin
- 1/2 tsp (2.5 ml) granulated or powdered garlic
- 1/2 tsp (2.5 ml) ground ginger
- 1/2 tsp (2.5 ml) ground cinnamon
- 1/4 tsp (1.25 ml) ground cardamom
- 1/4 tsp (1.25 ml) pepper
- 1/4 tsp (1.25 ml) salt
- 1/8 tsp (0.625 ml) chili powder
- 1/8 tsp (0.625 ml) ground clove

Poke bowl (2 servings)

- 2 sliced Lebanese cucumbers
- 1 medium carrot cut in julienne
- 1 sliced avocado
- 1 tomato cut into wedges
- 1/2 chopped red pepper in strips
- 2 cups (500 ml) chopped fresh spinach
- 2/3 cup (160 ml) grated red cabbage
- 1/2 cup (125 ml) minced fresh parsley
- Choice of sprouts
- Mixed salad or other such as wild or brown rice, buckwheat, quinoa, to fill the bottom of the bowls

Culinary creation:

1. Cut each piece of jackfruit into 3 or 4 pieces depending on their size. In a cauldron, bring water to a boil and cook the jackfruit for 30 minutes over medium high heat. Meanwhile, cut and prepare the vegetables, gather all the spices of the jackfruit shawarma in a small dish and make the Lebanese lemon tahini sauce, recipe below, reserve.

2. When the jackfruit is ready, strain it and put it back in the cauldron. Use a potato masher or fork to loosen and pull almost all the jackfruit. Add oil and spices and mix well.

3. In a skillet, heat a little oil and pour the jackfruit into it. Over medium low heat, dry and crisp the jackfruit for about 20 minutes, stirring occasionally. Meanwhile, prepare the bowls with the vegetables by spreading the ingredients of the poke bowl in 2 bowls.

4. When the jackfruit has the desired texture, i.e. crisp and/or with a drier effect, spread it in the 2 bowls. To taste, serve Lebanese lemon tahini sauce on the jackfruit shawarma only or on the whole poke bowl.

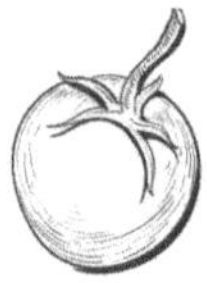

Variation: Use your favorite jackfruit recipe and raw vegetables to taste to create each time a new poke bowl, something to create a new delight, yum!

LEBANESE LEMON TAHINI SAUCE

- 2/3 cup (160 ml) unsweetened plant-based milk
- 2 tbsp + 1 tsp (35 ml) freshly squeezed lemon juice
- 2 tbsp (30 ml) minced garlic (6 cloves)
- 2 tbsp (30 ml) of tahini
- 1 tbsp (15 ml) nutritional yeast
- 1/4 tsp (1.25 ml) salt
- 1/8 tsp (0.625 ml) xanthan gum
- Pepper to taste

Culinary creation:

1. In a blender, add all ingredients and pulse until smooth and thick. Refrigerate. Can be kept 7 to 10 days in the refrigerator.

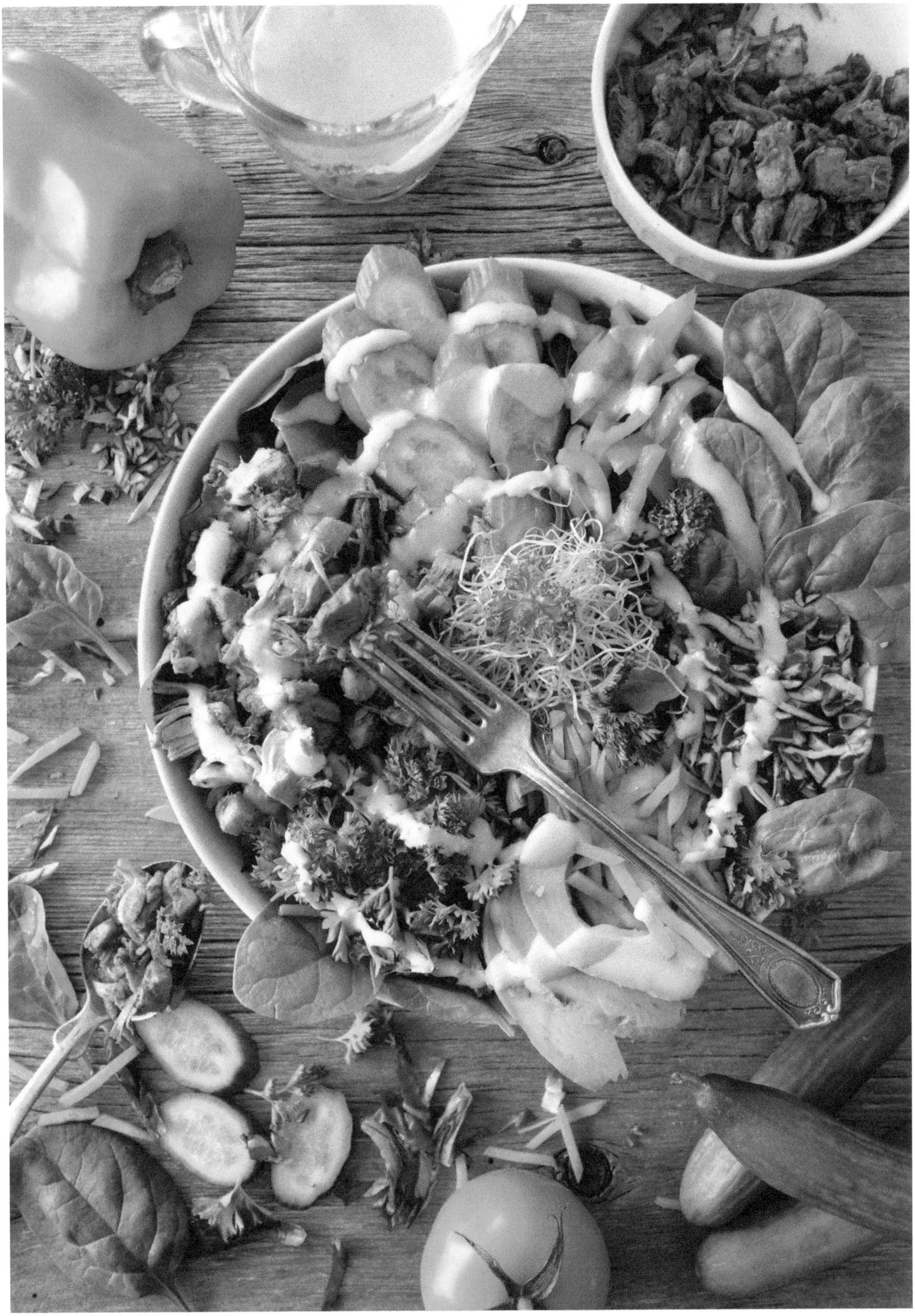

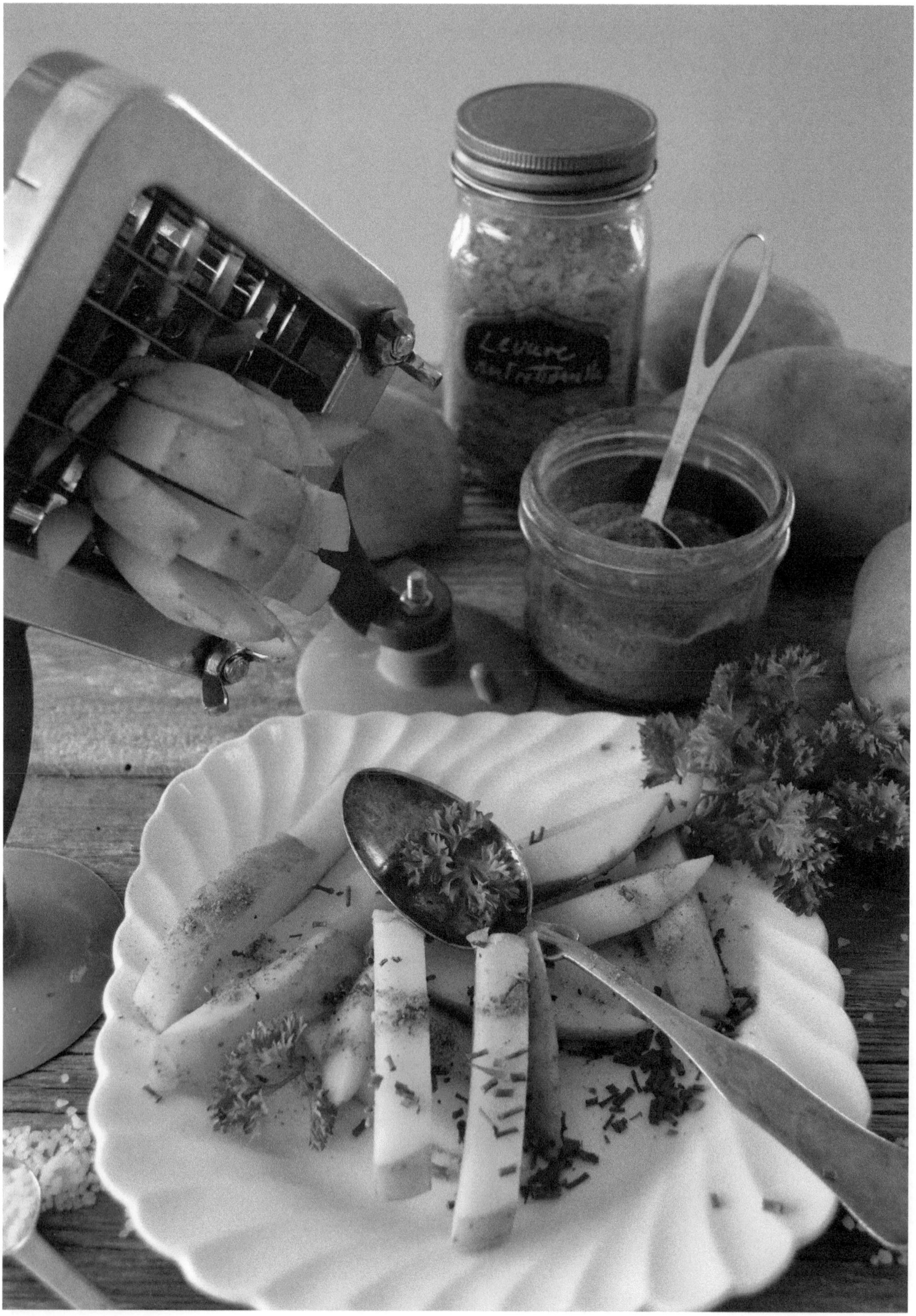
Levure

I am happy to present you my potato recipes that I have made over time! Here you will find recipes where the taste and texture are at the rendezvous. Everything is designed with a method that reduces the amount of oil used and ensure that the potatoes do not stick during cooking!

POTATOES & CO

GARLIC CUBES

- 8 cups (2000 ml) potatoes cut into thin cubes, peeled or not
- 2 tbsp (30 ml) avocado oil
- 2 tbsp (30 ml) freshly squeezed lemon juice
- 2 tbsp (30 ml) minced garlic (3 to 6 pods)
- 4 tsp (20 ml) granulated or powdered garlic
- 2 tsp (10 ml) onion powder
- 1 tsp (5 ml) salt
- Chopped parsley and lemon drizzle for serving (optional)

Culinary creation:

1. Preheat oven to 425°F. Place a parchment paper on a large baking sheet.

2. In a large pot, boil enough water to cover the potatoes. When the water boils, dip the potatoes and cook for about 3 to 4 minutes, starting to count the time when the water boils again. Here, we must especially remove them when a fork can start to fit in the cubes, but without breaking them.

3. After the cooking time, drain the cubes and put them back in the cauldron. Pour the oil and lemon juice everywhere on the potatoes while mixing with a large serving spoon to distribute. While continuing to mix, sprinkle the spices to distribute them evenly. Transfer to parchment and bake for about 45 min or more to taste, stirring 2 or 3 times during this time.

GARLIC CUBES potatoes are served with the following recipe:
- Shish taouk jackfruit plate on page 20

FRIES "NOT TOO SPICY"

- 12 cups (3000 ml) potatoes cut into French fries
- 1/4 cup (60 ml) avocado oil
- 1 tsp (5 ml) chili powder
- 3/4 tsp (3.75 ml) salt (more to taste)
- 3/4 tsp (3.75 ml) paprika
- 1/2 tsp (2.5 ml) ground cumin
- 1/4 tsp (1.25 ml) granulated or powdered garlic
- 1/4 tsp (1.25 ml) onion powder
- 1/4 tsp (1.25 ml) dried oregano
- 1/4 tsp (1.25 ml) ground black pepper

Culinary creation:

1. Preheat oven to 425°F. Place a parchment paper on a very large baking sheet. In a small dish, gather the spices, reserve.

2. In a large cauldron, boil enough water to cover the potatoes. When the water boils, dip the potatoes and cook for about 3 to 4 minutes, starting to count the time when the water starts to boil again. Here, we must especially remove the potatoes when a fork can begin to fit into the fries, but without breaking them.

3. After the cooking time, drain the fries and put them back in the cauldron. Pour the oil all over the potatoes while mixing with a large serving spoon to distribute it. While continuing to mix, sprinkle the spices and the salt to distribute them evenly on the potatoes. Transfer to the parchment and bake for about 45 minutes to 1 hour stirring fries 2 or 3 times during this time.

The FRIES "NOT TOO SPICY" potatoes are served with the following recipe:
- Bread garnished with cheese steak style jackfruit on page 54

FRITTERS STYLE CAKE

- 8 cups (2000 ml) grated potatoes
- 1 cup (250 ml) nutritional yeast
- 1/4 cup (60 ml) avocado oil
- 1/4 cup (60 ml) brown rice flour
- 3 tbsp (45 ml) onion powder
- 1 tbsp (15 ml) chopped fresh chives
- 1 tsp 1/4 (6.25 ml) salt
- 1/2 tsp (2.5 ml) pepper

Culinary creation:

1. Preheat oven to 425°F. Place a parchment paper on a large baking sheet.

2. Grate potatoes to get 8 cups, do not drip. Add to a bowl with all ingredients and mix to obtain a homogeneous mixture. With the equivalent of 1/4 cup (60 ml) of preparation, shape patties by hand by compacting them well to remove the excess liquid. Bake for 30 minutes, turning halfway through cooking. Makes 16 cakes.

The FRITTERS STYLE CAKE potatoes are served with the following recipe:
- Ribs of jackfruit BBQ on page 72

PEELS AU GRATIN

- 4 large elongated potatoes (about 1 kg)
- 2 sliced green onions
- 1/2 tsp (2.5 ml) onion powder
- 1/4 tsp (1.25 ml) salt
- 1/4 tsp (1.25 ml) smoked paprika
- 1 cup (250 ml) vegan cheddar to spread or toast, recipe on page 54
- 1/4 cup (60 ml) remaining jackfruit bacon, recipe on page 22 (optional)
- Vegan sour cream to taste, recipe on page 72

Culinary creation:

1. Preheat oven to 425°F. Place a parchment paper on a baking sheet.

2. Wash the potatoes, preserve the peel and make a long and deep incision in each potato lengthwise without cutting into 2. Wrap the potatoes in one large parchment paper as a papillote. Bake for 45 minutes directly on the grill. Omit this step if microwave cooking.

3. In a small dish, combine salt, onion powder and smoked paprika and set aside.

4. When the cooking time is complete, cut each potato in half and remove some potato to make a well. Sprinkle spices all over the potatoes, add the jackfruit bacon if desired and cover the surface with 1 to 2 tablespoons (15 to 30 ml) of vegan cheddar.

5. Bake for 15 minutes and grill for about 5 to 10 minutes to brown the vegan cheddar. Add green onions to serve and enjoy with vegan sour cream.

The PEELS AU GRATIN are served with the following recipe:
- Jackfruit roast beef blade style on page 74

CHEESE FLAVORED CRUSHED POTATOES

- 10 cups (2500 ml) peeled and cut yellow potatoes
- 1/4 cup (60 ml) avocado oil
- 1/4 cup (60 ml) water
- 1/4 cup (60 ml) nutritional yeast
- 1 tbsp (15 ml) minced garlic (3 cloves)
- 1 tbsp (15 ml) onion powder
- 1 tsp 1/2 (7.5 ml) salt

Culinary creation:

1. In a large cauldron, cook the potatoes in boiling water and drain when they are tender. Then crush and add the rest of the ingredients while mixing with the spatula.

The CHEESE FLAVORED CRUSHED POTATOES are served with the following recipe:
- Pulled jackfruit turkey-style on page 30

SEASONED QUARTERS

- 10 cups (2500 ml) potatoes quartered with peel (about 1.7 kilo)
- 3 tbsp (45 ml) avocado oil
- 1 tbsp (15 ml) paprika
- 1 tbsp (15 ml) onion powder
- 1 tsp (5 ml) granulated or powdered garlic
- 1 tsp (5 ml) salt
- 1/2 tsp (2.5 ml) chili powder

Culinary creation:

1. Preheat oven to 425°F. Place a parchment paper on a very large baking sheet. In a small dish, gather the spices, reserve.

2. In a large pot, boil enough water to cover the potatoes. When the water boils, dip the potatoes and cook for about 8 to 10 minutes, starting to count the time when the water starts to boil again. Here, we must especially remove the potatoes when a fork can begin to insert in the quarters, but without breaking them.

3. After the cooking time, drain the quarters and return them to the cauldron. Pour the oil all over the potatoes while mixing with a large serving spoon to distribute it. While continuing to mix, sprinkle the spices to evenly distribute them on the potatoes. Transfer to the parchment and bake for about 45 minutes to 1 hour, turning quarters 2 or 3 times during this time.

THE SEASONED QUARTERS are served with the following recipe:

- Greek-style jackfruit on gyros on page 38

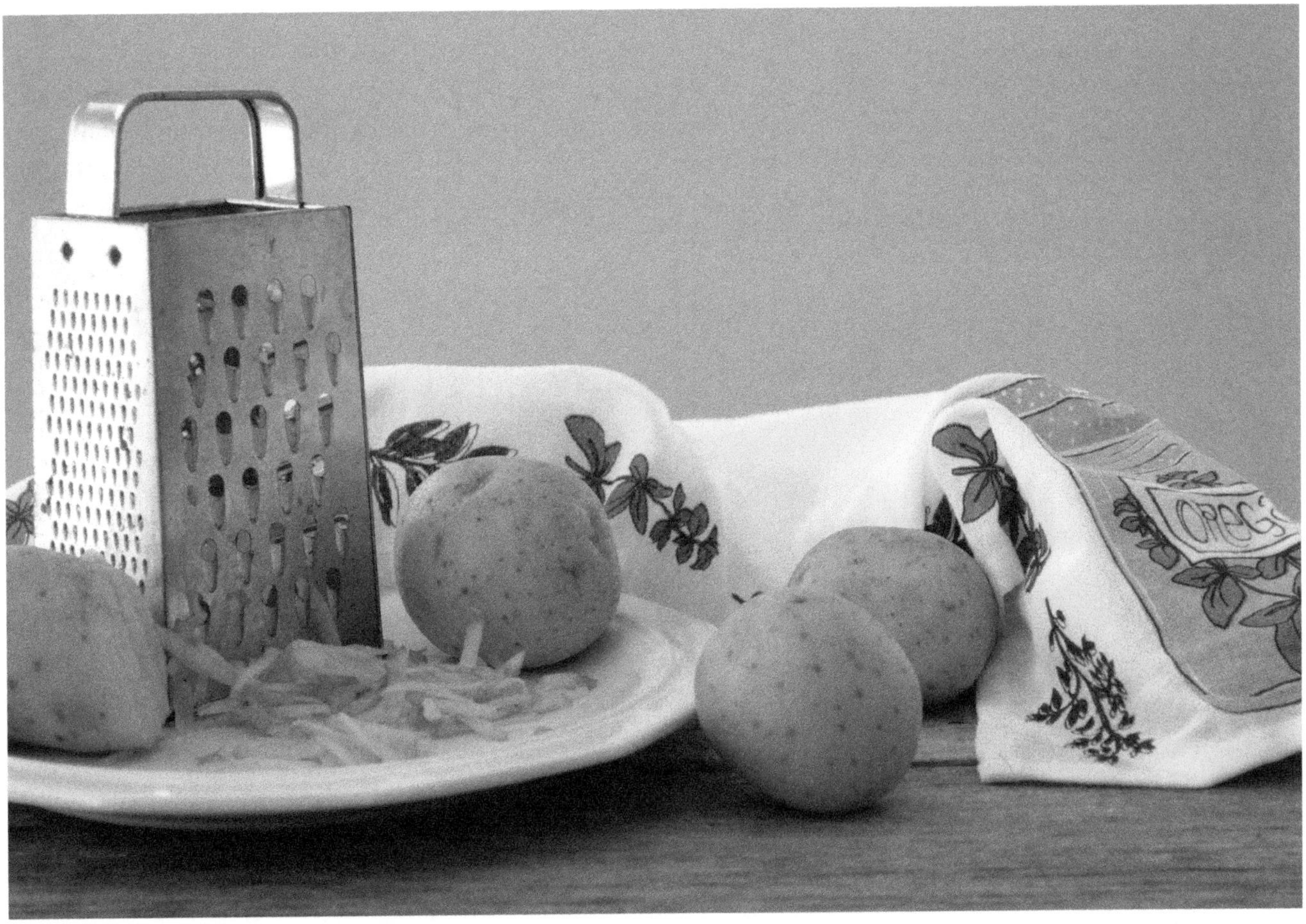
OREG

Whether you're the sauce type or not, or you simply choose the ketchup, mayonnaise or mustard to enjoy this recipe of jackfruit popcorn that will remind you of fried chicken so well, it's a safe bet that you will not be able resist it ... Another recipe to feast on!

FRIED CHICKEN STYLE JACKFRUIT POPCORN

Fried chicken style jackfruit

- 2 x 14 oz (400 ml) cans of green jackfruit in water or brine, rinsed and drained (for a total of 500 g jackfruit)
- 2 tbsp (30 ml) avocado oil
- 1 tsp (5 ml) smoked paprika
- 1/2 tsp (2.5 ml) onion powder
- 1/2 tsp (2.5 ml) granulated or powdered garlic
- 1/2 tsp (2.5 ml) salt
- 1/4 tsp (1.25 ml) thyme
- 1/4 tsp (1.25 ml) oregano
- 1/4 tsp (1.25 ml) chili powder
- 1/4 tsp (1.25 ml) black pepper

For the coating

- 1 cup 1/4 (310 ml) brown rice flour (to flour)
- 1 cup 1/4 (310 ml) brown rice flour
- 1 cup (250 ml) water
- 2 tsp (10 ml) onion powder
- 1 tsp (5 ml) granulated or powdered garlic
- 1/2 tsp (2.5 ml) salt
- 1/4 tsp (1.25 ml) pepper

Culinary creation:

1. Preheat oven to 300°F. Cut each piece of jackfruit into 2 pieces according to their size keeping the base that holds them together. In a cauldron, bring water to a boil and cook the jackfruit for 30 minutes over medium high heat. Meanwhile, gather the jackfruit spices in a small dish, set aside.

2. When the jackfruit is ready, strain it and pour it into a bowl. Here, we keep the whole jackfruit, we do not undo it to pull it. Add the oil and spices, sprinkling while mixing to coat, reserve to let the flavors enter the jackfruit.

3. Meanwhile, prepare 2 dishes or bowls for coating. In a first bowl, add the cup and 1/4 (310 ml) brown rice flour, onion and garlic powder, salt and pepper. Add water to this mixture and whisk until smooth, reserve at least 5 minutes before using to allow to thicken. In another bowl, add the other amount of brown rice flour that will serve to flour the jackfruit, reserve.

4. Use tongs to coat each piece in the liquid preparation first and then in the flour alone to completely coat with flour. Place each piece on a plate, while preparing all the pieces.

5. In a pot or pan, add enough oil to cover the jackfruit pieces, at least 3/4 inch (1 to 2 cm) high and heat the oil. Check that the oil is hot enough by dropping a small amount of dough into the pan. If it sizzles, the oil is ready for the jackfruit.

6. With a metal utensil, place the jackfruit pieces in the oil one by one and cook for 30 seconds on each side or until crisp and golden. Then put on a cloth to absorb the excess oil and keep in the oven while cooking the rest of the pieces. Serve immediately with your favorite sauce or mayo!

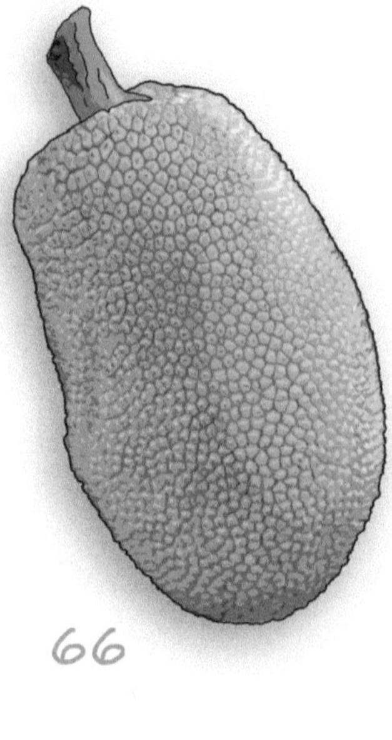

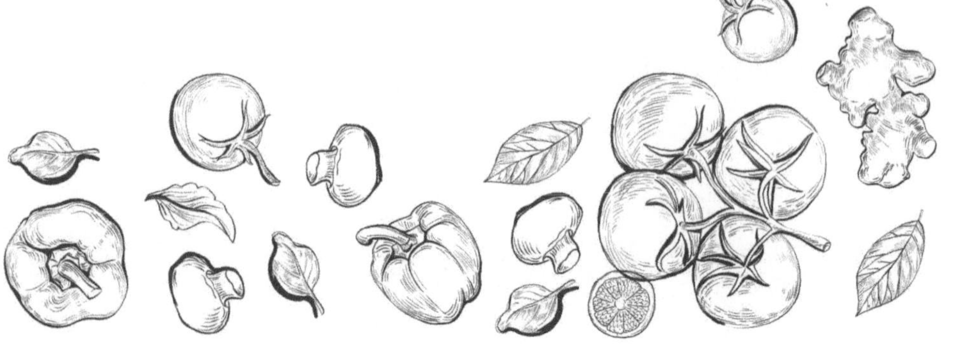

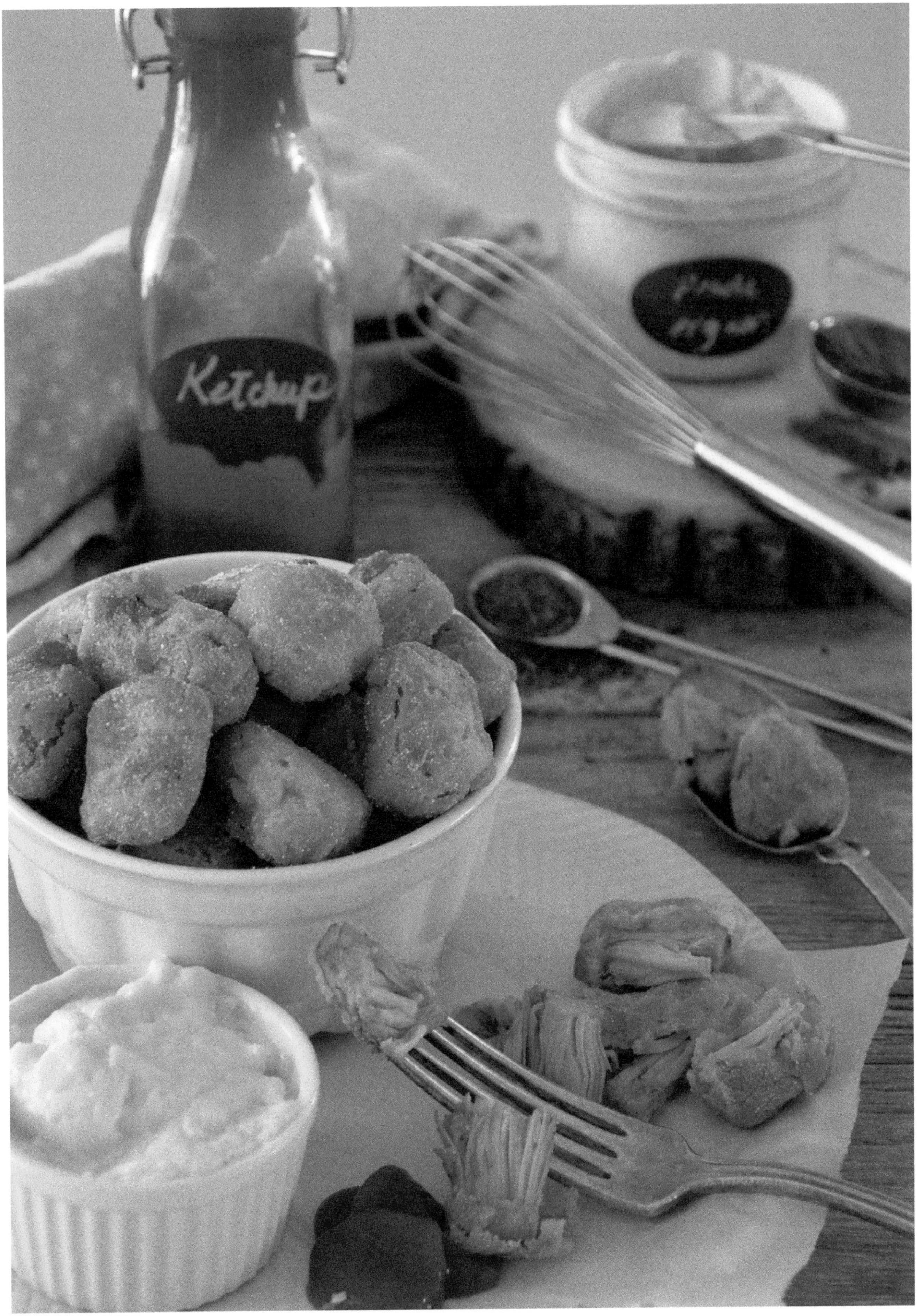
Ketchup

A traditional dish that warms the hearts is always welcome! Here is the traditional jackfruit stew that is most appreciated for its taste of yesteryear, its generous sauce and also because it perfectly accompanies pasta, potatoes, rice, quinoa or buckwheat. To savor all year long!

TRADITIONAL STEW WITH JACKFRUIT

- 1 x 14 oz (400 ml) can of green jackfruit in water or brine, rinsed and drained * (for a total of 250 g jackfruit)
- 2 red onions, diced
- 1 tray of 227 g sliced mushrooms
- 2 chopped celery stalks
- 2 sliced carrots
- 1 cup (250 ml) chopped turnip cubes
- 4 cups (1000 ml) water
- 1/3 cup (80 ml) nutritional yeast
- 2 tbsp (30 ml) balsamic vinegar
- 2 tbsp (30 ml) brown rice flour
- 1 tbsp (15 ml) minced garlic (3 cloves)
- 1 tsp 1/2 (7.5 ml) salt (more to taste)
- 1 tsp (5 ml) marjoram
- 1 tsp (5 ml) sage (not ground)
- 1/2 tsp (2.5 ml) thyme
- 1/2 tsp (2.5 ml) rosemary powder
- Pepper to taste

Culinary creation:

1. Preheat oven to 400°F. Prepare the jackfruit by rinsing, draining and cutting each piece of jackfruit into 3 to 4 pieces, set aside.

2. In a casserole (or in a large skillet if you are using a 9 x 13-inch baking dish after), sauté the onions, mushrooms and celery in a little oil for a few minutes. Add oil as needed. Meanwhile, combine the brown rice flour, salt, marjoram, sage, thyme and rosemary in a small dish, set aside.

3. When the vegetables are tender, add the minced garlic and spices, mix and cook for 30 seconds, enough time to bring out the flavor of the spices. Deglaze with the balsamic vinegar, add the water and remaining ingredients. Bring to a boil.

4. Cover and bake for about 1 hour 30 minutes, taking care, halfway through cooking, to pull the jackfruit as desired. Serve with pasta, rice, quinoa or crushed potatoes, recipe on page 63. Makes 4 servings.

* Note: It is not necessary to precook the jackfruit in this recipe, but it is possible to do it according to the basic method on page 12 to reduce the cooking time which is quite long.

Variation: Make a great jackfruit shepherd's pie by adding a second can of jackfruit to this recipe and baking for 1 hour in a 9 x 13-inch dish. Pull the jackfruit then remove the excess liquid and add crushed potatoes on top of the mixture. Bake for another 30 minutes and enjoy, yum!

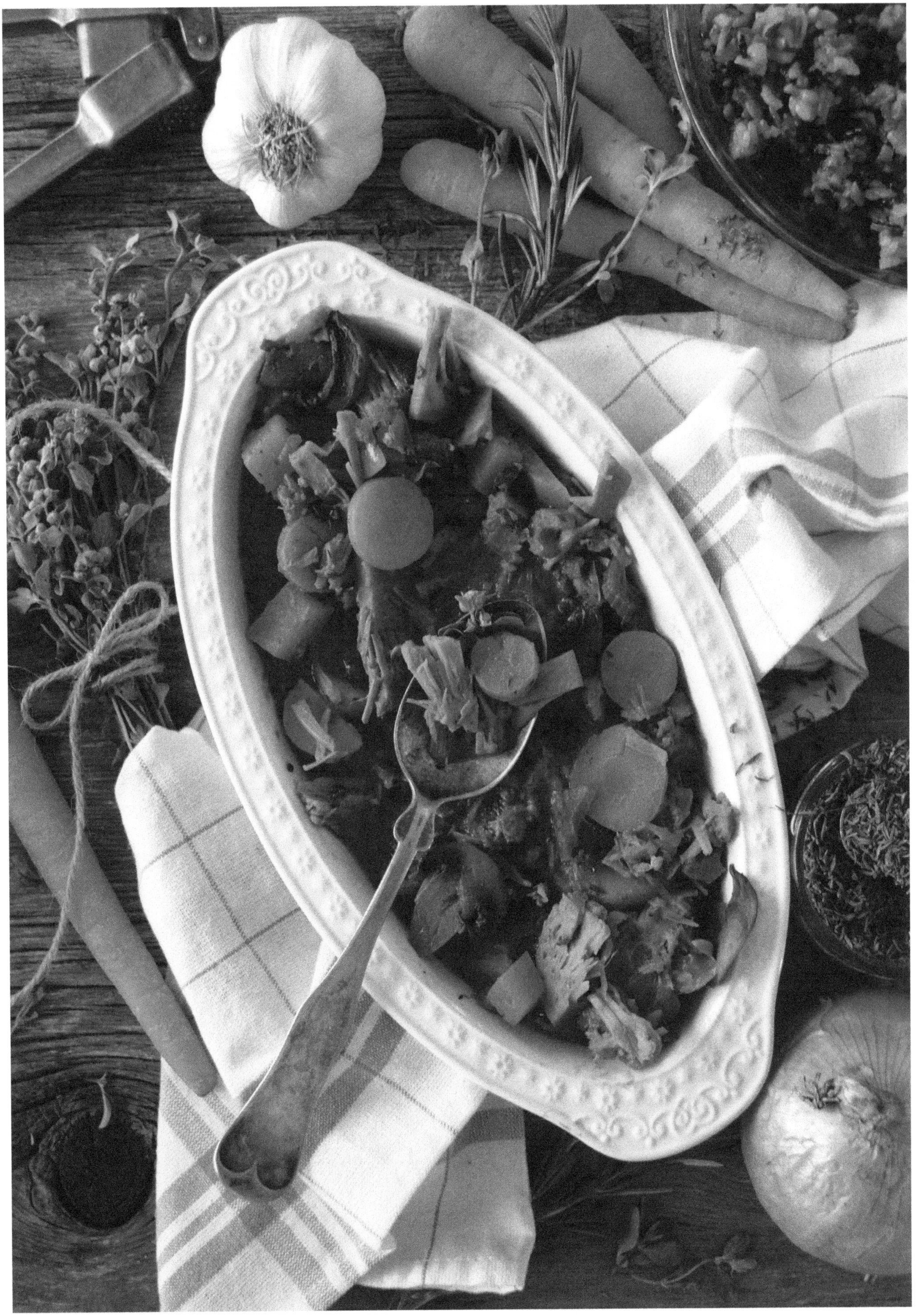

Here is one of my favorite dishes that I had the chance to "veganize" with the jackfruit, the quesadillas treat of jackfruit! What's more wonderful than finding, vegan way, the perfect taste of this classic! Only to close your eyes to savor and everything is there!

QUESADILLAS TREAT OF JACKFRUIT

Jackfruit chicken
- 2 x 14 oz (400 ml) cans of green jackfruit in water or brine, rinsed and drained (for a total of 500 g of jackfruit)
- 1/4 cup (60 ml) nutritional yeast
- 2 tbsp (30 ml) avocado oil
- 2 tsp (10 ml) onion powder
- 2 tsp (10 ml) granulated or powdered garlic
- 1/2 tsp (2.5 ml) salt

Quesadillas
- 4 tortillas, recipe on page 48
- Vegan cheddar to spread or toast, recipe on page 54
- 1/2 cup (125 ml) sliced black olives
- 4 minced green onions
- Salsa of the market to taste
- Guacamole if desired, recipe below

Culinary creation:

1. Cut each piece of jackfruit into 3 or 4 pieces depending on their size. In a cauldron, bring water to a boil and cook the jackfruit for 30 minutes over medium high heat. Meanwhile, gather the spices and nutritional yeast in a small dish, set aside.

2. When the cooking time has finished, drain the jackfruit and put it back in the cauldron. Use a potato masher or fork to loosen and pull the jackfruit. Then add spices, nutritional yeast and avocado oil by sprinkling and mixing well to coat.

3. Pour the jackfruit into a pan and a little oil. While preparing the remaining ingredients, adjust cooking over low heat to dry and crisp the jackfruit for about 20 minutes, stirring occasionally. When the jackfruit has a drier appearance, it is ready.

4. Make quesadillas by first spreading vegan cheddar on each tortilla over the entire surface (or vegan grated cheese only on half of the surface). Transfer to a skillet over low heat and garnish. First, add about 1/3 cup (80 ml) of jackfruit on only half of the tortilla. To taste, add black olives, green onions and about 2 tablespoons (30 ml) salsa (and if vegan grated cheese is used, finish with this over salsa).

5. Close the quesadilla in 2 and cook on low heat in the pan for 1 to 2 minutes on each side. Cut in 2 to serve. Repeat for each quesadilla. Serve with guacamole if desired. Makes about 4 quesadillas.

EASY GUACAMOLE

- 3 big avocados
- 1/4 tsp (1.25 ml) ground cumin
- 1/4 tsp (1.25 ml) onion powder
- 1/4 tsp (1.25 ml) ground cilantro
- 1/4 tsp (1.25 ml) pepper
- 1/8 tsp (0.625 ml) salt (more to the taste)
- A drizzle of lime or lemon juice to taste (optional)

Culinary creation:

1. In a bowl, crush the avocados and add the remaining ingredients. Mix well and serve immediately.

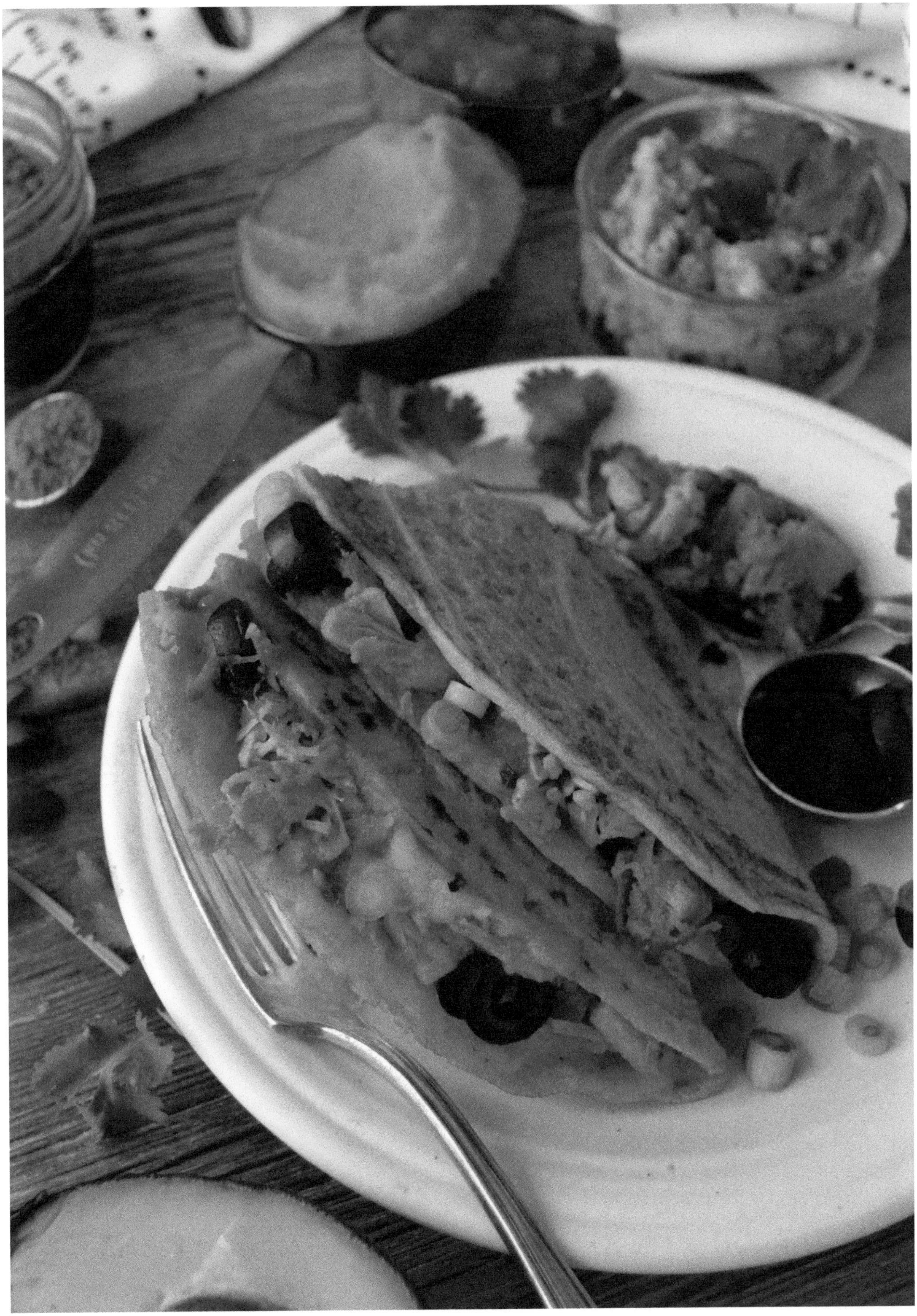

When you can eat with your hands, it's a treat! You will be doubly served here with these ribs of jackfruit BBQ which are accompanied by two other recipes that are also eaten with the hands. Everything to ask again and again!

RIBS OF JACKFRUIT BBQ

- 2 x 14 oz (400 ml) cans of green jackfruit in water or brine, rinsed and drained (for a total of 500 g jackfruit)
- 1 cup (250 ml) vegan BBQ sauce, recipe on page 80
- 1 cup (250 ml) brown rice already cooked
- 1/3 cup (80 ml) potato starch
- 1/3 cup (80 ml) nutritional yeast
- 2 tbsp (30 ml) ground flaxseed

- 2 tbsp (30 ml) chia seeds
- 1 tbsp (15 ml) minced garlic (3 cloves)
- 1 tbsp (15 ml) smoked paprika
- 1 tbsp (15 ml) onion powder
- 2 tsp (10 ml) liquid smoke
- 1 tsp (5 ml) granulated or powdered garlic
- 3/4 tsp (3.75 ml) salt

Culinary creation:

1. Precook and prepare the jackfruit according to the basic method explained on page 12, then reserve to let cool. Meanwhile, in a blender or coffee grinder, grind the chia seeds and gather in a bowl with remaining ingredients except BBQ sauce, mix and set aside.

2. Preheat oven to 425°F and place a parchment in a 9 x 13-inch baking dish. When the jackfruit is cooled a little, cut it finely on a cutting board with a large knife.

3. Add the jackfruit in the bowl with remaining ingredients, mix well. By hand, knead and compact the entire mixture until a large ball is formed. Divide mixture into 2 and using plastic wrap or parchment paper, form 2 rectangles approximately 9 x 4 inches by 3/4 inch high (22 x 10 x 2 cm) by hand. Before placing in the dish, spread 1 tablespoon (15 ml) BBQ sauce on one side of each rectangle that will become the bottom, place in the dish using the parchment to transfer it.

4. With a knife, draw 8 to 10 lines on each rectangle to create a "ribs" effect without cutting the ribs. Then spread 2 to 3 tablespoons of BBQ sauce on top and sides, reserve the rest for basting before serving or dipping the ribs.

5. For a glaze effect, cover and bake for 35 minutes. For a drier effect, cover, bake for 20 minutes and then cook uncovered for 15 minutes. To serve, cut the ribs of jackfruit with the knife following the lines drawn and if desired, baste to taste with the remaining sauce. Makes 3 to 4 servings.

WESTERN CABBAGE SALAD

- 3 cups (750 ml) grated green cabbage
- 1 dill pickle cut into slices with a mandolin
- 1/3 cup (80 ml) chopped fresh parsley
- 2 tbsp (30 ml) avocado oil

- 1/2 tsp (2.5 ml) maple syrup
- 1/4 tsp (1.25 ml) apple cider vinegar
- Salt and pepper to taste

Culinary creation:

1. In a bowl, mix all ingredients, salt, pepper to taste and serve.

VEGAN SOUR CREAM

- 1/2 cup (125 ml) reduced fat coconut milk
- 1/4 cup (60 ml) avocado oil
- 1 tbsp (15 ml) nutritional yeast
- 1 tbsp (15 ml) lemon juice

- 1 tbsp (15 ml) apple cider vinegar
- 1/8 tsp (0.625 ml) salt
- 1/8 tsp (0.625 ml) xanthan gum

Culinary creation:

1. In a large measuring cup, pulse with a blender stand for 30 seconds all ingredients except oil and xanthan gum. Then, still blending, add the oil in a thin stream followed by the xanthan gum. Pulse until the cream has a little thickened. Refrigerate at least 1 hour before serving. Can be kept 7 days in the refrigerator.

FRITTERS STYLE CAKE

Recipe on page 64 in the section "Potatoes & Co"

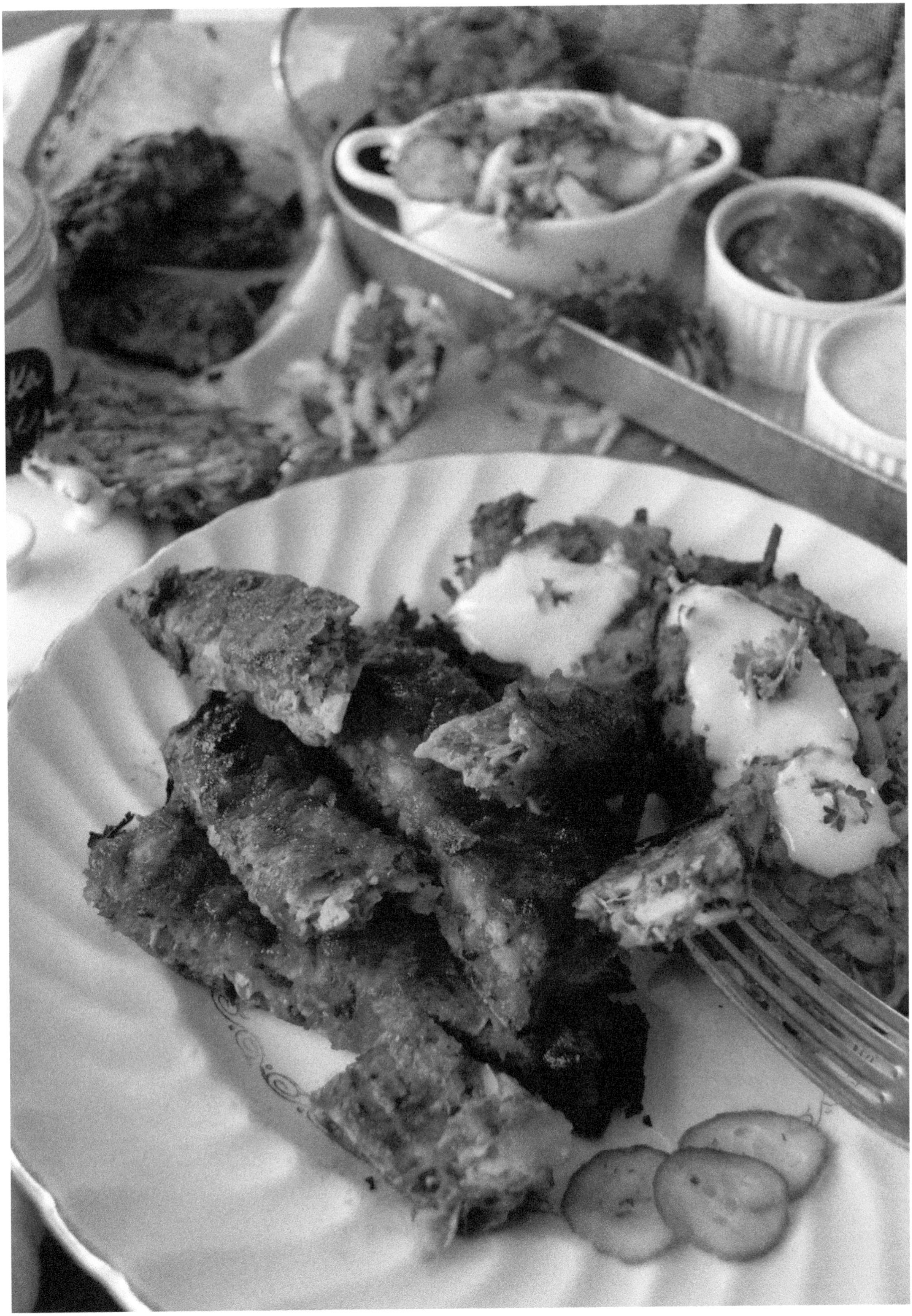

Here is a dish where the jackfruit is quite reminiscent of the blade roast! This dish that warms the heart will be enjoyed quickly with the brown sauce and peels au gratin that accompany it. Perfect for long cold winter evenings and why not at all times too!

JACKFRUIT ROAST BEEF BLADE STYLE

- 3 x 14 oz (400 ml) cans of green jackfruit in water or brine, rinsed and drained * (for a total of 750 g jackfruit)
- 2 onions cut into strips
- 5 cups (1250 ml) water
- 1/3 cup (80 ml) dehydrated onions
- 1/4 cup (60 ml) nutritional yeast

- 1/4 cup (60 ml) soy-like sauce, recipe on page 44
- 1 tbsp (15 ml) coconut sugar
- 2 tsp (10 ml) onion powder
- 2 tsp (10 ml) granulated or powdered garlic
- 1 tsp (5 ml) balsamic vinegar
- 1/4 tsp (1.25 ml) salt

Culinary creation:

1. Preheat oven to 400°F. Prepare the jackfruit by rinsing, draining and cutting into 2 to 3 pieces, set aside.

2. In a casserole (or in a large skillet if you are using a 9 x 13-inch baking dish after), sauté the onions in a little oil for a few minutes. Add oil as needed.

3. When the onions are tender, add the jackfruit and sprinkle the onion and garlic powder all over, mixing to distribute them. Cook for 30 seconds, time to bring out the flavor of the spices. Deglaze with water and balsamic vinegar, add remaining ingredients. Bring to a boil.

4. Cover and bake for 1 hour. Then use a fork or potato masher to loosen and pull the jackfruit. Cook another 30 minutes. If desired, serve with vegan brown sauce on pasta, rice, quinoa or potatoes of your choice. Makes 4 servings.

* Note: It is not necessary to precook the jackfruit in this recipe, but it is possible to do it according to the basic method on page 12 to decrease the cooking time which is quite long.

VEGAN BROWN SAUCE

- 2 cups (500 ml) water
- 1/4 cup (60 ml) brown rice flour
- 2 tbsp (30 ml) avocado oil
- 4 tsp (20 ml) onion powder
- 2 tsp 1/2 (12.5 ml) coconut sugar
- 2 tsp (10 ml) balsamic vinegar

- 1 tsp (5 ml) salt
- 1 tsp (5 ml) smoked paprika
- 1/2 tsp (2.5 ml) cocoa
- 1/4 tsp (1.25 ml) thyme
- 2 pinches of sage (not ground)
- Pepper to taste

Culinary creation:

1. In a cauldron over low heat, whisk the brown rice flour in the oil. When the flour begins to bubble, add thyme and sage, whisk again and cook a few more seconds. Add the water and remaining ingredients, pepper if desired. Bring to a boil while whisking constantly until the sauce thickens. Boil for a few seconds, remove from heat and serve. For a slightly lighter sauce, add 2 tablespoons (30 ml) of water.

PEELS AU GRATIN

Recipe on page 63 in the section "Potatoes & Co"

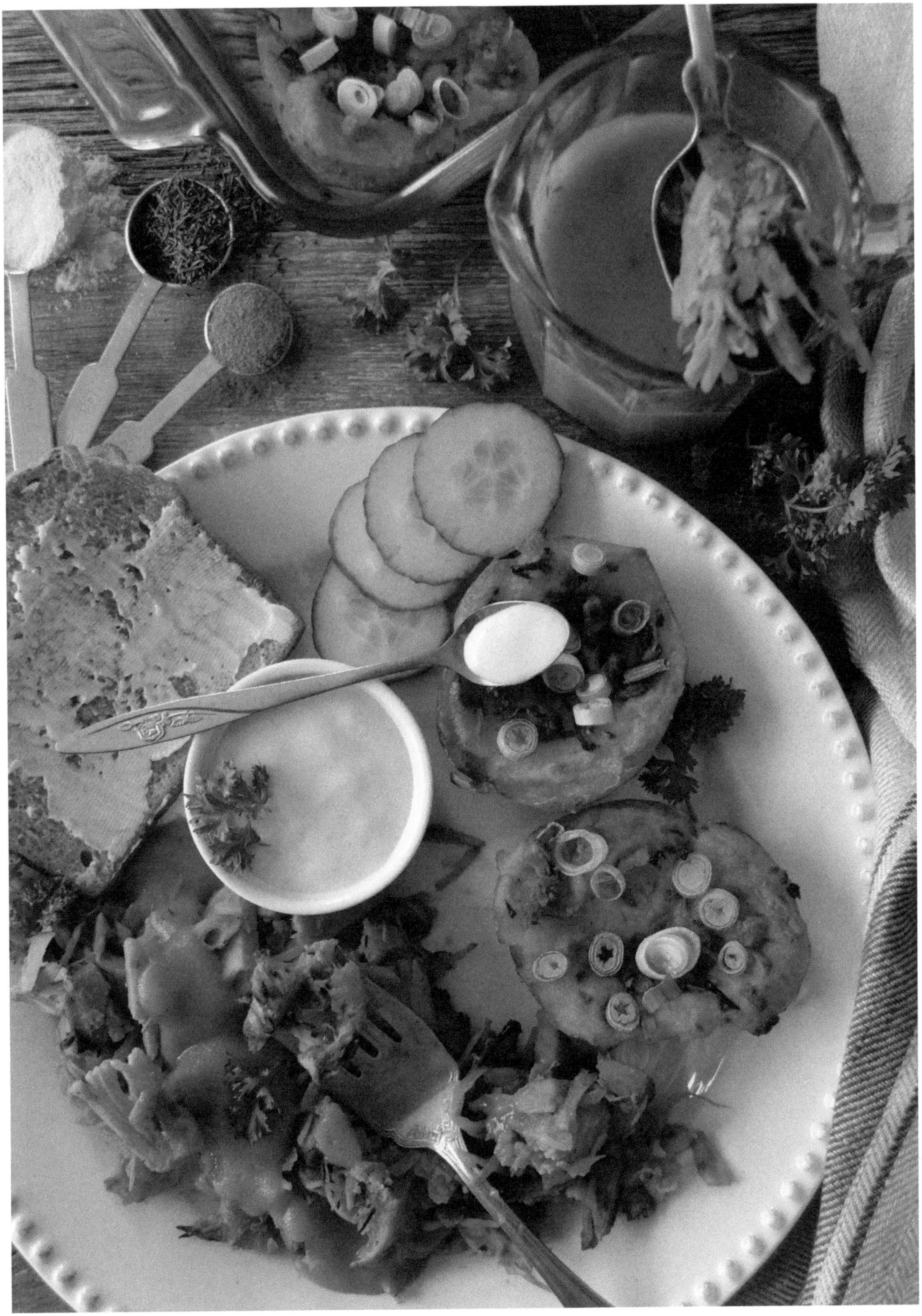

No matter which cracker, bread or tortilla you add to these jackfruit toppings and no matter whether these fillings are served as appetizers or as a meal, you'll find each time with these 3 versions of toppings a happy blend where the flavors make the joy of eating grow! The jackfruit, simply a great ally!

JACKFRUIT ROLLS 3 WAYS
ROLLS with garnish of JACKFRUIT CHICKEN

- 1 x 14 oz (400 ml) can of green jackfruit in water or brine,
- rinsed and drained (for a total of 250 g jackfruit)
- 1/3 cup (80 ml) vegan mayo, recipe on page 22
- 2 tbsp (30 ml) nutritional yeast
- 2 tbsp (30 ml) chopped fresh parsley
- 1 tsp (5 ml) onion powder

- 1/2 tsp (2.5 ml) granulated or powdered garlic
- 1/4 tsp (1.25 ml) salt
- 1/8 tsp (0.625 ml) ground cumin
- 1/8 tsp (0.625 ml) smoked paprika
- 1-2 leaves of curly lettuce by rolled
- 2 tortillas, recipe on page 48

Culinary creation:

1. Precook and prepare the jackfruit according to the basic method explained on page 12. Allow to cool completely in the refrigerator for about 2 hours. Meanwhile, gather dry spices, salt and nutritional yeast in a small dish, set aside.

2. When cooled, cut the jackfruit thinly enough on a chopping board with a large knife. Then add in a bowl with the vegan mayo and spices. Mix well. If desired, add additional vegan mayo on the tortilla before continuing (the tortilla is at room temperature so that it does not break when rolled). Garnish each tortilla, roll and wrap with plastic wrap. Refrigerate at least 1 hour before serving or slicing.

ROLLS with garnish of JACKFRUIT AND HERBS

- 1 x 14 oz (400 ml) can of green jackfruit in water or brine, rinsed and drained (for a total of 250 g jackfruit)
- 1/3 cup (80 ml) vegan mayo, recipe on page 22
- 1 green onion cut thinly
- 1 celery stalk, very finely chopped

- 1 tbsp (15 ml) chopped cilantro
- 1 tbsp (15 ml) chopped dill
- Salt and pepper to taste
- Alfalfa and/or shoots of your choice
- 2 tortillas, recipe on page 48

Culinary creation:

1. Precook and prepare the jackfruit according to the basic method explained on page 12. Allow to cool completely in the refrigerator for about 2 hours. Meanwhile, prepare the vegetables and herbs, reserve.

2. When cooled, cut the jackfruit thinly on a cutting board with a large knife, then place in a bowl with remaining ingredients (except alfalfa or shoots). Mix well. If desired, add additional vegan mayo on the tortilla before continuing (the tortilla is at room temperature so that it does not break when rolled). Garnish each tortilla, roll and wrap with plastic wrap. Refrigerate at least 1 hour before serving or slicing.

ANTIPASTI ROLLS with garnish of PESTO JACKFRUIT

Antipasti rolls
- 1 x 14 oz (400 ml) can of green jackfruit in water or brine, rinsed and drained (for a total of 250 g jackfruit)
- 1/3 cup (80 ml) pesto, recipe on the right
- 6 to 8 strips of roasted peppers in pots and/or 6 to 8 tomatoes dried in oil cut into pieces
- 1/4 cup (60 ml) sliced Kalamata olives
- 3 to 4 pepperoncini peppers cut into slices
- 2 tortillas, recipe on page 48

Pesto
- 1 cup (250 ml) freshly chopped basil
- 1 cup (250 ml) freshly chopped parsley
- 2/3 cup (160 ml) avocado oil
- 1/2 cup (125 ml) nutritional yeast
- 2 tbsp (30 ml) minced garlic (4 to 6 pods)
- 1/2 tsp (2.5 ml) salt
- Pepper to taste

Culinary creation:

1. Precook and prepare the jackfruit according to the basic method explained on page 12. Allow to cool completely in the refrigerator for 2 hours. Meanwhile, prepare the pesto by pulsing all the ingredients in a blender until smooth, reserve.

2. When cooled, cut the jackfruit thinly on a cutting board with a large knife, then add to a bowl with 1/3 cup (80 ml) pesto, mix well (remaining pesto can be frozen). Before continuing, take care that the tortilla is at room temperature so that it does not break when rolled. Divide the jackfruit and ingredients in each tortilla, roll and wrap with plastic wrap. Refrigerate at least 1 hour before serving or slicing.

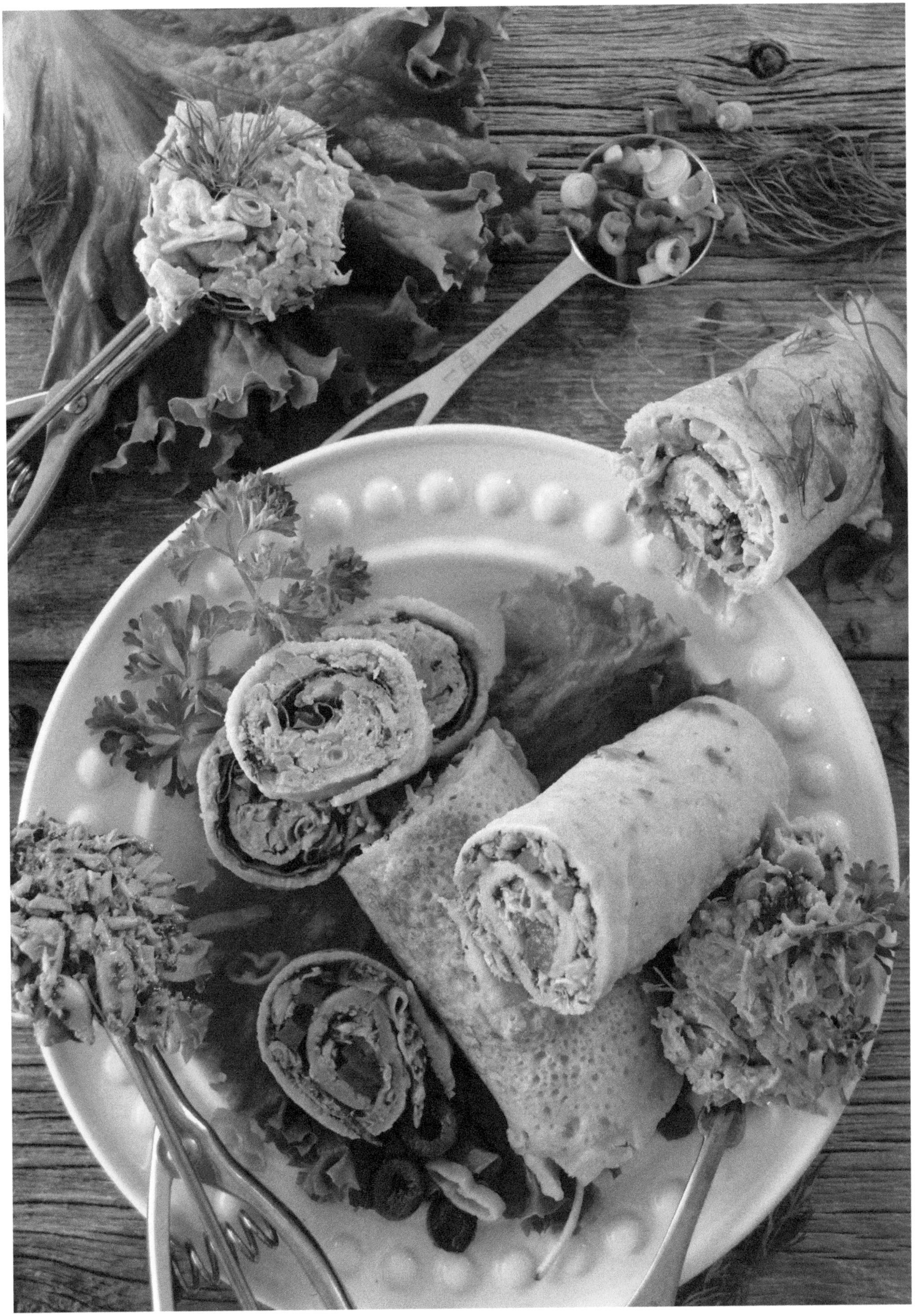

Here is one of the dishes that I particularly liked before becoming vegan, the submarine! Here you will find 2 versions of submarines and 2 different vinaigrettes to accompany them and create some of the most delicious variations!

JACKFRUIT CHICKEN SUBMARINE DELIGHT

Smoked chicken jackfruit

- 2 x 14 oz (400 ml) cans of green jackfruit in water or brine, rinsed and drained (for a total of 500 g jackfruit)
- 1/4 cup (60 ml) nutritional yeast
- 2 tbsp (30 ml) avocado oil
- 1 tbsp (15 ml) onion powder
- 1 tsp (5 ml) granulated or powdered garlic
- 1/2 tsp (2.5 ml) salt
- 1/2 tsp (2.5 ml) liquid smoke

For a gardener submarine, also add:

- 1 green pepper and 1 red pepper cut into small slices
- 1/3 cup (80 ml) sliced green olives
- 1/4 cup (60 ml) pesto, recipe on page 76

Submarine garnish

- 4 submarine breads of 7 inches
- Vegan mayo recipe on page 22
- 1 tray of 227 g sliced mushrooms
- 1 onion cut into strips
- 3 cups (750 ml) iceberg lettuce chopped very finely
- Vinaigrette of your choice below (or any other vinaigrette)
- 1 to 2 sliced tomatoes

Culinary creation:

1. Precook and prepare the jackfruit according to the basic method explained on page 12. Meanwhile, fry the mushrooms and onion in a pan with a little oil until tender. For the gardener version, add the peppers and olives as well and towards the end of the cooking, add the pesto. Set aside in the oven to prepare the rest of the ingredients.

2. After the jackfruit has been practically all pulled according to the basic method, add avocado oil and liquid smoke and by sprinkling, add spices and nutritional yeast. Mix well to coat.

3. Transfer the jackfruit to a skillet over medium low heat with a little oil. During the time to prepare the remaining ingredients, dry and crisp the jackfruit for about 20 minutes, stirring occasionally.

4. Meanwhile, toss to taste the vinaigrette chosen with lettuce, reserve. A few minutes before the assembly grill the submarines inside to warm them up a bit.

5. Make the submarines by first spreading on each vegan mayo, add the jackfruit by dividing it into 4 equal parts, add the vegetables, lettuce and tomatoes. Serve immediately. Makes 4 submarines.

HOMEMADE RANCH DRESSING

- 1 cup (250 ml) water
- 1/2 cup (125 ml) avocado oil
- 3 tbsp (45 ml) nutritional yeast
- 2 tbsp (30 ml) minced garlic in jar
- 1 tbsp 1/2 (22.5 ml) apple cider vinegar
- 2 tsp (10 ml) onion powder
- 1/2 tsp (2.5 ml) parsley
- 1/2 tsp (2.5 ml) salt
- 1/2 tsp (2.5 ml) dried dill
- 1/4 tsp (1.25 ml) xanthan gum
- 1/4 tsp (1.25 ml) pepper

Culinary creation:

1. In a blender, add all ingredients and pulse until smooth and thick. Refrigerate. Can be kept 7 to 10 days in the refrigerator.

SUPER SUBMARINE VINAIGRETTE

- 1/2 cup (125 ml) avocado oil
- 2 tbsp (30 ml) balsamic vinegar
- 1 tbsp (15 ml) oregano
- 1 tsp (5 ml) minced garlic (1 clove)
- 1/2 tsp (2.5 ml) salt
- Pepper to taste

Culinary creation:

1. In a small dish, add all ingredients and whisk until smooth. Refrigerate.

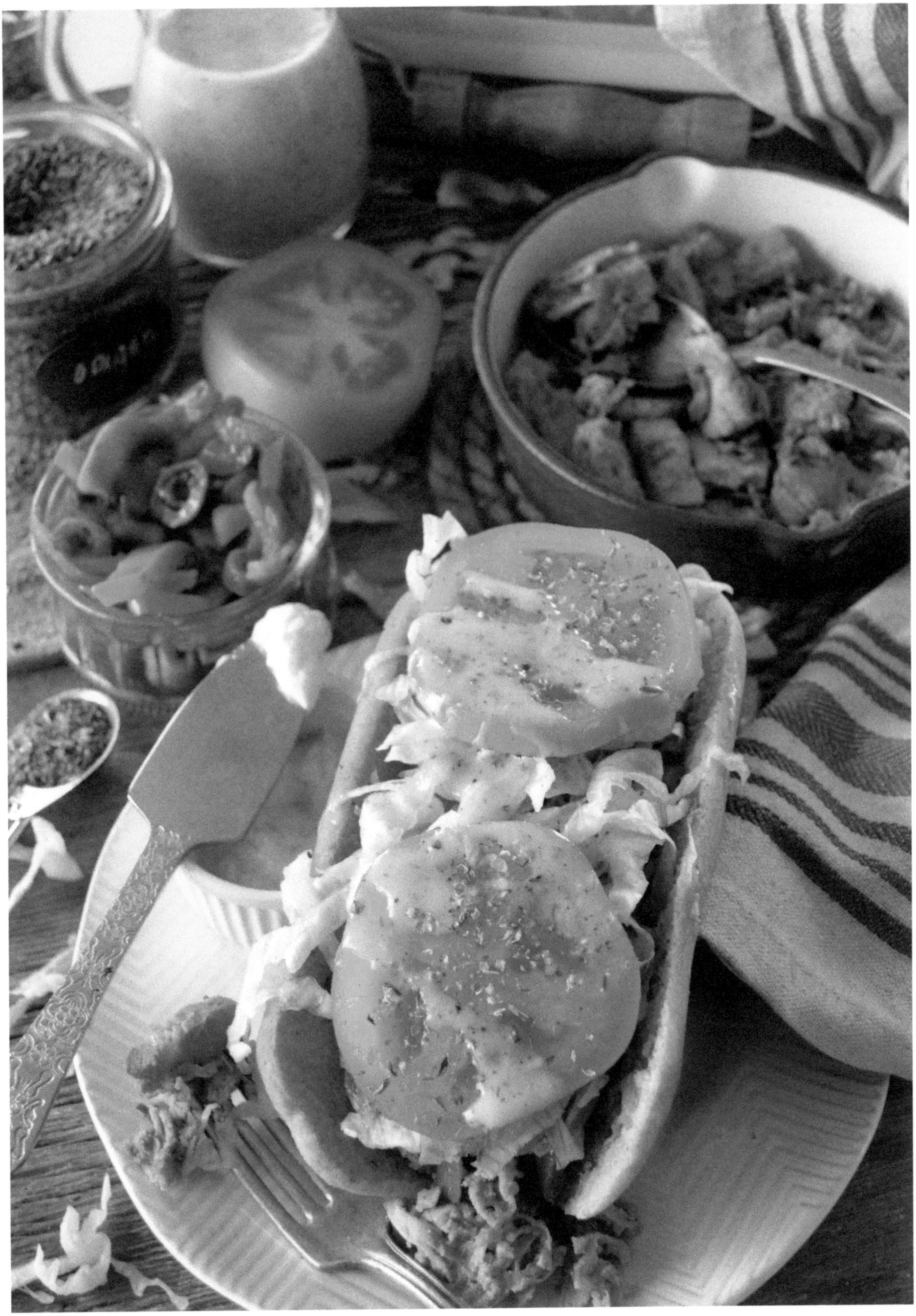

Here is a recipe, an essential classic, where the jackfruit is at its best, the jackfruit BBQ pulled pork. What's more wonderful than tasting this fruit that has everything to please everyone! In addition to being vegan and gluten free! Here, we can really say that to try it is to adopt it!

SUBLIME JACKFRUIT BBQ PULLED "PORK" VERSION

Jackfruit BBQ pulled "pork" version
- 2 x 14 oz (400 ml) cans of green jackfruit in water or brine, rinsed and drained (for a total of 500 g jackfruit)
- 1 cup (250 ml) vegan BBQ sauce, recipe below
- 1 tbsp (15 ml) maple syrup
- 1 tbsp (15 ml) minced garlic (3 cloves)
- 1 tsp (5 ml) smoked paprika
- 1/2 tsp (2.5 ml) chili powder
- 1/2 tsp (2.5 ml) cumin
- 1/2 tsp (2.5 ml) salt

Hamburger fillings
- 6 hamburger buns
- Salad leaves to choose
- Red cabbage salad, recipe below
- Mayo vegan, recipe on page 22

Culinary creation:

1. Precook and prepare the jackfruit according to the basic method explained on page 12. Then, in a skillet heated over medium heat with a little oil (which will be covered with a lid), add the jackfruit with the rest of the ingredients of the jackfruit BBQ. Mix to completely coat with sauce and spices.

2. Cover and simmer 10 to 15 minutes, stirring occasionally, to prepare the rest of the ingredients. (It is also possible to bake this recipe in the oven at 400°F for 30 minutes in a covered 8 x 8 inch dish, stirring 2 to 3 times during this time.)

3. When the cooking time is over, make the burgers. Makes 6 servings.

VEGAN BBQ SAUCE

- 1 chopped onion very finely
- 1 can of 156 ml of tomato paste (2/3 cup)
- 1/4 cup (60 ml) water
- 3 tbsp (45 ml) maple syrup
- 1 tbsp (15 ml) apple cider vinegar
- 1 tbsp (15 ml) Worcestershire sauce, recipe on page 46
- 1 tbsp (15 ml) minced garlic (3 cloves)

- 1 tsp (5 ml) onion powder
- 1 tsp (5 ml) smoked paprika
- 1/4 tsp (1.25 ml) ground cumin
- 1/4 tsp (1.25 ml) chili powder
- 1/4 tsp (1.25 ml) ground chipotle
- 1/4 tsp (1.25 ml) salt

Culinary creation:

1. In a saucepan with a little oil, sauté the onion over low heat until translucent. Add oil as needed. Add the minced garlic and cook 1 more minute. Add the tomato paste, water and the rest of the ingredients. Mix and simmer for 5 minutes covered. Remove from heat and refrigerate when chilled if sauce is not used immediately. Makes about 1 cup (250 ml) of vegan BBQ sauce.

RED CABBAGE SALAD WITH CUMIN

- 3 cups 1/2 (875 ml) grated red cabbage
- 3 tbsp (45 ml) avocado oil
- 1 tbsp (15 ml) maple syrup
- 1 tsp (5 ml) balsamic vinegar

- 1 tsp (5 ml) cumin grains
- 1/2 tsp (2.5 ml) oregano
- 1/4 tsp (1.25 ml) salt (more to the taste)

Culinary creation:

1. In a bowl, add all ingredients and mix well, refrigerate.

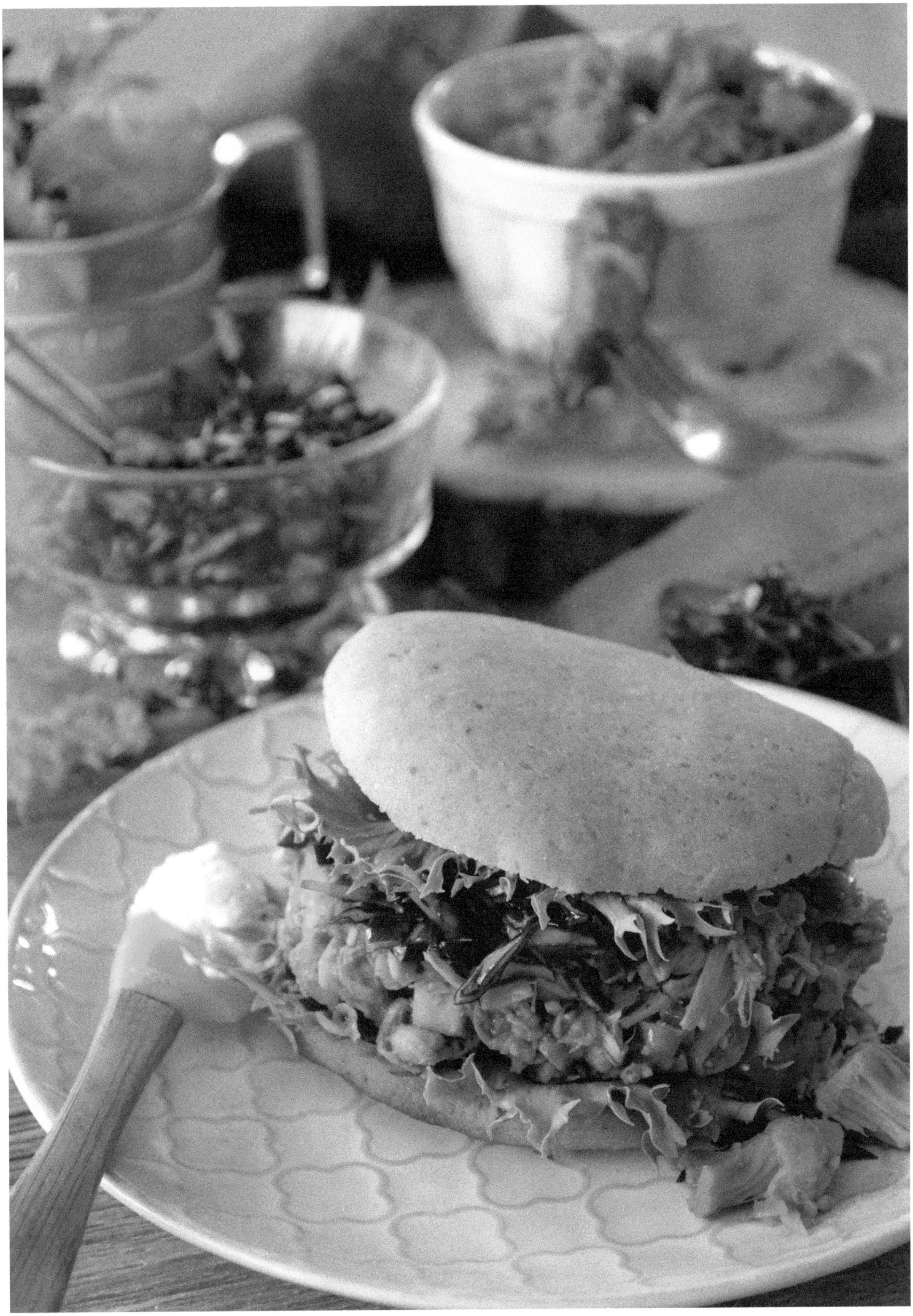

On the practical side, because the jackfruit is a great idea for lunches and express dinners, and that, because it can also be prepared in advance, it is a safe bet that you will want to double this spread recipe next time to make the pleasure last!

JACKFRUIT SPREAD, HAM TASTE

- 1 x 14 oz (400 ml) can of green jackfruit in water or brine, rinsed and drained (for a total of 250 g jackfruit)
- 1/3 cup (80 ml) vegan mayo, recipe on page 22
- 2 tsp (10 ml) nutritional yeast
- 1/2 tsp (2.5 ml) smoked paprika
- 1/2 tsp (2.5 ml) granulated or powdered garlic
- 1/2 tsp (2.5 ml) liquid smoke
- 1/4 tsp (1.25 ml) maple syrup
- 1/4 tsp (1.25 ml) balsamic vinegar
- 1/4 tsp (1.25 ml) salt
- 1 tbsp (15 ml) relish (optional)
- 4 express naan breads, recipe on page 48

Culinary creation:

1. Cut each piece of jackfruit into 3 or 4 pieces depending on their size. In a cauldron, bring water to a boil and cook the jackfruit for 30 minutes over medium high heat. When the jackfruit is ready, strain it and put it back in the cauldron. Use a potato masher or fork to loosen and pull almost all the jackfruit, refrigerate for at least 2 hours to cool completely.
2. When cooled, cut the jackfruit finely on a chopping board with a large knife. In a bowl, add the jackfruit with remaining ingredients and mix. Serve over naan express breads or any other bread or cracker. If desired, add hints of pesto, recipe on page 76. Makes 4 servings on naan breads.

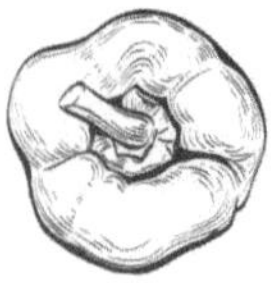

Variation: Omit the mayonnaise and relish and use the jackfruit prepared with the rest of the ingredients to garnish a homemade pizza to your taste, yum!

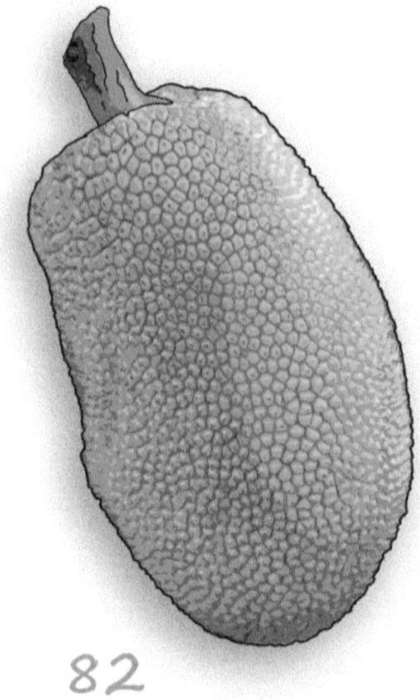

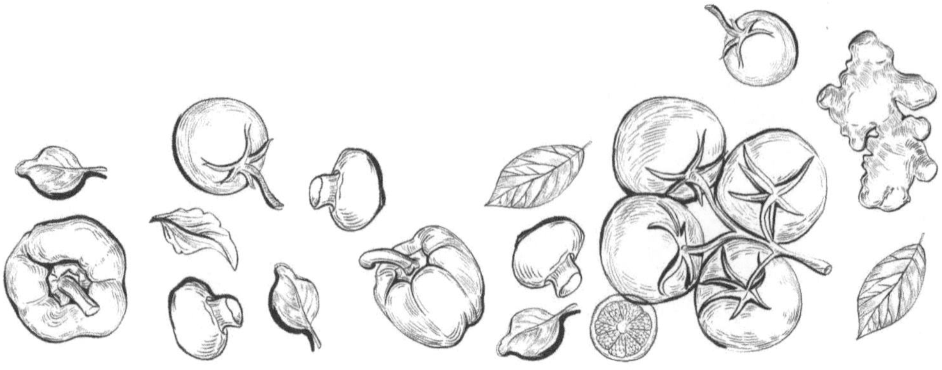

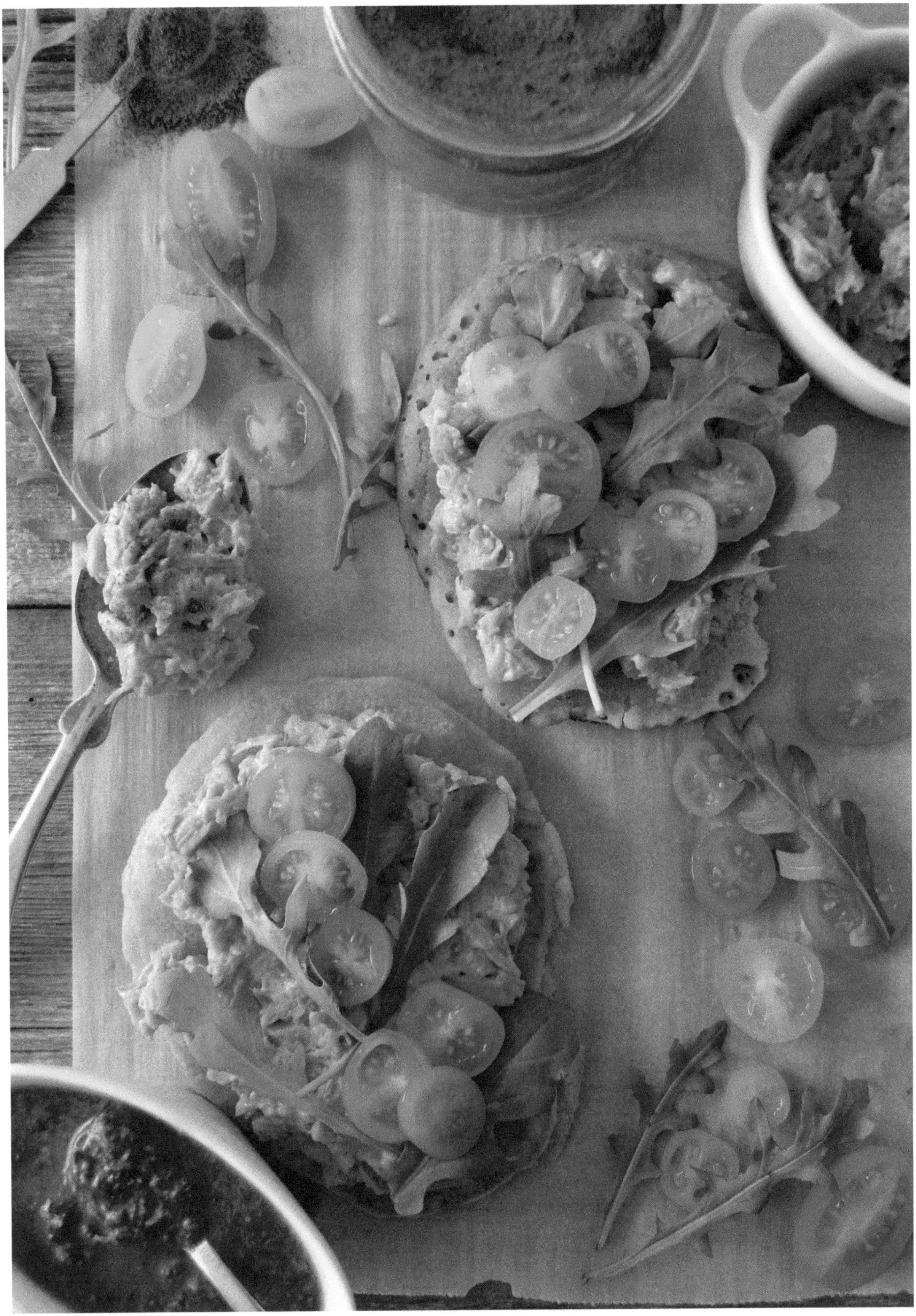

To start a good evening or to finish it, here are two recipes to put on the table. One being cold and one hot, these recipes will be perfect for snacking, celebrating or simply to feast on! To serve on crackers of your choice, on tortillas and why not in your favorite bread?

TRADITIONAL JACKFRUIT TERRINE

- 1 x 14 oz (400 ml) can of green jackfruit in water or brine, rinsed and drained (for a total of 250 g jackfruit)
- 1 minced onion
- 1 cup 1/4 (310 ml) water
- 1 tbsp (15 ml) chopped fresh parsley
- 1 tbsp (15 ml) chopped fresh chives
- 1 tbsp (15 ml) minced garlic (3 cloves)

- 2 tsp (10 ml) onion powder
- 3/4 tsp (3.75 ml) agar-agar powder *
- 1/2 tsp (2.5 ml) granulated or powdered garlic
- 1/2 tsp (2.5 ml) salt
- 1 to 2 pinches of ground cloves
- Pepper to taste

Culinary creation:

1. Cut each piece of jackfruit into 3 or 4 pieces depending on their size. In a cauldron, bring water to a boil and cook the jackfruit for 40 minutes over medium high heat. When the jackfruit is ready, strain it and put it back in the cauldron. Use a potato masher or fork to loosen and pull the whole jackfruit. Then place the jackfruit on a cutting board and chop it coarsely with a large knife, set aside.

2. In a skillet with a little oil, fry the onions until completely cooked, adding oil as needed. Then add the minced garlic and cook for another minute.

3. Pour the water and bring to a boil. Reduce the intensity of the heat, add the agar-agar and let simmer for 1 to 2 minutes to activate the agar-agar. Then add the onion powder, garlic powder, salt, clove and finally the jackfruit. Leave to boil gently for a few minutes until almost no liquid remains. Add salt and pepper to taste.

4. Allow the mixture to cool to room temperature and, mixing to distribute, add the parsley and chives. Pour into a container by compacting the jackfruit so that there is no more empty space. Before serving, refrigerate 2 to 3 hours to allow the terrine to set. Makes about 2 cups (500 ml).

* Note: without the agar-agar, this recipe becomes 2 servings of what was once called in my family, an old-fashioned pork stew, then we serve this hot dish with the same ingredients, delicious served with potatoes and brown sauce, yum!

HOT DIP OF JACKFRUIT BUFFALO STYLE

- 2 x 14 oz (400 ml) cans of green jackfruit in water or brine, rinsed and drained (for a total of 500 g jackfruit)
- 1 onion cut into cubes
- 1 cup (250 ml) diced potatoes already boiled
- 1/2 cup (125 ml) water
- 1/2 cup (125 ml) reduced fat coconut milk
- 1/3 cup (80 ml) Buffalo hot pepper sauce
- 1/4 cup (60 ml) tapioca flour

- 1 tbsp (15 ml) minced garlic (3 cloves)
- 1 tbsp (15 ml) nutritional yeast
- 2 tsp (10 ml) onion powder
- 1 tsp (5 ml) apple cider vinegar
- 3/4 tsp (3.75 ml) salt
- 1/2 tsp (2.5 ml) parsley
- 1/2 tsp (2.5 ml) dill
- Pepper to taste

Culinary creation:

1. Preheat oven to 375°F. Cut each piece of jackfruit into 3 or 4 pieces depending on their size. In a cauldron, bring water to a boil and cook the jackfruit for 30 minutes over medium high heat. Cook the potatoes if they are not already cooked. When the jackfruit is ready, strain it and put it back in the cauldron. Use a potato masher or fork to loosen and pull almost all the jackfruit, reserve.

2. In a large skillet, sauté the onion until translucent. Meanwhile, in a blender, pulse all ingredients except the onion, jackfruit and hot pepper sauce until very smooth. Transfer to the pan with the onions when they are ready. Bring to a boil while whisking constantly, the mixture will thicken.

3. When the mixture has thickened, add jackfruit and chili sauce. Mix well and pour into a baking dish. Bake for 30 minutes. Makes about 4 cups (1000 ml) of hot dip with medium spicy taste.

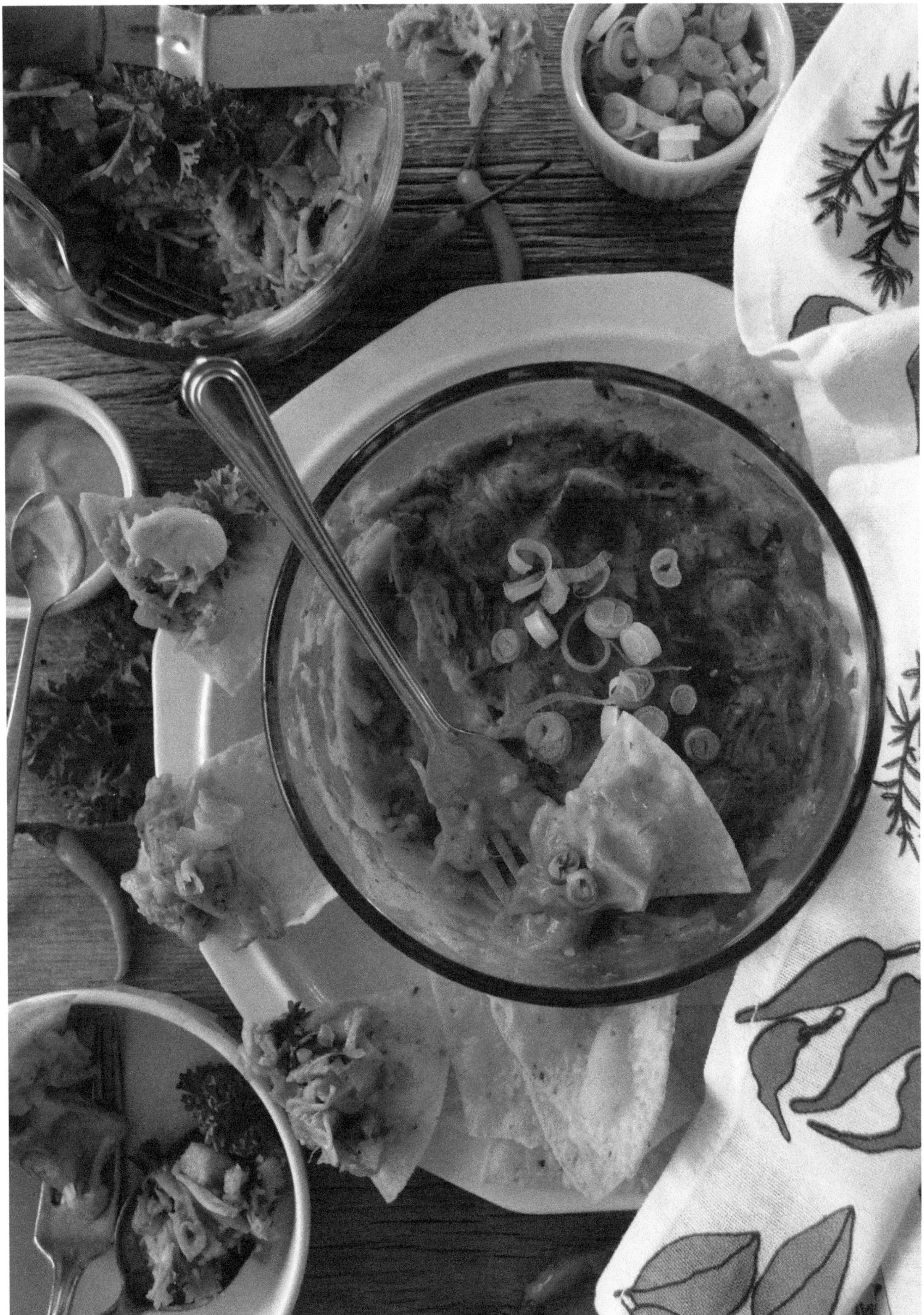

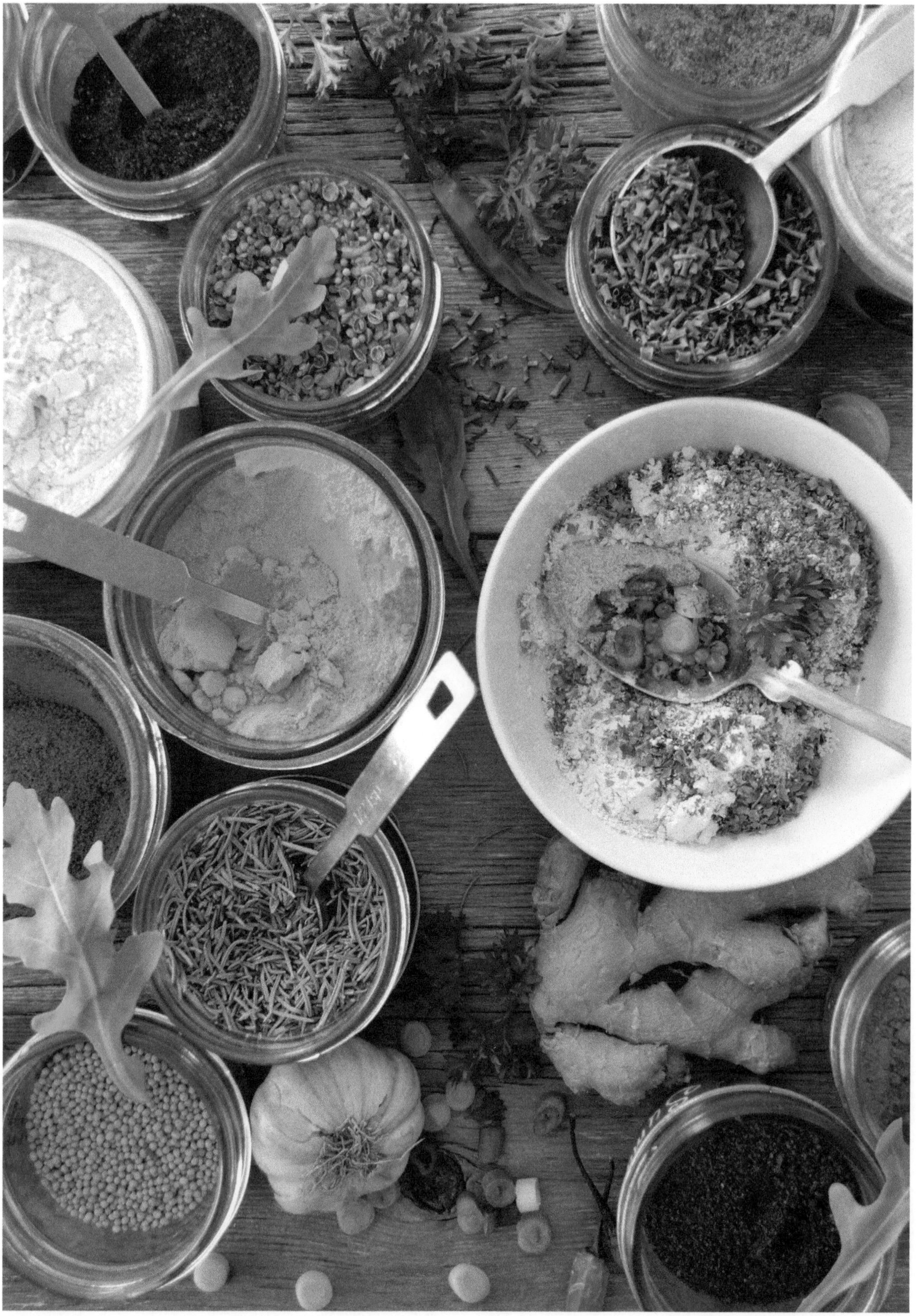

TIPS AND TRICKS WITH THE JACKFRUIT

In this page, I share some tips and tricks that I use every day to cook in order to make pleasant and easy everything I do. To this end, here are some avenues to explore that are quite effective.

Make ahead

To add to your kitchen in general, it can be really useful and practical to make in advance what can be. As throughout this book, it is often advisable to gather the spices in a small dish while the jackfruit boils. Here, to get ahead, it is possible **to gather in advance the spices of a recipe**. Although at first glance this information may seem really simplistic, it remains that this way of proceeding is most helpful. Spices can be prepared the day before when planning the meal to come or a little at any time.

And even when preparing the spices of a recipe, **you can make several mixtures of spices at once.** This is also what I do when I gather my spices for cooking: I use a small dish to gather my spices for my recipe in question and I also take the opportunity to make additional spice mixtures that I keep in some well-identified small Mason jars. So, if I cook, let's say Indian jackfruit, I prepare the spices for the next two or three times. So, the next time when I cook the Indian jackfruit again, I just have to take out my spice mixture which is already done, easy!

On this subject, here are some recipes where you can use this method to do it in advance:

- Shish taouk Jackfruit plate
- Burritos delight of lime-chipotle jackfruit
- Pulled jackfruit turkey-style
- Greek Jackfruit on gyros
- Jackfruit Indian "butter chicken" style
- Fries "not too spicy"

As spices can be gathered in advance, **recipes with flour mixes can also be prepared in advance.** I thus proceed in this way with the recipes preparations registered in the gluten-free corner. When I have free time or when cooking a particular recipe, I always prepare two or three other flour mixes kept in Mason jars. In this way, just as with the spices, I save time for the next times to come and also, I avoid having to get out all the spices or flours every time. I also avoid having to clean the subsequent times, especially with the flours that still leave their traces!

Cook large amounts of jackfruit

If, like me, you become a fan of jackfruit, you will also find that it is really interesting to cook it in large quantities using the basic method explained on page 12. For my part, I always boil several cans of jackfruit according to this method, because I like to always have it at hand. It's convenient and quick to make any recipe from the book, especially knowing that it will keep for 7 to 10 days in the refrigerator after being cooked.

And it's here that having a scale to weigh the jackfruit becomes interesting, because if you use 20-ounce cans of jackfruit for cooking, you weigh it when it comes out of cans and then you calculate the weight to find the equivalent in cans of 14 ounces. By experience, because I've also cooked a few times with 20-ounce cans, you often need 7 cans of 20 ounces to get the weight of 8 cans of 14 ounces (2000 grams). However, I recommend weighing and calculating every time you cook in large quantities, as the weight of the jackfruit in 20-ounce cans is variable.

After the jackfruit has been weighed, it can be cooked. Knowing that there is for example the equivalent of 8 cans of 14 ounces in the cauldron, we weigh again the weight obtained after cooking (because it changes) and divide it into 8 to obtain the new weight for a can. With this new weight obtained, it is multiplied by 2 or 3 according to the chosen recipe (or not at all if the recipe requires 1 can) and we take the equivalent to cook. For my part, I always leave a note on the dish that contains the rest of the jackfruit to tell me how many cans are left in this dish. So I can easily make another recipe afterwards.

Another little trick here, when you boil the jackfruit, I recommend oiling the inside of the cauldron, especially the top part of the cauldron, where the water stops or ends, because the jackfruit releases latex while cooking. So for ease, oiling this part avoids having to scour the latex that accumulates in this place in the pan. Long live the ease!

HOW TO GO FURTHER WITH THE JACKFRUIT?

There are probably thousands of ways to cook jackfruit, as there are incredible amounts of recipes. In this section, I share different alternatives to help you go further with the jackfruit to enjoy it!

Sandwiches, rolls and everything else!

One of the best ways to use leftover jackfruit and cook it for that purpose is to add it to a sandwich, hamburger or roll. Embellished with salad to taste or vegetables such as avocados, slices of tomatoes and cucumbers and a sauce or condiment to choose, everything is there to savor fully and in another way the jackfruit.

Moreover, I myself often reused the remaining of certain dishes to put them in rolls. I'm thinking here of the Indian "butter chicken" style jackfruit, the traditionnal jackfruit terrine or the General Tao jackfruit. It's such a nice way to extend the pleasure!

Pasta, everything is in the sauce!

Whether your favorite pasta dishes are Alfredo linguine, spaghetti with tomato sauce or pesto penne (of course all vegans and with or without vegetables), the jackfruit will become your favorite ally to create an unforgettable wow effect! Use the chicken-flavored jackfruit (page 70) or the bacon-flavored jackfruit (page 22) to make all your pasta dishes memorable!

Poutine and pizza, your best friends!

Homemade poutines and pizzas are often a source of happiness and comfort and will be even more so now with jackfruit! Use Greek-style jackfruit (page 38), Lebanese (page 20), bacon flavor (page 22) or General Tao (page 50) to enjoy a poutine or pizza with a different flavor! Guaranteed happiness to fill small and big appetites!

Long live the bowls!

Whether in Buddha style bowls or poke bowl, the jackfruit will stand out for its great resemblance to meat, but without it being. Accompanied by raw and fresh vegetables, all laid on rice of choice, quinoa, buckwheat or on different lettuce and shoots to choose, the bowls with the jackfruit are a preferred choice to get the maximum of nutrients from the raw vegetables.

I have often reproduced these bowls like the poke bowl with jackfruit shawarma (page 60) because I am a big fan of raw vegetables and salads. As there is an infinite number of possibilities, we can vary the jackfruit in bowls inspired by the recipes of this book. For example, you can create a Greek bowl with Greek jackfruit. We add vegetables that are "Greek" and you're done. And why not create an Asian bowl with sprouted beans, carrots, avocados all sprinkled with sesame seeds? Long live the bowls with the jackfruit!

Cook the sweet jackfruit

Since jackfruit is primarily a fruit, it can be interesting to cook it as such. With its distinctive taste when it is ripe, it can be added to virtually any dessert or lunch to taste its flavor.

Moreover, in some Asian grocery stores, it is found fresh, already prepared, which is rather helping because there is a certain challenge to cut the whole jackfruit! The only thing that is necessary to do before cooking is to remove the seeds from each aril. In short, the sweet version of the jackfruit is a whole world to discover!

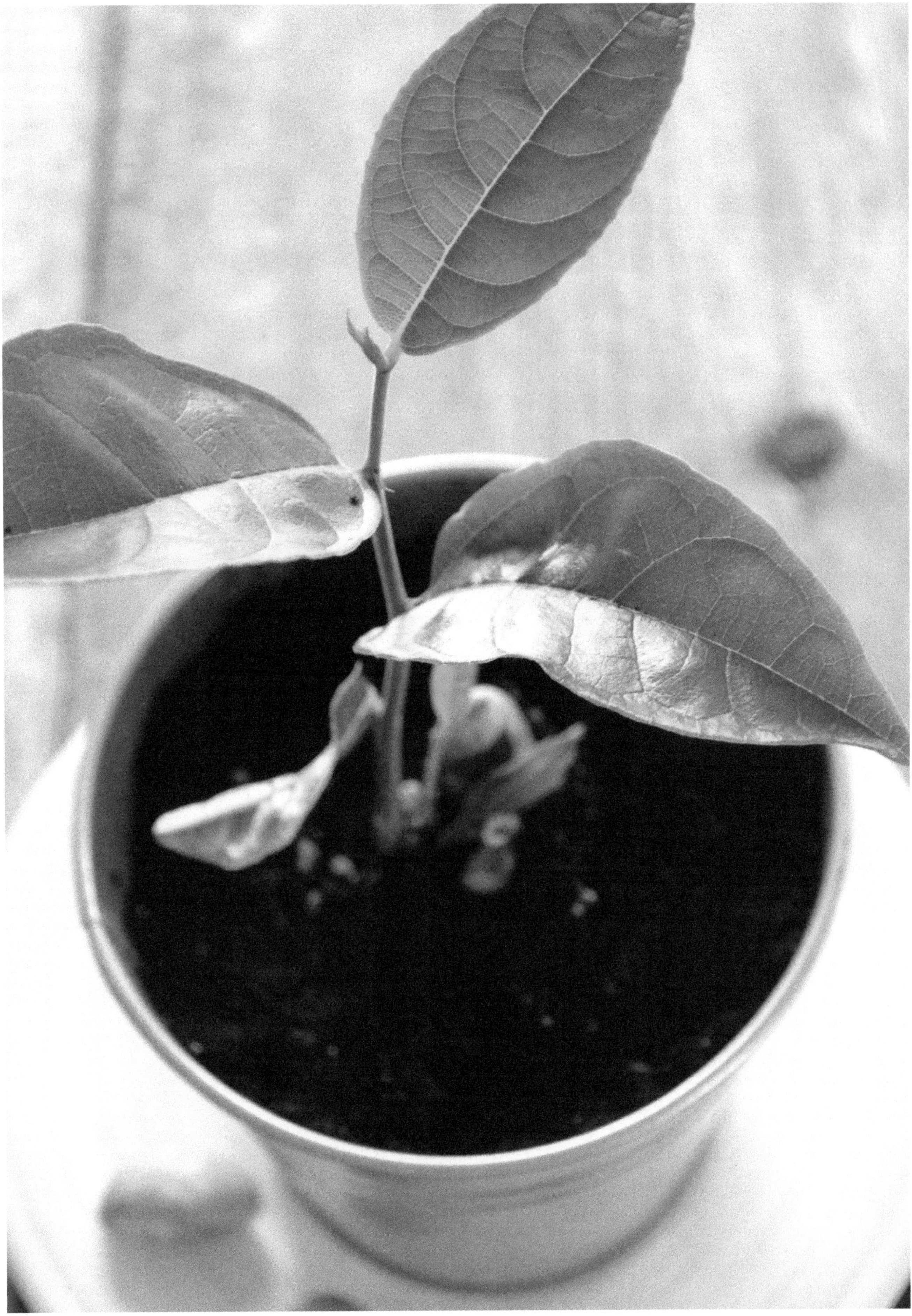

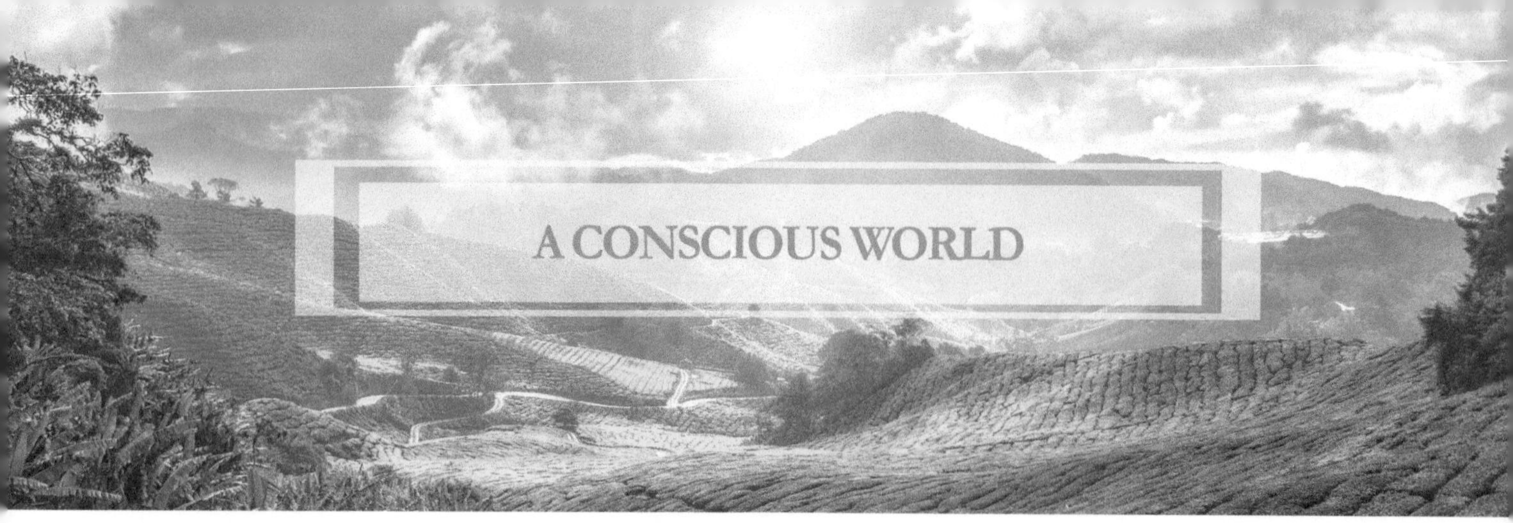

A CONSCIOUS WORLD

A Conscious World is a non-profit organization whose mission is to share the Consciousness by publishing books that touch the human being in its daily life. Autism, veganism and spirituality occupy a prominent place in our editorial line.

Whether the different topics are to become more Conscious, to live in a better world or to create renewal, our books share points of view that contribute to reflection and that sometimes challenge the ways of living and thinking within the society.

The organization is actively involved in promoting veganism and promoting a new vision of autism and the unexplored potential that is an integral part of this condition.

By consulting the website, you will be able to:

- Directly order copies of books
- Get "Vegan for Life" items
- To financially support the distribution of Consciousness by donating
- Subscribe to the newsletter
- Click "Like" to follow us on Facebook
- Discover why we are a "green and ecologist" publisher

To learn more about the author, we also invite you to get her other books by visiting:
www.aconsciousworld.org

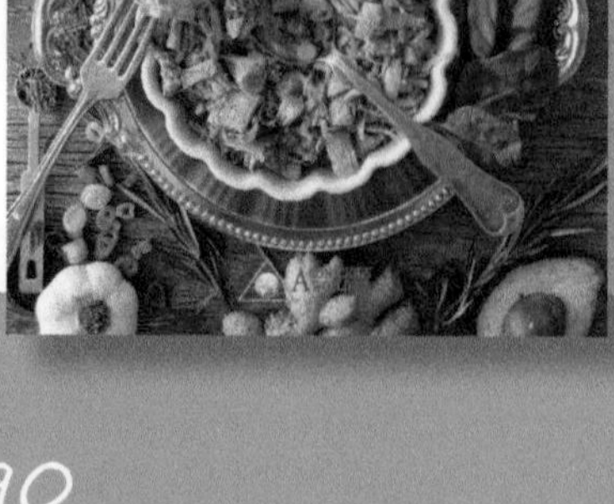
Nadine Primeau
The VEGAN and AMAZING recipes of JACKFRUIT
gluten free · soy free · nut free

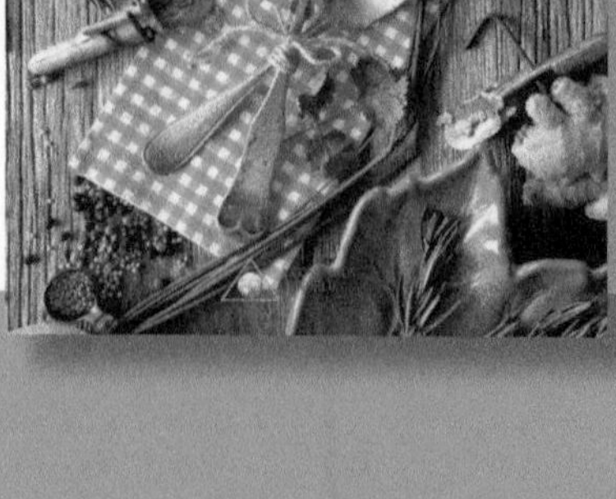
Nadine Primeau
Recipes from the VEGAN SUGAR SHACK
gluten-free | soy-free | nut-free

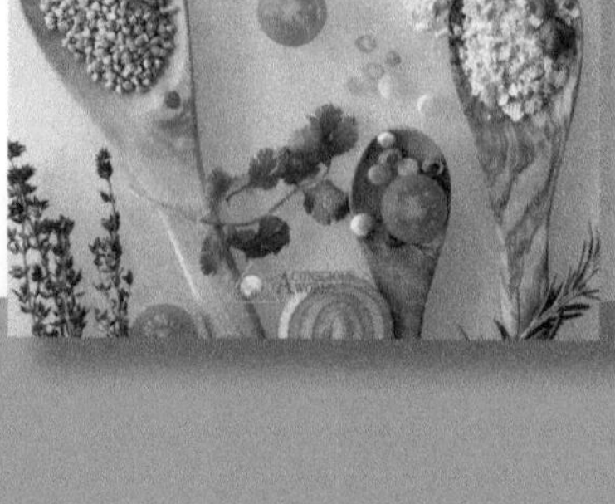
Nadine Primeau
The VEGAN BUCKWHEAT delivers you its recipes
Delicious · Vegan · Gluten-free
And also:
Nut-free
Leguminous-free
Soy-free
Dairy-free
Egg-free

Other original books are waiting for you at A Conscious World, visit us!

A CONSCIOUS WORLD

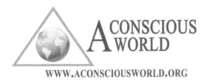

WWW.ACONSCIOUSWORLD.ORG

Nadine Primeau
INITIATIC
AND MAGIC TALES
To transform the heart and contact the soul
A CONSCIOUS WORLD

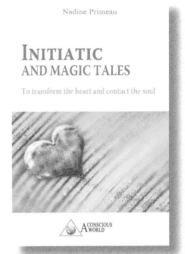

Nadine Primeau
BEYOND
THE LIMITS OF AUTISM
The Quest and the revelations of a mother
A CONSCIOUS WORLD

PIERRE-ANDRÉ PELLETIER
AUTISM, REVIEWED AND CORRECTED BY
A MAN WITH ASPERGER SYNDROME
CONTROVERSIAL TESTIMONY FROM A CONSCIOUS GENIUS
A CONSCIOUS WORLD

Rev. G. J. Ouseley
Jesus said NO to meat
in The Gospel of the Holy Twelve
THE GOSPEL OF THE HOLY TWELVE, UNCOVERED AND UNCENSORED
A CONSCIOUS WORLD

PIERRE-ANDRÉ PELLETIER
SHOCK BOOK:
GET OUT OF THE
ILLUSION AND FIND GOD
WRITTEN BY A MYSTIC WITH ASPERGER SYNDROME
A CONSCIOUS WORLD

PIERRE-ANDRÉ PELLETIER
FREE YOURSELF
FROM THE ROOT OF EVIL
WRITTEN BY A MYSTIC WITH ASPERGER SYNDROME
THE TEACHINGS OF CONSCIOUSNESS
A CONSCIOUS WORLD

PIERRE-ANDRÉ PELLETIER
MAY THE LIGHT
OF GOD BE
WRITTEN BY A MYSTIC WITH ASPERGER SYNDROME
THE TEACHINGS OF CONSCIOUSNESS
A CONSCIOUS WORLD

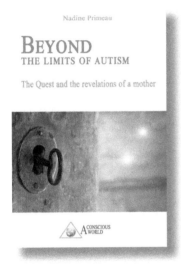

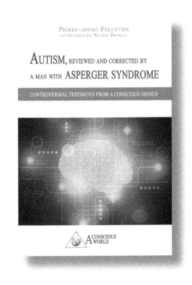

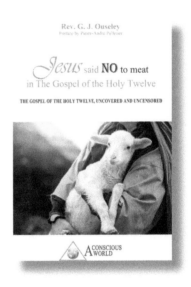

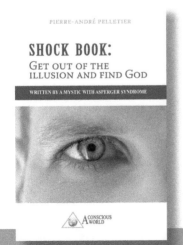

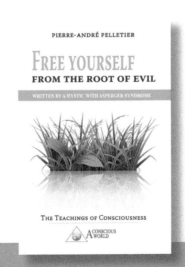

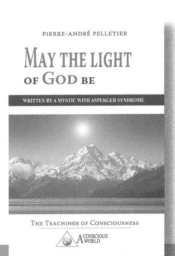

Lightning Source UK Ltd.
Milton Keynes UK
UKHW050301210622
404696UK00005BA/44

FOR ALL THE STORIES THAT WERE NEVER TOLD ...

THE MAN WITH A HOLLOW CHEST

Author: D. Hurd

Historian: Mark Bando

Artist: Kim Fujiwara

Creative & Production: C.O. & Company

www.hollowchest.com

75th Anniversary of D-Day Edition

Profits benefit veteran support groups

Copyright © 2019 by D. Hurd

All rights reserved. This book or any portion thereof may not be
reproduced or used in any manner whatsoever without the
express written permission of the publisher
except for the use of brief quotations in a book review.

Printed in the United States of America

First Printing, 2019

ISBN 978-1-7330598-0-0

THE MAN WITH A HOLLOW CHEST

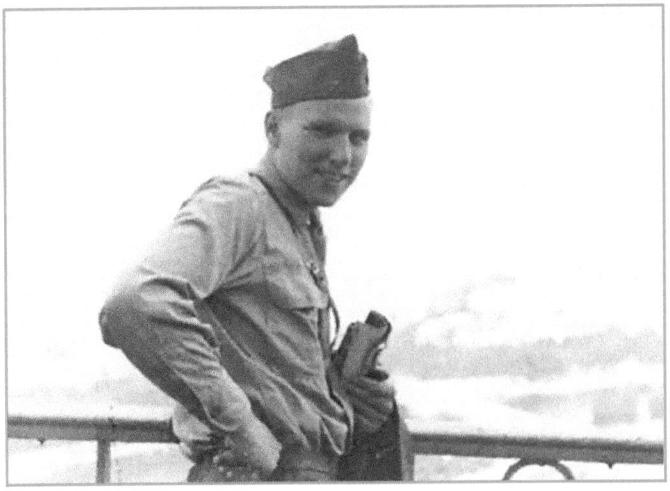

The true story of L. Allen Hurd Jr., Private First Class, 101st Airborne Division, 501st Parachute Infantry Regiment, 2nd Battalion, Headquarters Company, S-2 Section Scout. Told by his daughter, Denise Hurd.

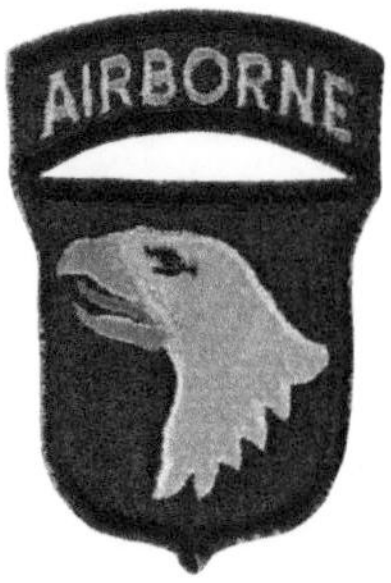
AIRBORNE

HOW THIS STORY CAME TO BE

In 2017, the doorbell rang and a stranger holding a book under his arm announced he was looking for Denise Hurd. To further the mystery, he stated he was sent by her father, who died in 2009. This stranger turned out to be Mark Bando, the well-known historian for the 101st Airborne Division. He was sent by Denise's father with instructions to share his WW II experiences with her after his death. Although Denise had talked with her father about his wartime service, he was not able to share the details of actual combat.

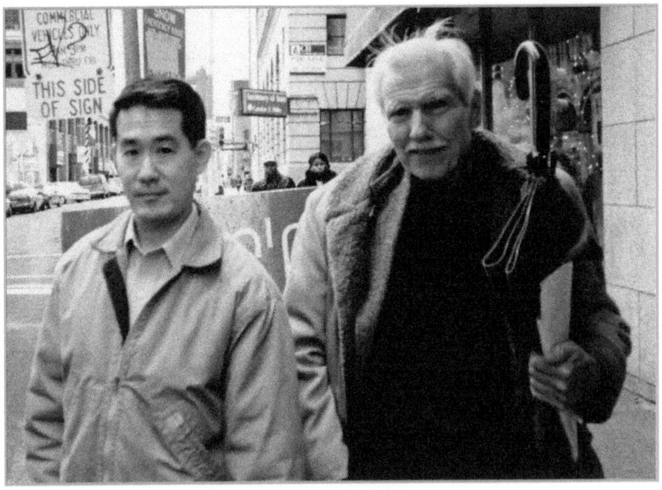
THIS SIDE
OF SIGN

Mark Bando and Allen Hurd in Detroit, 1990s.

In 1968, Mark Bando was a history major at Wayne State University in Detroit, Michigan. He began collecting and documenting the stories of WW II veterans in the Detroit area and continues his efforts today. He got to know many veterans, including Allen, attended their local reunions, and captured their stories which otherwise would have been lost.

Although he befriended Allen and was able to learn much about the war through the letters home he had saved, Allen never told his combat stories to anyone. He was troubled by his experiences and did not want to tell the kind of "war stories" that might encourage young men to see war as a heroic adventure instead of the hell it actually is. Over the years, he threw away his medals, uniform, and letters. In sharing these stories of Allen Hurd, Mark makes it clear "...most of what I know about what he did was not told to me by him, it was told to me by people who knew him."

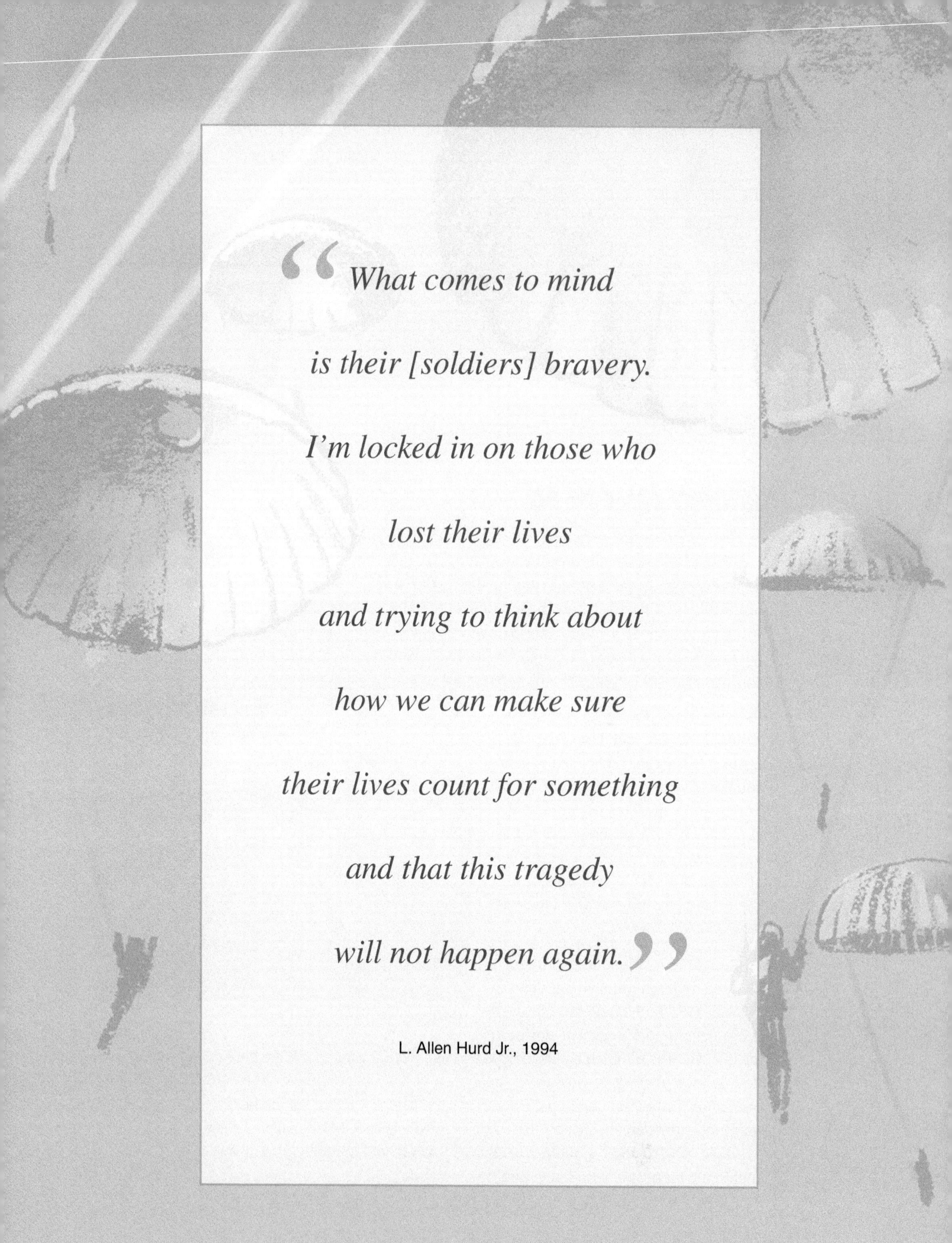

"What comes to mind

is their [soldiers] bravery.

I'm locked in on those who

lost their lives

and trying to think about

how we can make sure

their lives count for something

and that this tragedy

will not happen again."

L. Allen Hurd Jr., 1994

MARCH 16, 1922 - THE STORY BEGINS

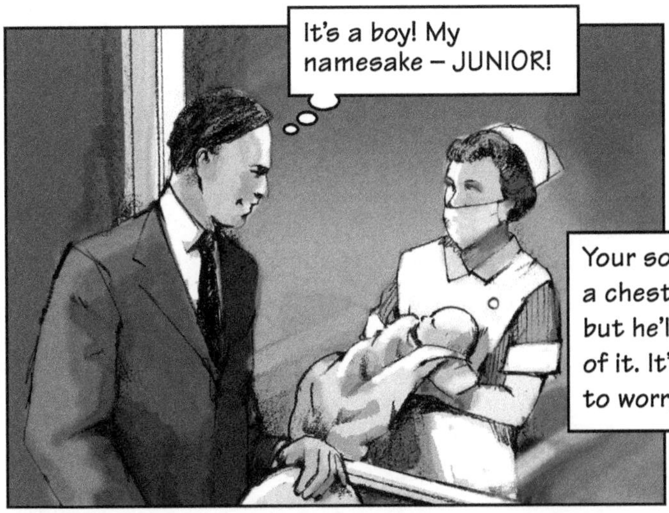

It's a boy! My namesake – JUNIOR!
Your son has a chest deformity but he'll grow out of it. It's nothing to worry about!

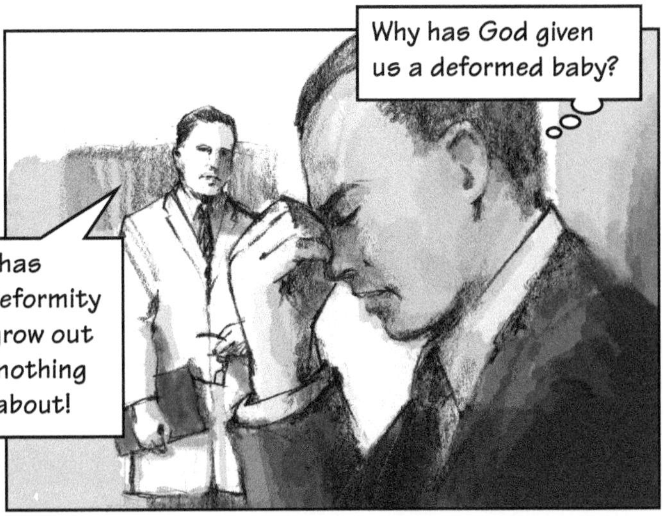

Why has God given us a deformed baby?

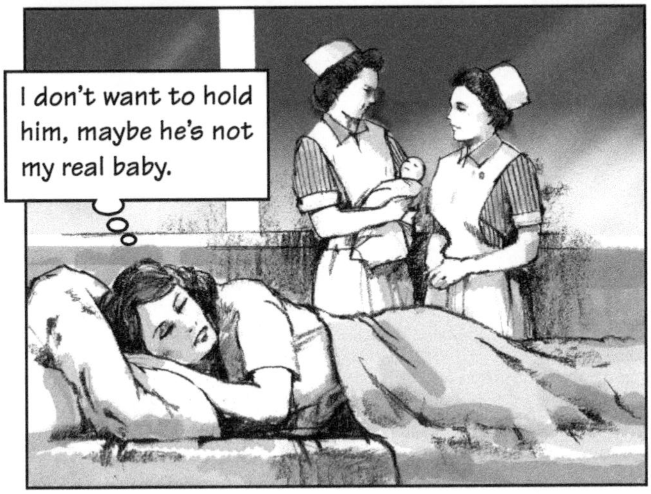

I don't want to hold him, maybe he's not my real baby.

Pectus Excavatum is Latin for "hollowed chest." In this birth defect, the growth of bone and cartilage in the chest wall is abnormal, creating a sunken or hollow appearance. In severe cases, it looks as if the center of the chest has been scooped out. It can impair cardiac and respiratory functions. Children and adults may suffer feelings of embarrassment, social anxiety, and depression.

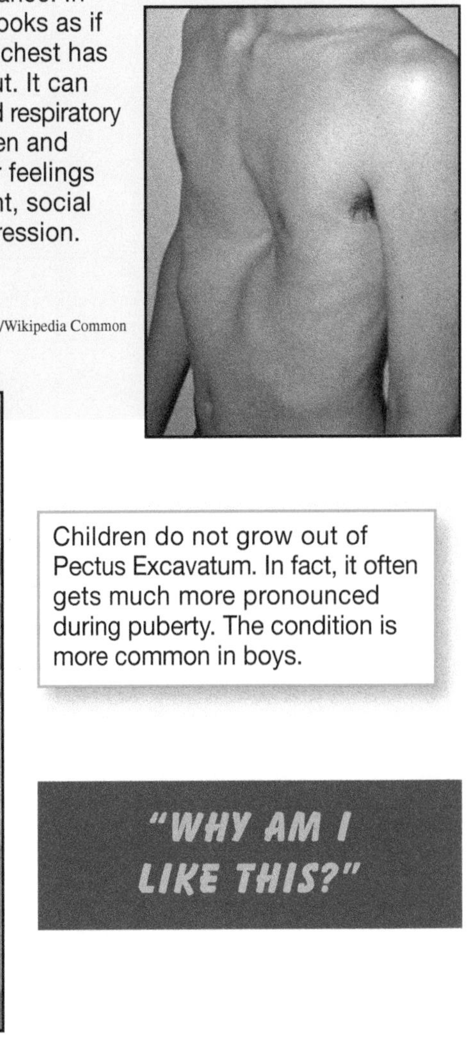

Wikimedia/Wikipedia Common

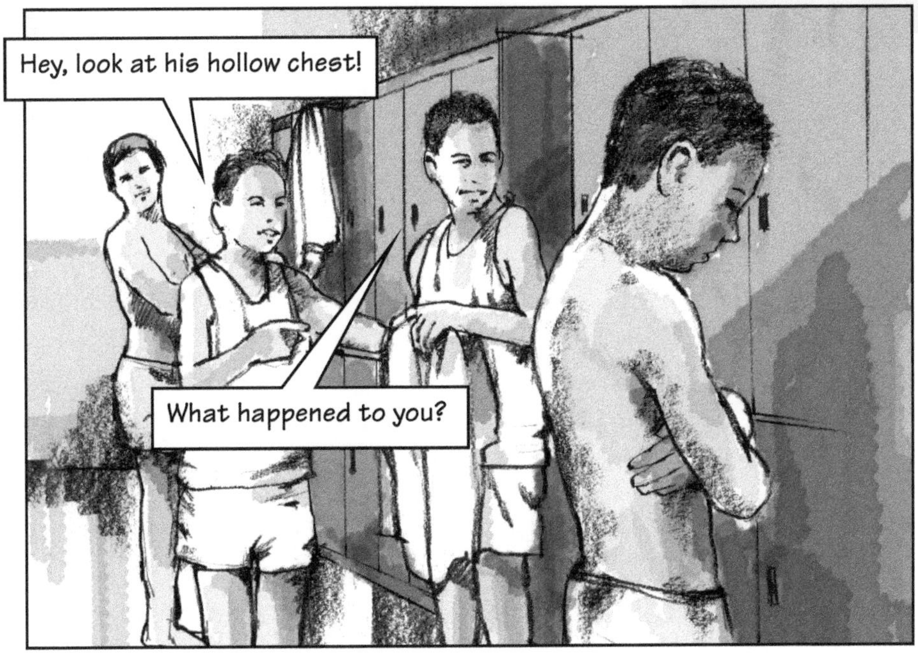

Hey, look at his hollow chest!
What happened to you?

Children do not grow out of Pectus Excavatum. In fact, it often gets much more pronounced during puberty. The condition is more common in boys.

"WHY AM I LIKE THIS?"

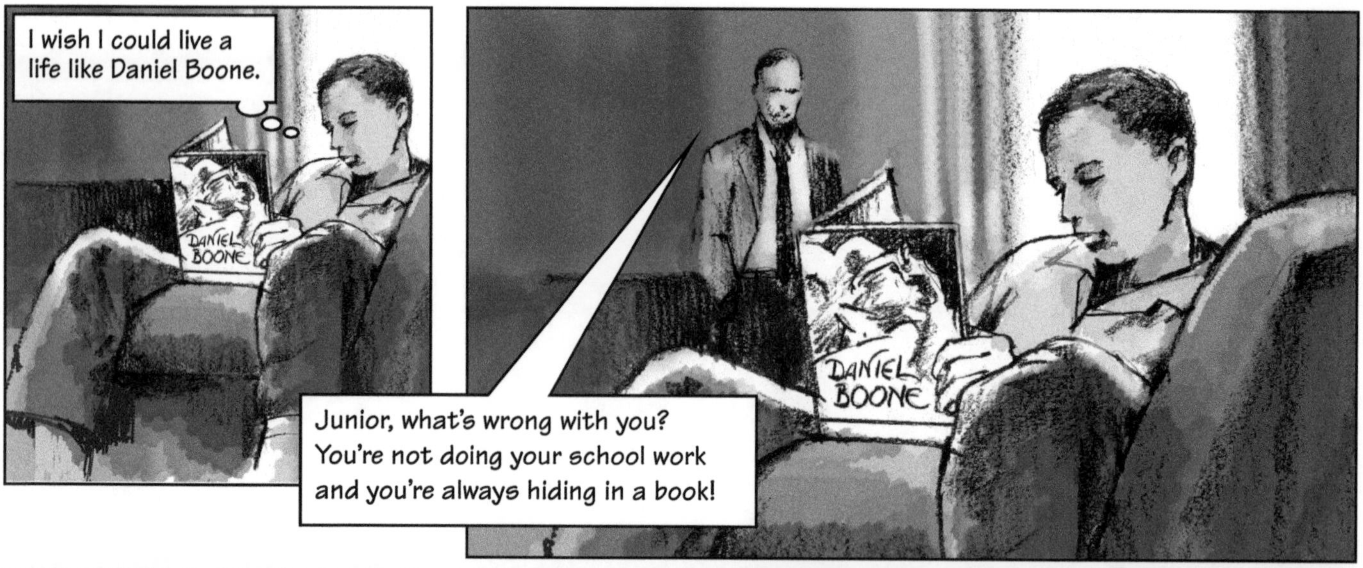
I wish I could live a life like Daniel Boone.
DANIEL BOONE
Junior, what's wrong with you? You're not doing your school work and you're always hiding in a book!
DANIEL BOONE

"I HATE BEING CALLED JUNIOR!"

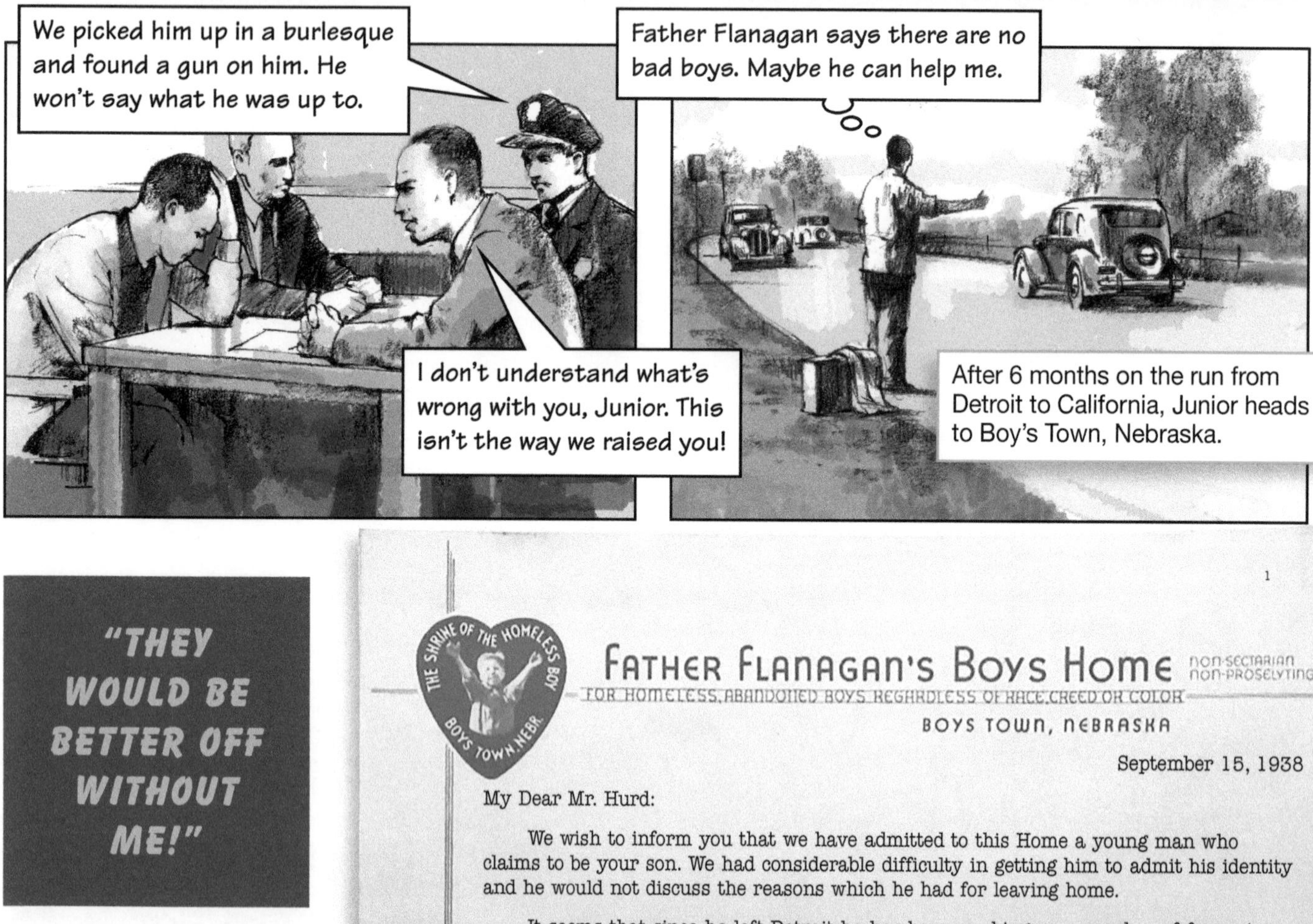
We picked him up in a burlesque and found a gun on him. He won't say what he was up to.
I don't understand what's wrong with you, Junior. This isn't the way we raised you!
Father Flanagan says there are no bad boys. Maybe he can help me.
After 6 months on the run from Detroit to California, Junior heads to Boy's Town, Nebraska.

"THEY WOULD BE BETTER OFF WITHOUT ME!"

1

THE SHRINE OF THE HOMELESS BOY — BOYS TOWN, NEBR.

FATHER FLANAGAN'S BOYS HOME NON-SECTARIAN NON-PROSELYTING

FOR HOMELESS, ABANDONED BOYS REGARDLESS OF RACE, CREED OR COLOR

BOYS TOWN, NEBRASKA

September 15, 1938

My Dear Mr. Hurd:

We wish to inform you that we have admitted to this Home a young man who claims to be your son. We had considerable difficulty in getting him to admit his identity and he would not discuss the reasons which he had for leaving home.

It seems that since he left Detroit he has been working on a number of farms to support himself. He came here today having hitch-hiked from California. He seems to realize he has made some mistakes, which he would not discuss, but now wants to get a clean start in life. We will do everything possible to help him as long as he is contented to remain here and makes a satisfactory adjustment.

Rev. L. J. Demers
Welfare Department

[1]Actual letters from Boys Town files. Father Flanagan was a priest and social reformer who advocated for children's rights and opened the Boys Home (later Town) for troubled or homeless boys in 1917.

Detroit, Michigan

Sept. 18, 1938

Dear Sir:

I must begin this letter by expressing our appreciation of your kindness to our son. I believe Junior's case to be an exceptional one and that at the time you took him in he needed the help you have to offer possibly as much as anyone in the school. What would have happened to him had he not found this opportunity is difficult to imagine. **No doubt if he were brought home now the problem would still be unsolved and the chance to make a real man and useful citizen out of him would be lost.**

Gratefully yours,
Lyman A. Hurd Sr.

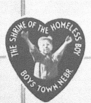

ONE WEEK LATER

THE SHRINE OF THE HOMELESS BOY — BOYS TOWN, NEBR.

FATHER FLANAGAN'S BOYS HOME NON-SECTARIAN NON-PROSELYTING
FOR HOMELESS, ABANDONED BOYS REGARDLESS OF RACE, CREED OR COLOR
BOYS TOWN, NEBRASKA

September 26, 1938

My Dear Mr. Hurd:

I wish to advise you that Lyman, Jr.[2] will leave Omaha by bus tomorrow morning and is due to arrive in Detroit Wednesday morning at 9:40 A.M. Lyman Jr. informed me last Saturday or Friday that he was homesick and wanted to return to you, but he did not tell me that he had already phoned you and bought bus tickets, I only learned of that this morning.

Because he left our premises without our permission, he will be compelled to attend our Court this evening to explain why he took it upon himself to make arrangements for his return to Detroit instead of relying on our ability to make these arrangements for him.

We are glad to have been of help to Junior and trust that his absence will make him appreciate his own home more than he, evidently, has in the past.

Most Sincerely yours,
Reverend L. J. Demers

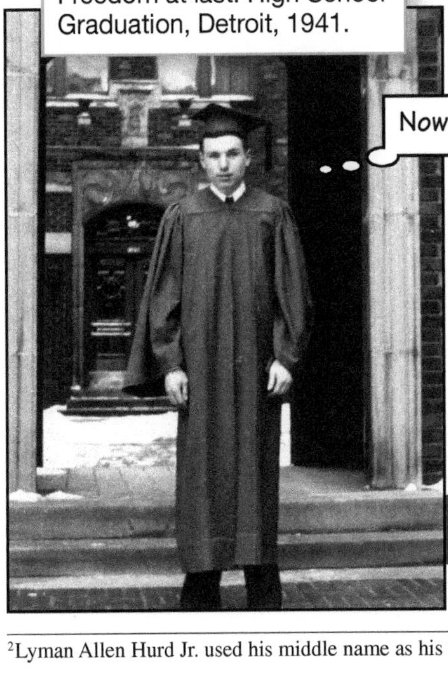
Freedom at last. High School Graduation, Detroit, 1941.
Now what?

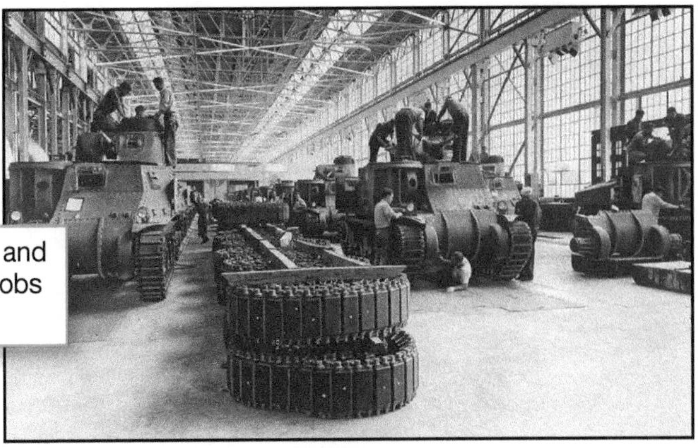
The world is at war and there are plenty of jobs in Detroit.

National Automotive History Collection, Detroit Public Library

...DRAFTED!

[2]Lyman Allen Hurd Jr. used his middle name as his first name.

TRAINING FOR BATTLE

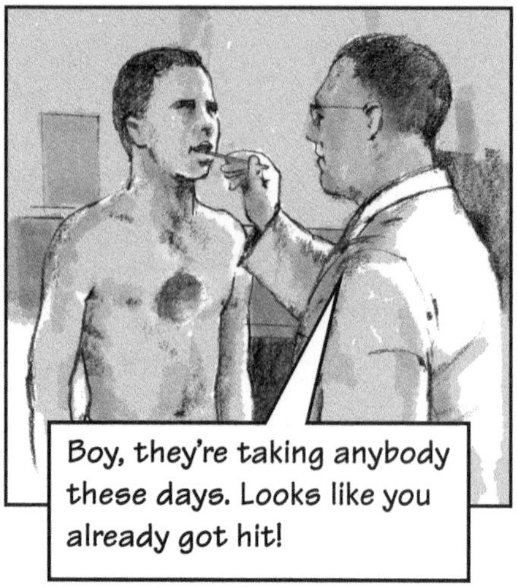
Boy, they're taking anybody these days. Looks like you already got hit!

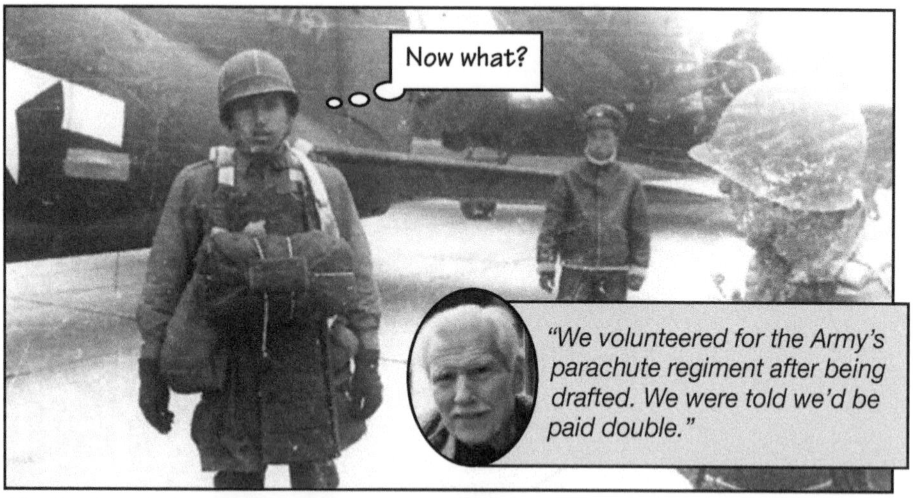
Now what?
"We volunteered for the Army's parachute regiment after being drafted. We were told we'd be paid double."

Allen Hurd, ready for practice jump, Camp Mackall, 1943.[3]

State-side training for the PIR (Parachute Infantry Regiment) volunteers was especially rigorous. Most soldiers had no previous military or jump experience. Training was designed to wash out the mentally and physically unfit and prepare the remaining for the difficult battles to come.

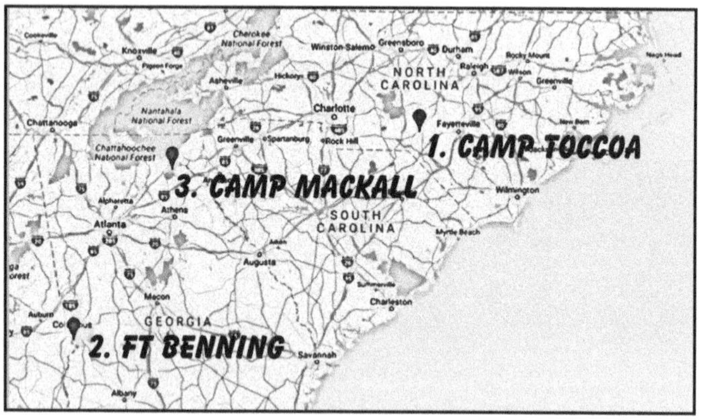
Knoxville
Asheville
Winston-Salem
Greensboro
Durham
NORTH CAROLINA
Charlotte
Fayetteville
1. CAMP TOCCOA
Greenville
Spartanburg
Rock Hill
3. CAMP MACKALL
Wilmington
SOUTH CAROLINA
Athens
Atlanta
Augusta
Charleston
Macon
GEORGIA
2. FT BENNING
Savannah

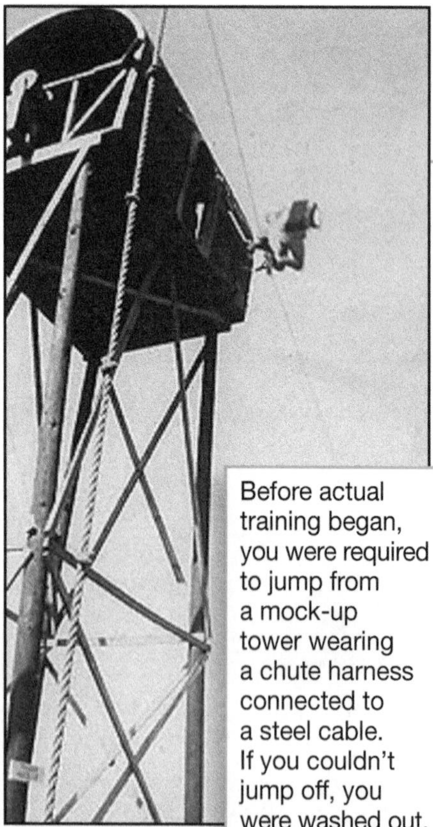

Before actual training began, you were required to jump from a mock-up tower wearing a chute harness connected to a steel cable. If you couldn't jump off, you were washed out.

JANUARY 1943 - BASIC TRAINING, CAMP TOCCOA, GEORGIA

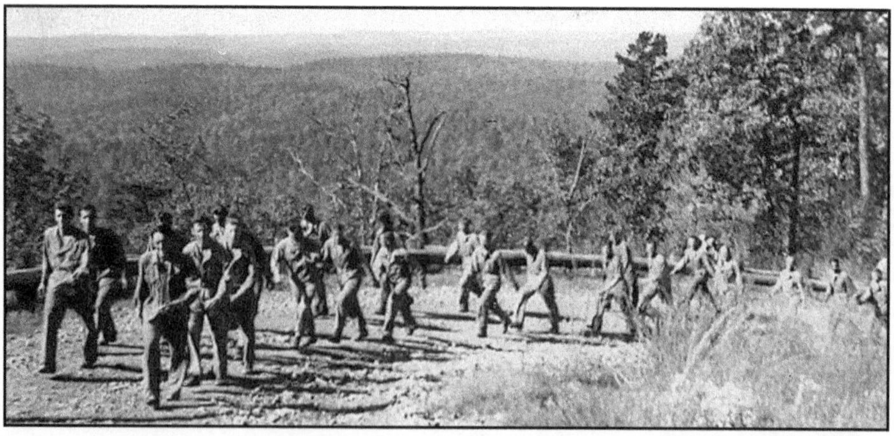

Running three miles up and back on Currahee Mountain. Handout/Currahee Military Museum

"Jumpy" Johnson, the Colonel in charge of the 501st PIR, believed in extreme physical fitness conditioning, especially long distance running. Almost half of the parachute volunteers did not make it.

[3]From WW II reminiscences and photos shared in an interview with daughter in 2004.

MAY 1943 - JUMP SCHOOL, FT. BENNING, GEORGIA

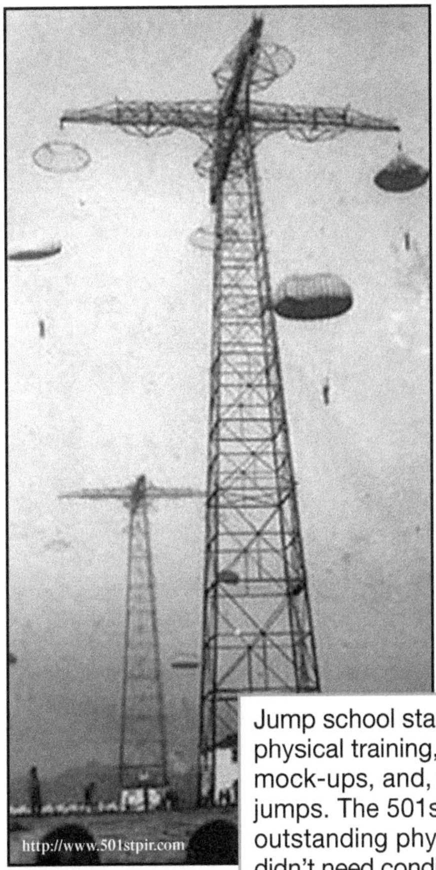
http://www.501stpir.com

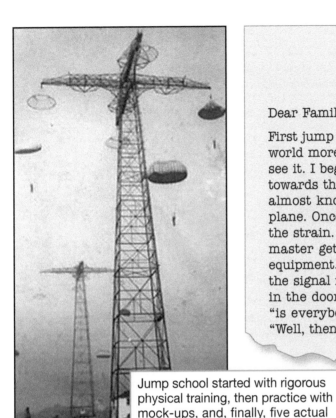

Hoisted up the 250-foot jump tower and then released.

PARATROOPS
FORT BENNING, GA

[4]

Dear Family,

First jump completed. What a thrill. If there's anything in this world more exciting than a parachute jump, I don't want to see it. I began to get a little nervous when we started to walk towards the plane. The motors were roaring and the prop blast almost knocks you over as you mount the little stairs to the plane. Once inside we try to sing and make merry to ease the strain. It doesn't work any too well. Before long the jump master gets up and yells "Stand up and hook up, check equipment." After this he yells "Stand in the doors." This is the signal for the first man (an officer) to take his position in the door. After he is set, he looks back at us and says "is everybody happy?" We all commit a lie and say "Yes!" "Well, then lets go" he shouts, and out we tumble.

Allen

Jump school started with rigorous physical training, then practice with mock-ups, and, finally, five actual jumps. The 501st were in such outstanding physical shape they didn't need conditioning and started right in on jump training.

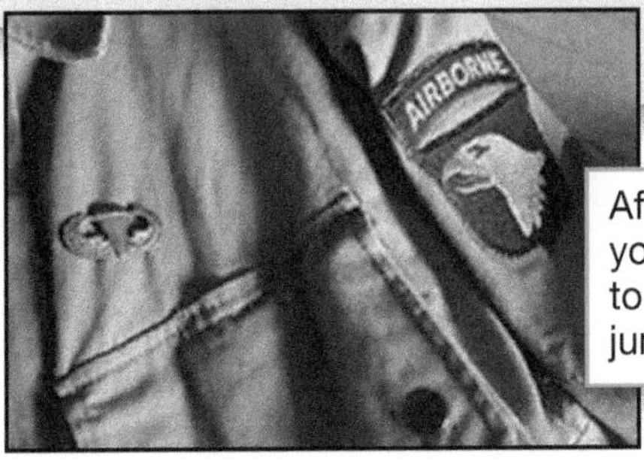
AIRBORNE

After the fifth jump, you earned the right to wear the prized jump wings.

JUNE 1943 - CAMP MACKALL, NORTH CAROLINA

Camp Mackall was Airborne Command's home base during large unit training and maneuvers in North Carolina, Tennessee, and Louisiana.

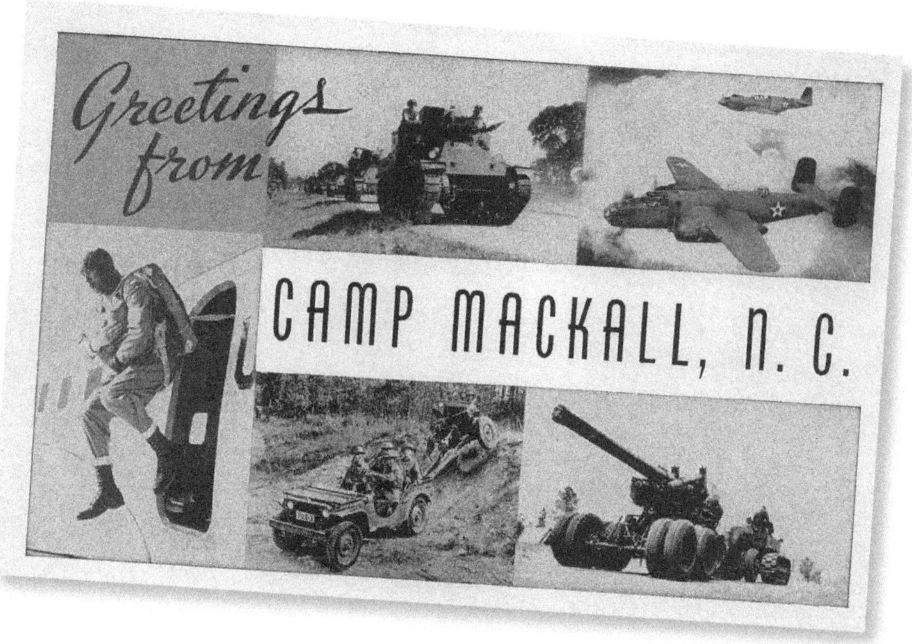
Greetings from
CAMP MACKALL, N. C.

[4]Letter home, 1943.

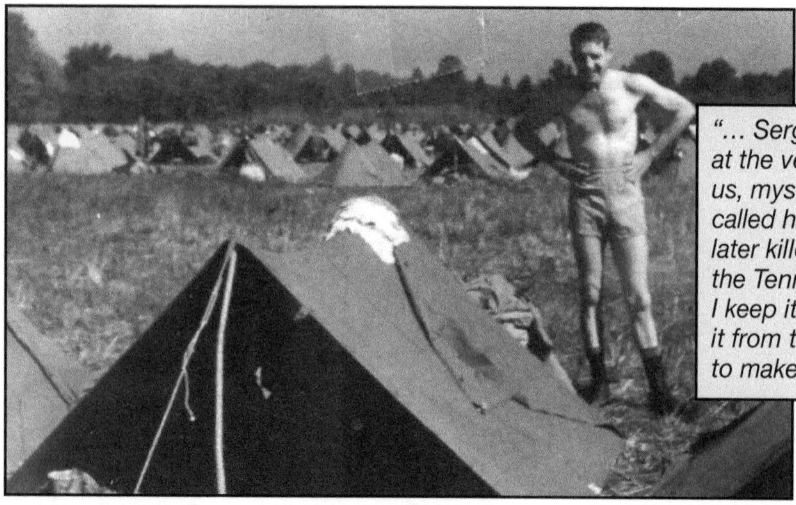

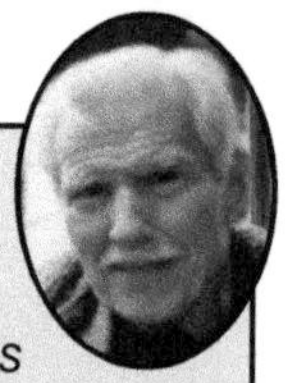

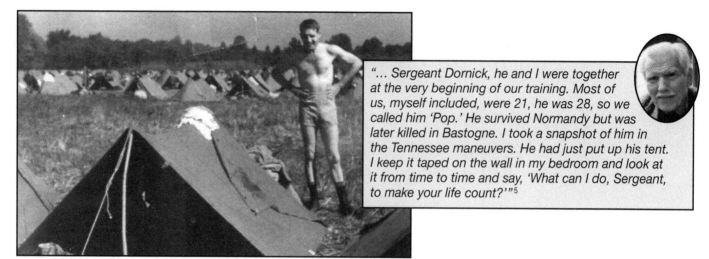

"... Sergeant Dornick, he and I were together at the very beginning of our training. Most of us, myself included, were 21, he was 28, so we called him 'Pop.' He survived Normandy but was later killed in Bastogne. I took a snapshot of him in the Tennessee maneuvers. He had just put up his tent. I keep it taped on the wall in my bedroom and look at it from time to time and say, 'What can I do, Sergeant, to make your life count?'"[5]

Sergeant "Pop" Dornick on maneuvers in Tennessee, 1943.

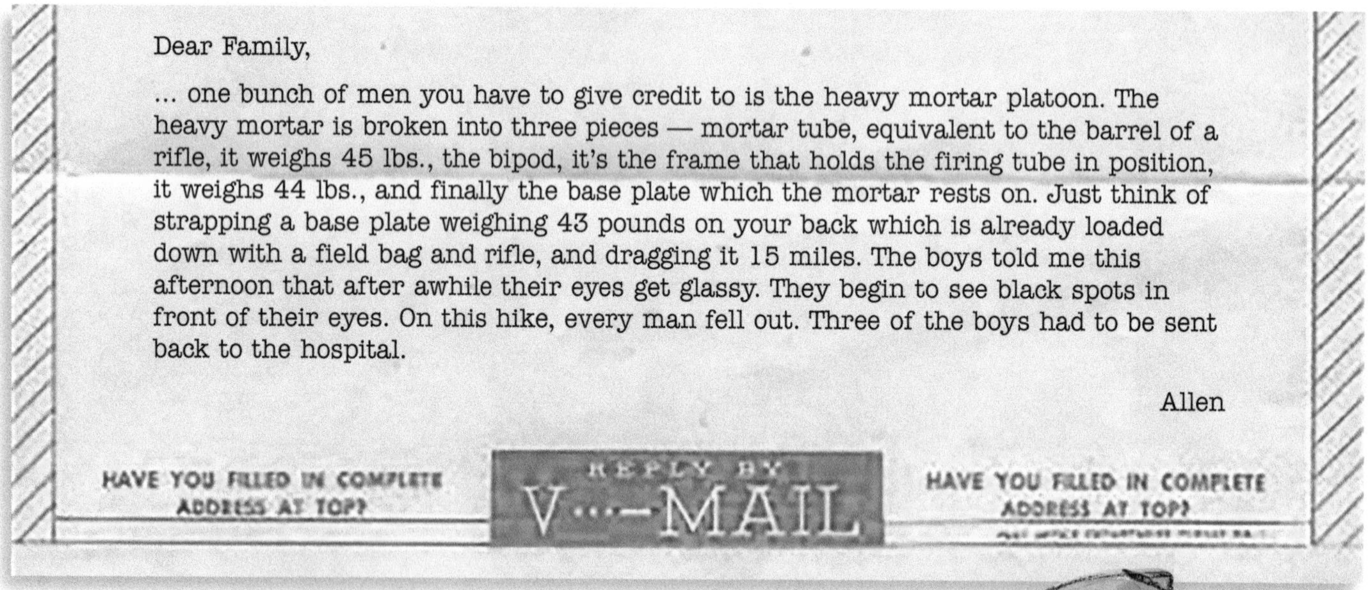

Dear Family,

... one bunch of men you have to give credit to is the heavy mortar platoon. The heavy mortar is broken into three pieces — mortar tube, equivalent to the barrel of a rifle, it weighs 45 lbs., the bipod, it's the frame that holds the firing tube in position, it weighs 44 lbs., and finally the base plate which the mortar rests on. Just think of strapping a base plate weighing 43 pounds on your back which is already loaded down with a field bag and rifle, and dragging it 15 miles. The boys told me this afternoon that after awhile their eyes get glassy. They begin to see black spots in front of their eyes. On this hike, every man fell out. Three of the boys had to be sent back to the hospital.

Allen

HAVE YOU FILLED IN COMPLETE ADDRESS AT TOP?

REPLY BY V—MAIL

HAVE YOU FILLED IN COMPLETE ADDRESS AT TOP?

DECEMBER 1943 - ON TO EUROPE

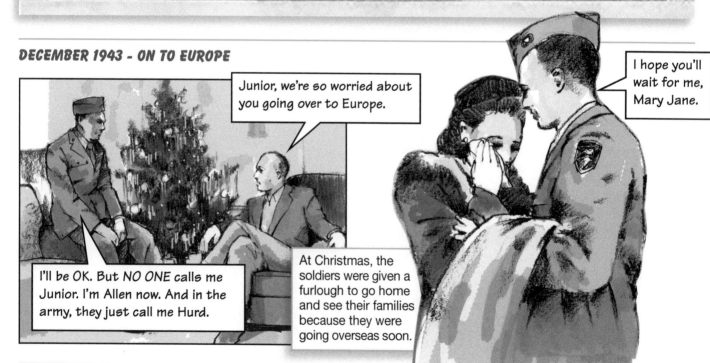

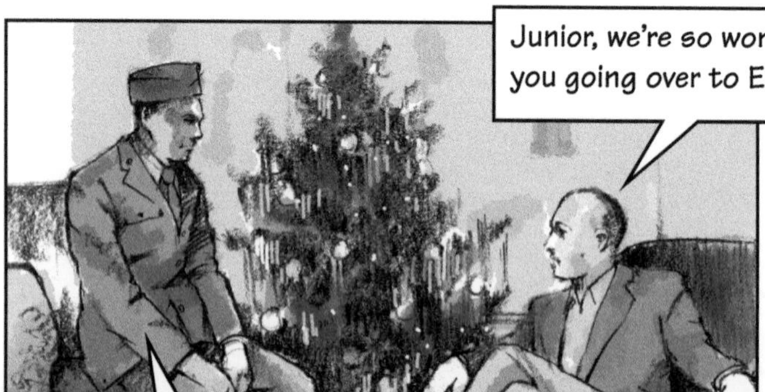
Junior, we're so worried about you going over to Europe.
I'll be OK. But NO ONE calls me Junior. I'm Allen now. And in the army, they just call me Hurd.

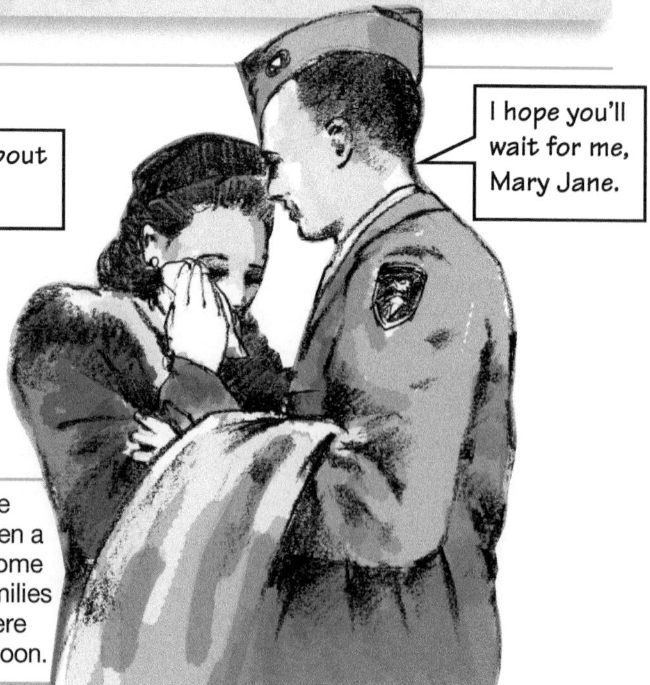
I hope you'll wait for me, Mary Jane.

At Christmas, the soldiers were given a furlough to go home and see their families because they were going overseas soon.

[5]From June 6, 1994 Face-to-Face interview with Rich Fisher on Channel 2 Detroit News. The occasion was Allen's donation of a flag to the Detroit Library in honor of those who died at Normandy.

In January 1944, the 501st 2nd battalion sailed across the Atlantic aboard the US army transport ship the George W. Goethals. After landing in Glasgow, Scotland, they went by train to Newbury, England, for more training.

January, 1944

Dear Family,

My sea voyage is almost over. Man! The waves on this man's ocean are something to see. Huge, rolling mountains of water. We enlisted men are packed like sardines in the hold of the ship. Good place to store cargo... if the cargo isn't too fragile. To kill time I'm forced to read 10 year old National Geographic magazines which is just about rock bottom in the sphere of human activities.

Allen

HAVE YOU FILLED IN COMPLETE ADDRESS AT TOP?

HAVE YOU FILLED IN COMPLETE ADDRESS AT TOP?

JANUARY-MAY 1944 - TRAINING IN NEWBURY, ENGLAND

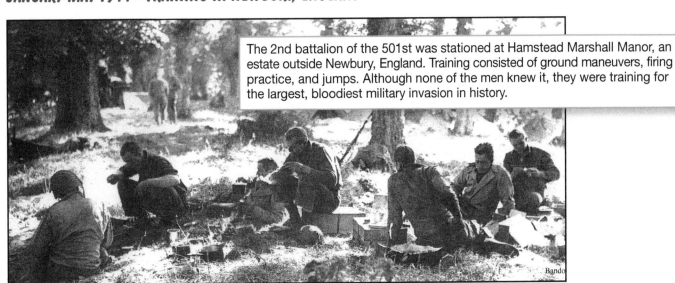

The 2nd battalion of the 501st was stationed at Hamstead Marshall Manor, an estate outside Newbury, England. Training consisted of ground maneuvers, firing practice, and jumps. Although none of the men knew it, they were training for the largest, bloodiest military invasion in history.

501st at Newbury, 1944.

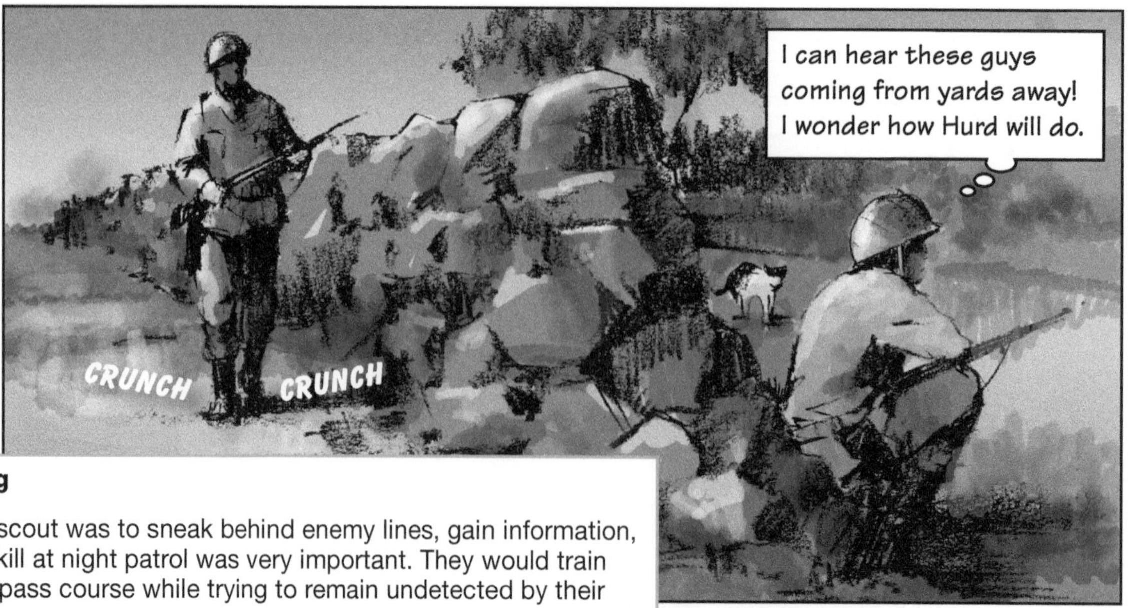
CRUNCH
CRUNCH
I can hear these guys coming from yards away! I wonder how Hurd will do.

Scouts in Training

The job of the PIR scout was to sneak behind enemy lines, gain information, and report back. Skill at night patrol was very important. They would train by following a compass course while trying to remain undetected by their commanding officer.

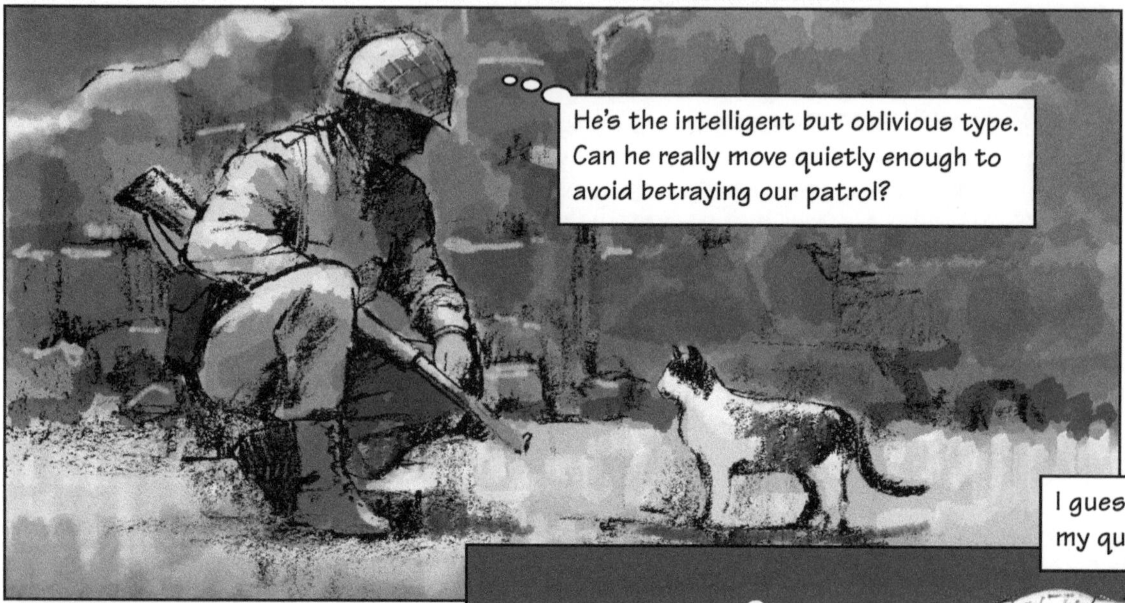
He's the intelligent but oblivious type. Can he really move quietly enough to avoid betraying our patrol?

6, 7

WHAT WOULD DANIEL BOONE DO?

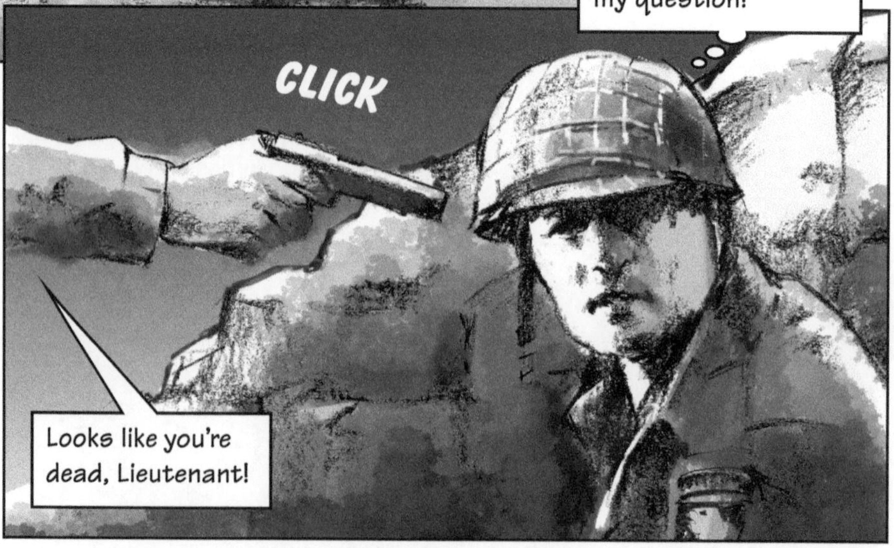
I guess that answers my question!
CLICK
Looks like you're dead, Lieutenant!

[6] Story from Lt. G. William Sefton, *It Was My War* (Sunflower University Press, 1994), p. 42-43. Allen was able to sneak up on his Lieutenant because he had wrapped his boots in gunny sacks.

[7] "In one of the letters he destroyed, I did not transcribe it, he [Allen] said, 'the more I become like my childhood hero, Daniel Boone, the more effective I will be.'" Interview with Mark Bando, 2017.

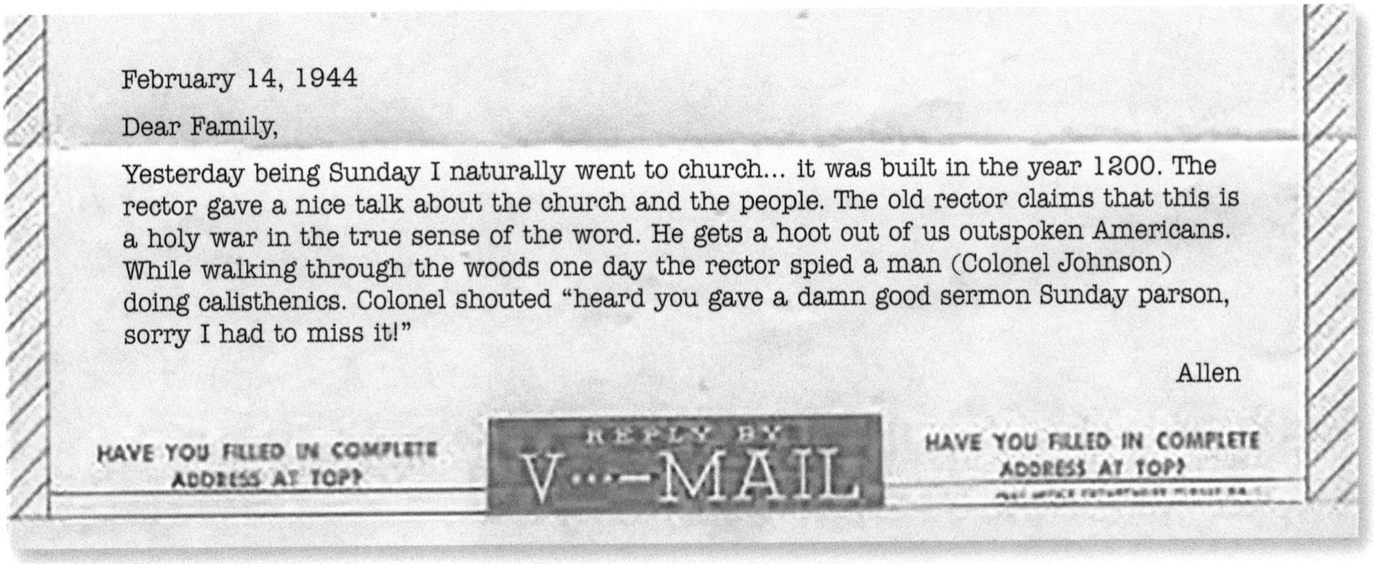

February 14, 1944

Dear Family,

Yesterday being Sunday I naturally went to church... it was built in the year 1200. The rector gave a nice talk about the church and the people. The old rector claims that this is a holy war in the true sense of the word. He gets a hoot out of us outspoken Americans. While walking through the woods one day the rector spied a man (Colonel Johnson) doing calisthenics. Colonel shouted "heard you gave a damn good sermon Sunday parson, sorry I had to miss it!"

Allen

HAVE YOU FILLED IN COMPLETE ADDRESS AT TOP?

REPLY BY V---MAIL

HAVE YOU FILLED IN COMPLETE ADDRESS AT TOP?

JUNE 1944 - INTO BATTLE

By 1944, Germany controlled much of Europe. Millions of people had been killed or forced into slavery. The allied Operation Overlord on D-Day began the liberation of the people of France and Western Europe.

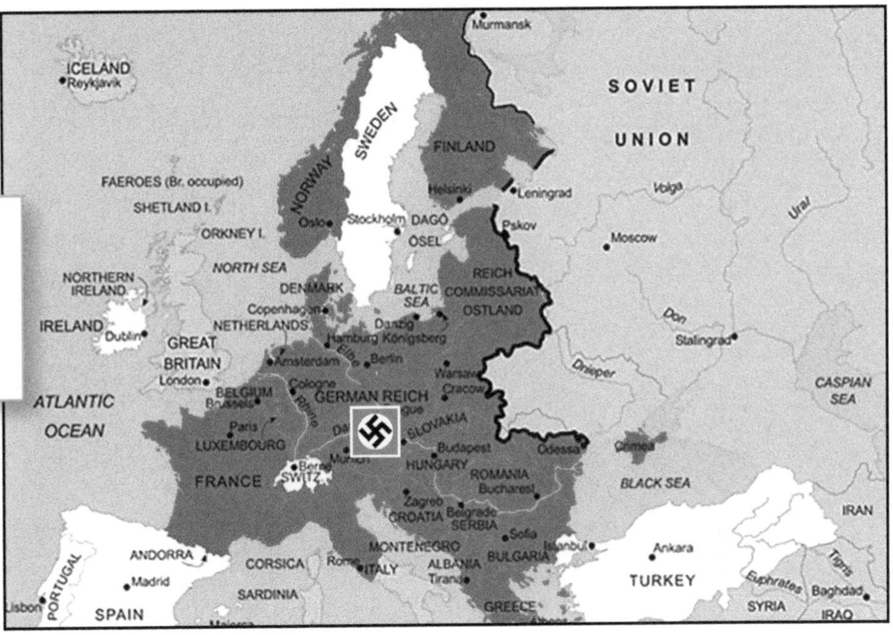

Murmansk
ICELAND
Reykjavik
SOVIET
UNION
SWEDEN
NORWAY
FINLAND
FAEROES (Br. occupied)
SHETLAND I.
Helsinki
Leningrad
Volga
Ural
Oslo
Stockholm
DAGO
OSEL
Pskov
Moscow
ORKNEY I.
NORTH SEA
NORTHERN IRELAND
DENMARK
BALTIC SEA
REICH COMMISSARIAT OSTLAND
Copenhagen
IRELAND
Dublin
NETHERLANDS
Danzig
Hamburg
Königsberg
Don
Stalingrad
GREAT BRITAIN
Amsterdam
Berlin
London
Warsaw
Dnieper
CASPIAN SEA
BELGIUM
Brussels
Cologne
GERMAN REICH
Cracow
ATLANTIC OCEAN
Paris
LUXEMBOURG
SLOVAKIA
Budapest
Odessa
Crimea
Munich
HUNGARY
Berne
SWITZ
FRANCE
ROMANIA
Bucharest
BLACK SEA
Zagreb
CROATIA
Belgrade
SERBIA
IRAN
Sofia
MONTENEGRO
BULGARIA
Istanbul
Ankara
ANDORRA
CORSICA
Rome
ITALY
ALBANIA
Tirana
PORTUGAL
Madrid
TURKEY
Euphrates
Tigris
Baghdad
SARDINIA
Lisbon
SPAIN
GREECE
SYRIA
IRAQ

OPERATION OVERLORD – D-DAY

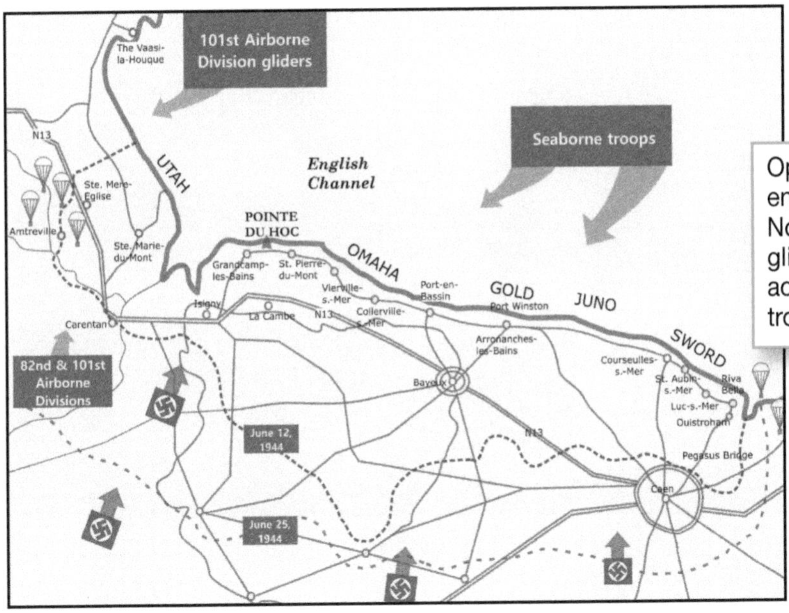

101st Airborne Division gliders
The Vaasi-la-Houque
N13
Seaborne troops
UTAH
English Channel
Ste. Mere-Eglise
Amtreville
POINTE DU HOC
Ste. Marie-du-Mont
OMAHA
Grandcamp-les-Bains
St. Pierre-du-Mont
Vierville-s.-Mer
Port-en-Bassin
GOLD
JUNO
Isigny
La Cambe
N13
Colleville-s.-Mer
Port Winston
Carentan
Arromanches-les-Bains
SWORD
82nd & 101st Airborne Divisions
Courseulles-s.-Mer
St. Aubin-s.-Mer
Riva Bella
Bayeux
Luc-s.-Mer
Ouistreham
June 12, 1944
N13
Pegasus Bridge
Caen
June 25, 1944

Operation Overlord combined allied forces in an enormous assault on the enemy in occupied Normandy, France. The airborne paratroopers and gliders were sent in first to secure crucial roads across the marshes at Utah beach for the seaborne troops coming ashore at dawn.

Eisenhower Library, National Archives

"One morning, we were awakened and told we would be addressed by General Eisenhower. So we polished our boots exceptionally and got out into a country meadow and waited, as you so often do in the military, so our thoughts ranged all over the place. Finally, the band strikes up a particular instrumentality called Hail to the Chief and we can see in the distance that a jeep has left the road and was headed toward us – of course, that was Eisenhower. It was quite stirring because we had been waiting so long and then suddenly called to attention. I can get kind of emotional about it because he was our chief and whatever he said, we would do [chokes up]. We were trained to respond to the chief and finally he was here. Our first contact with General Eisenhower![8]"

ON TO MERRYFIELD AIRFIELD

Orig-Press-Photo

US soldier enjoys eggs at abandoned farm.

"We were shipped from Newbury to the coast and given special food. Quite a fun thing – all the eggs you could eat. Of course, we knew it was kind of like the prisoner being taken to the electric chair, but it was still fun to have all that wonderful food. And then close to midnight we were rounded up and got into the planes."

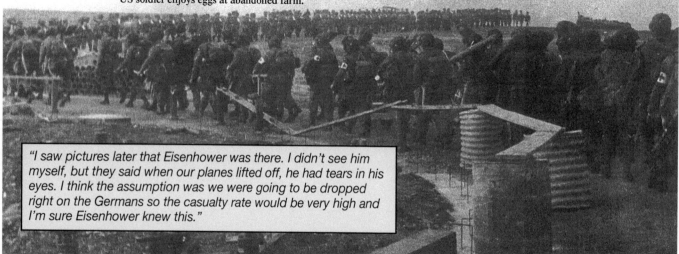

"I saw pictures later that Eisenhower was there. I didn't see him myself, but they said when our planes lifted off, he had tears in his eyes. I think the assumption was we were going to be dropped right on the Germans so the casualty rate would be very high and I'm sure Eisenhower knew this."

501st at Merryfield before jump.

Bando

[8] Hurd's story as told to his daughter, Denise Hurd, in 2004.

JUNE 5, 1944 - CLOSE TO MIDNIGHT

The 501st PIR took off for their first combat jump from Merryfield Airport close to midnight, June 5, 1944. Their target was Drop Zone D. The goal of the 2nd Battalion was to destroy the Carentan Bridges over the Douve River and secure the town of St. Come-du-Mont.

However, low clouds and anti-aircraft fire forced the planes out of formation and most of the paratroopers landed outside the drop zone. Many were killed by enemy fire or by being forced to land in trees or water.

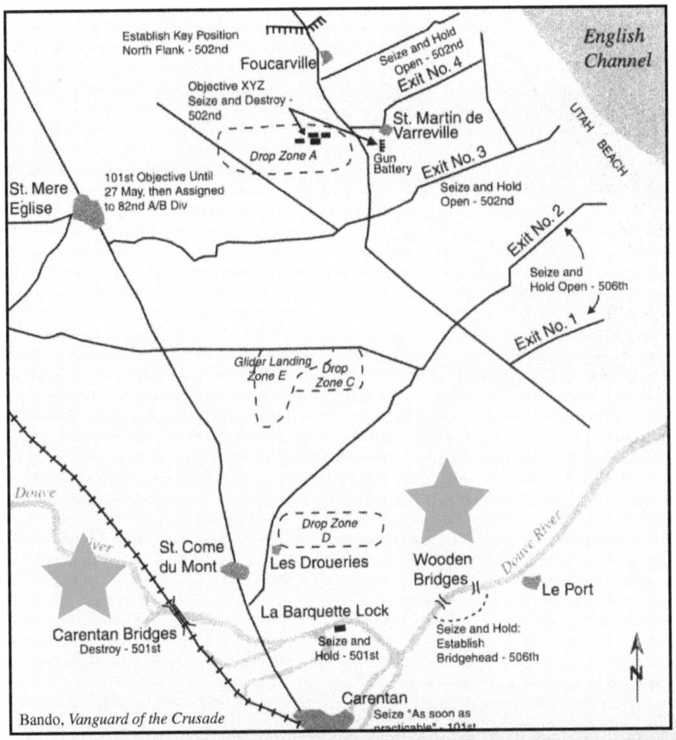

Establish Key Position North Flank - 502nd
Foucarville
Seize and Hold Open - 502nd
Exit No. 4
English Channel
Objective XYZ Seize and Destroy - 502nd
St. Martin de Varreville
Drop Zone A
Gun Battery
Exit No. 3
UTAH BEACH
St. Mere Eglise
101st Objective Until 27 May, then Assigned to 82nd A/B Div
Seize and Hold Open - 502nd
Exit No. 2
Seize and Hold Open - 506th
Exit No. 1
Glider Landing Zone E
Drop Zone C
Douve
St. Come du Mont
Drop Zone D
Les Droueries
Wooden Bridges
Douve River
Le Port
La Barquette Lock
Carentan Bridges Destroy - 501st
Seize and Hold - 501st
Seize and Hold: Establish Bridgehead - 506th
Carentan
N

Bando, *Vanguard of the Crusade*

101st takes off on D-Day.

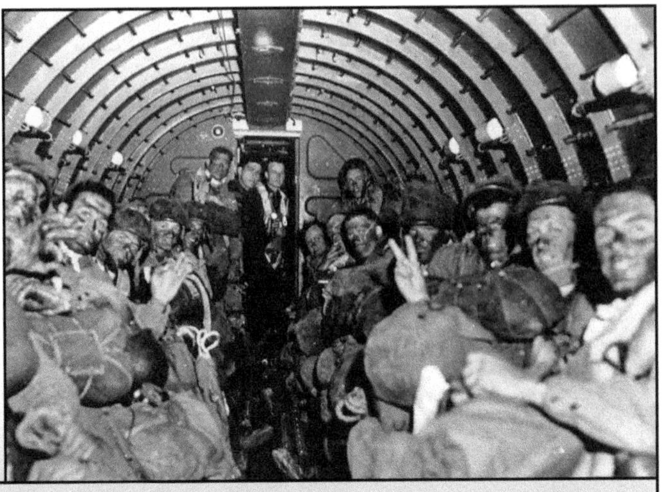

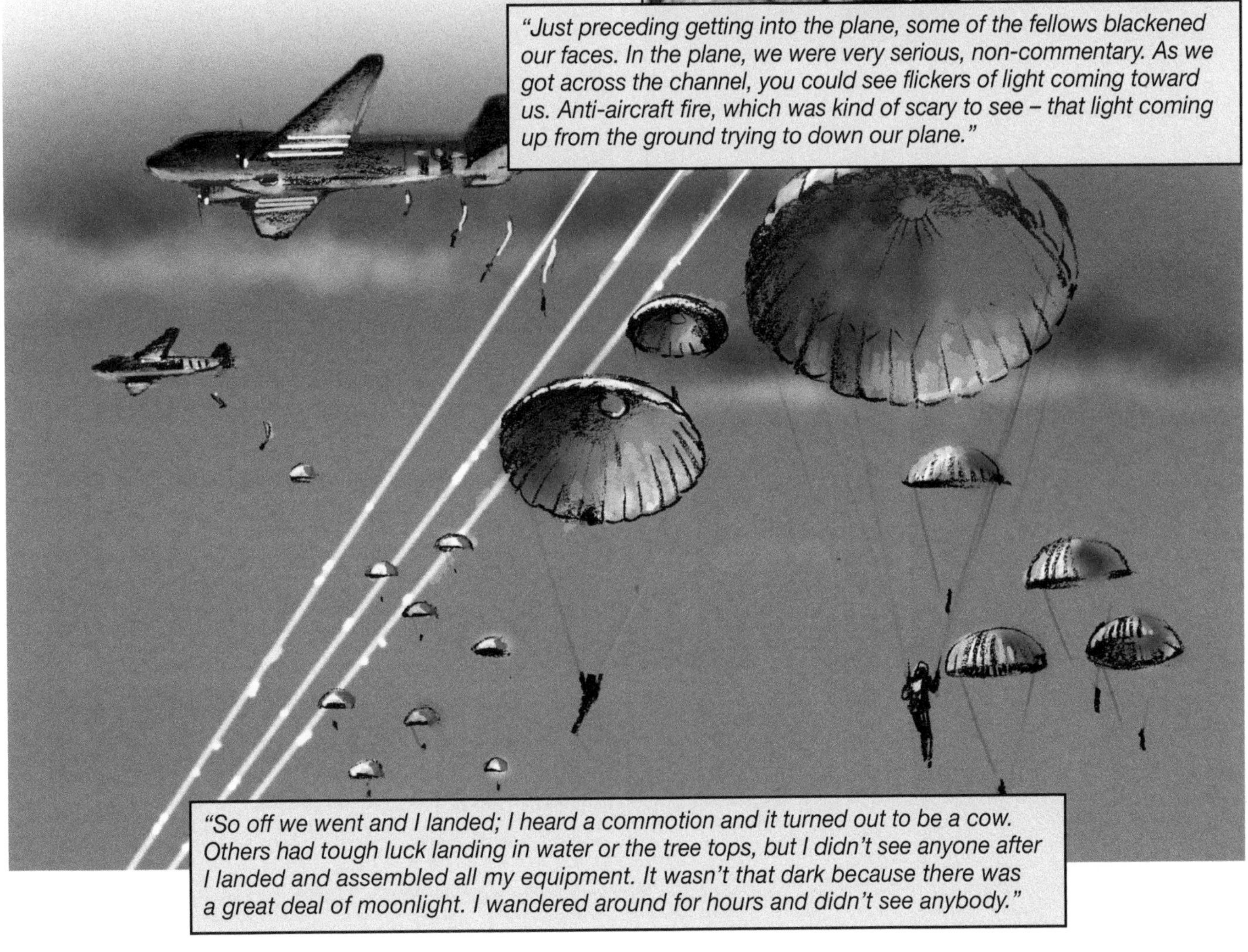

"Just preceding getting into the plane, some of the fellows blackened our faces. In the plane, we were very serious, non-commentary. As we got across the channel, you could see flickers of light coming toward us. Anti-aircraft fire, which was kind of scary to see – that light coming up from the ground trying to down our plane."

"So off we went and I landed; I heard a commotion and it turned out to be a cow. Others had tough luck landing in water or the tree tops, but I didn't see anyone after I landed and assembled all my equipment. It wasn't that dark because there was a great deal of moonlight. I wandered around for hours and didn't see anybody."

"As dawn broke, a few of us got together, still not our complete company. My first observations walking along the road, besides seeing a lot of cattle killed, were we saw young Germans our age killed by aircraft fire before they could get off the road into a ditch. So we see them and the expressions on their faces and the contortions of their legs. The shock of seeing their faces! We were about exactly the same age, between 20 and 22, and I had never seen a young fellow dead, let alone with that expression on his face, so that was a particularly vivid memory."

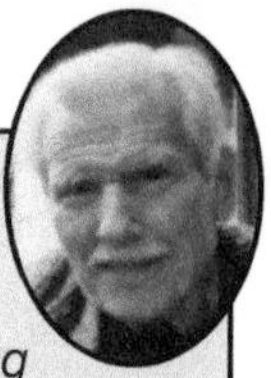

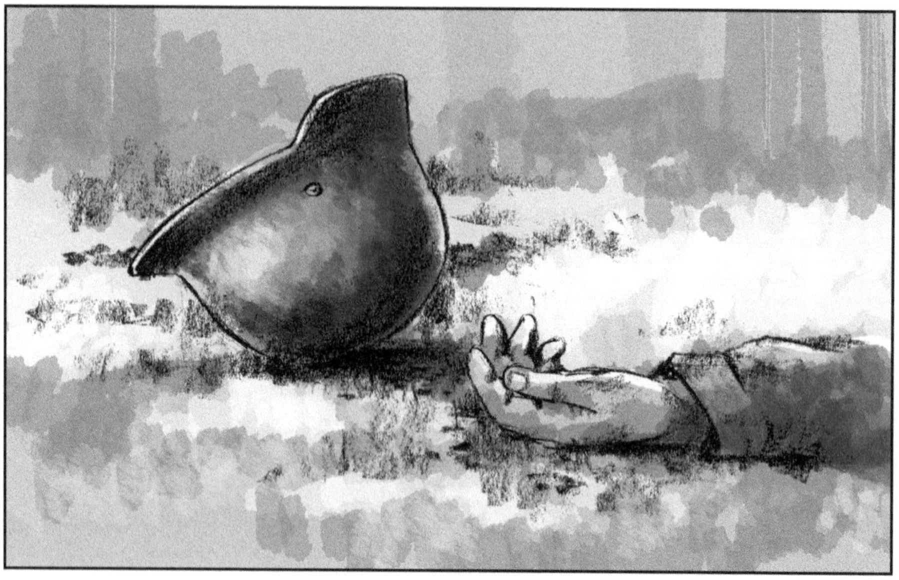

JUNE 7 & 8, 1944

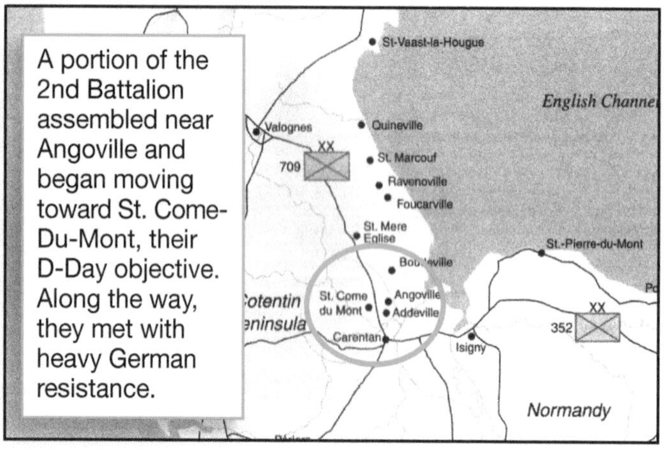
A portion of the 2nd Battalion assembled near Angoville and began moving toward St. Come-Du-Mont, their D-Day objective. Along the way, they met with heavy German resistance.
St-Vaast-la-Hougue
English Channel
Valognes
Quineville
XX
709
St. Marcouf
Ravenoville
Foucarville
St. Mere Eglise
St.-Pierre-du-Mont
St. Come du Mont
Angoville
Addeville
Carentan
XX
352
Isigny
Normandy

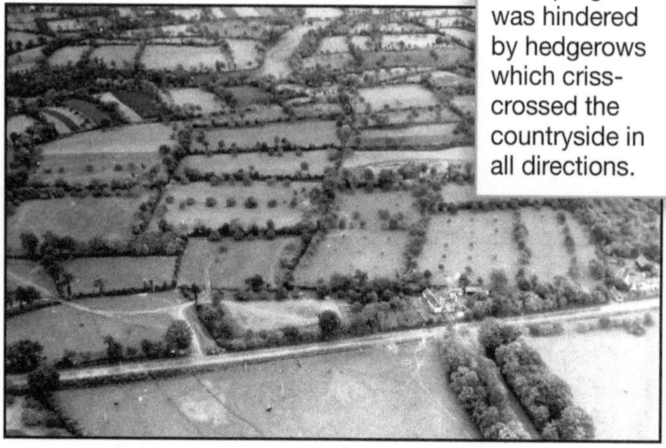
Their progress was hindered by hedgerows which criss-crossed the countryside in all directions.

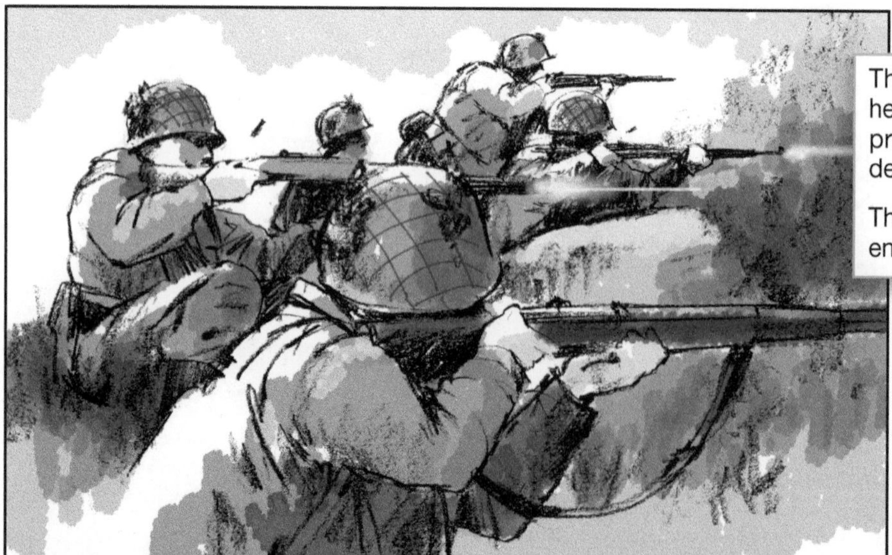

The 2nd Battalion was stopped at a hedgerow by Germans shooting from the protection of the mounded earth and dense undergrowth.

The battalion was pinned down by fierce enemy fire.

A STALEMATE!

WHAT WOULD DANIEL BOONE DO?

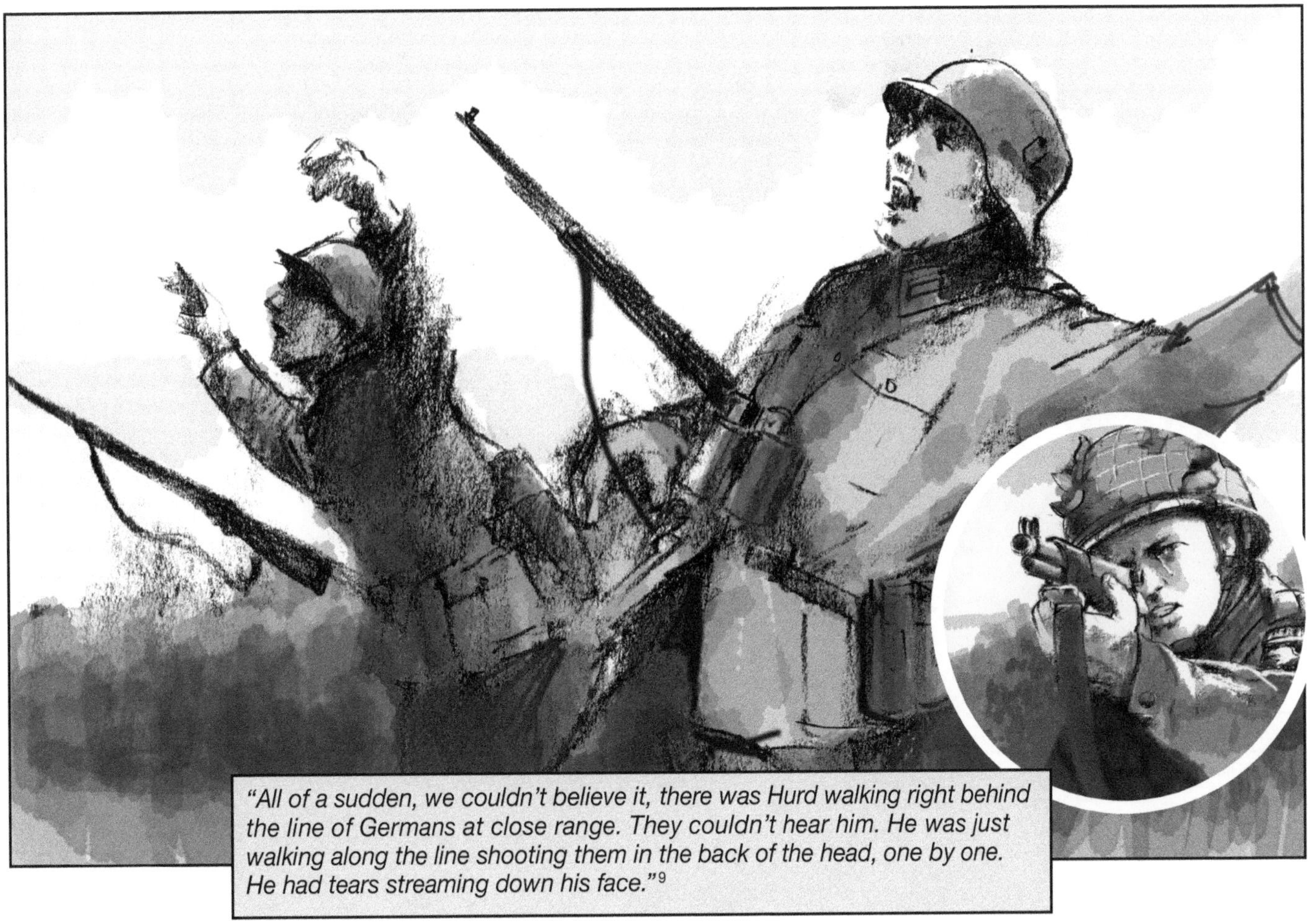
"All of a sudden, we couldn't believe it, there was Hurd walking right behind the line of Germans at close range. They couldn't hear him. He was just walking along the line shooting them in the back of the head, one by one. He had tears streaming down his face."[9]

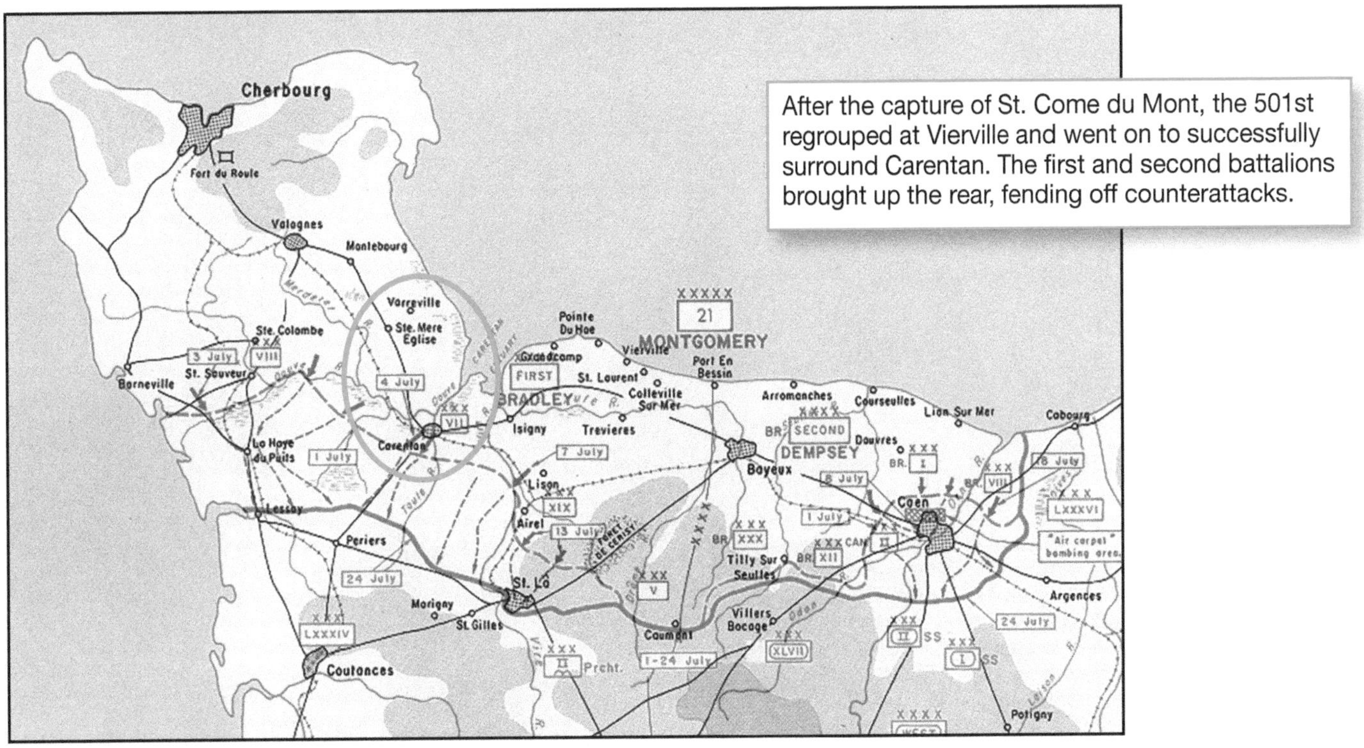
After the capture of St. Come du Mont, the 501st regrouped at Vierville and went on to successfully surround Carentan. The first and second battalions brought up the rear, fending off counterattacks.
Cherbourg
Fort du Roule
Valognes
Montebourg
Varreville
Ste. Mere Eglise
Ste. Colombe
St. Sauveur
Barneville
La Haye du Puits
Carentan
Lessay
Periers
Coutances
Marigny
St. Gilles
St. Lo
Pointe Du Hoe
Vierville
Grandcamp
St. Laurent
Colleville Sur Mer
Port En Bessin
Isigny
Trevieres
Lison
Airel
21
MONTGOMERY
FIRST
BRADLEY
Arromanches
Courseulles
Lion Sur Mer
Cabourg
SECOND
DEMPSEY
Douvres
Bayeux
Caen
Tilly Sur Seulles
Villers Bocage
Caumont
Argences
Potigny
"Air carpet" bombing area
3 July
4 July
1 July
7 July
13 July
24 July
8 July
1-24 July
18 July
VIII
VII
XIX
XXX
XII
LXXXIV
LXXXVI
XLVII

[9]As told to Mark Bando by Lt. Bill Sefton of the 501st 2nd Battalion.

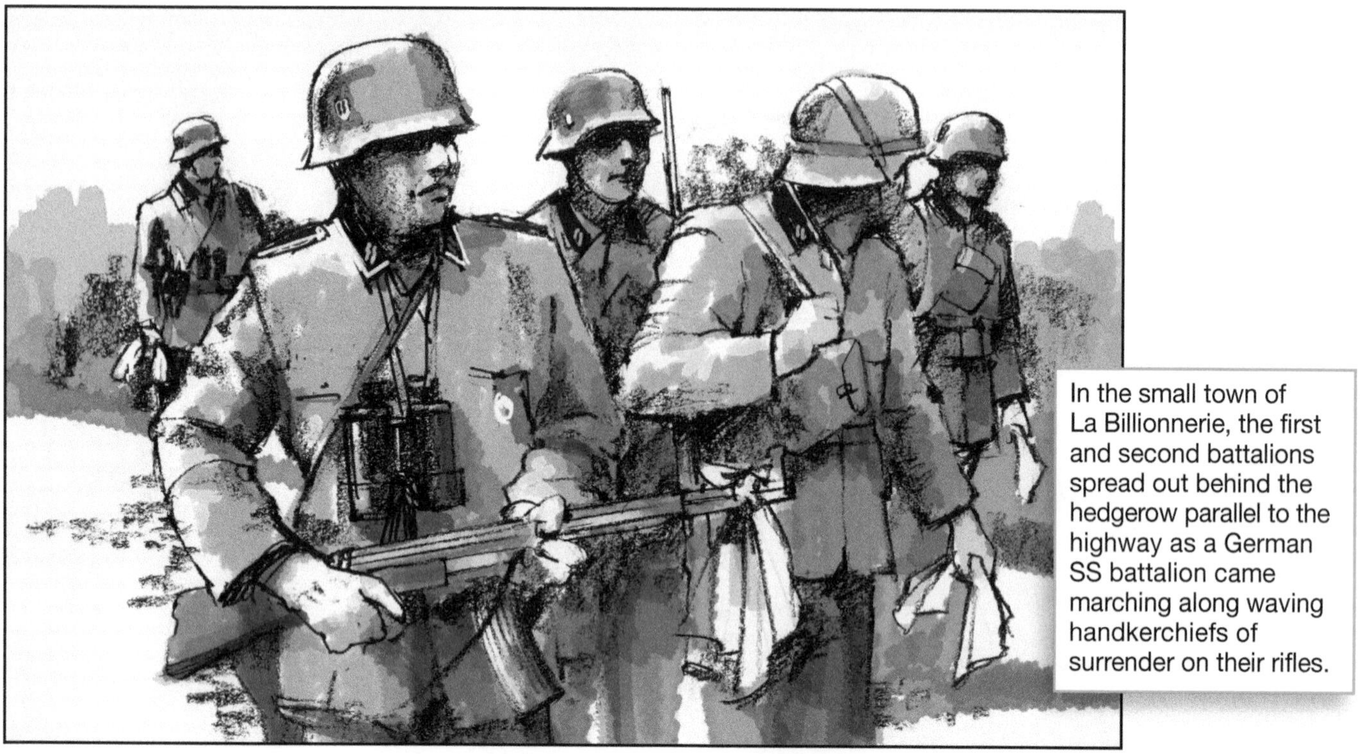
In the small town of La Billionnerie, the first and second battalions spread out behind the hedgerow parallel to the highway as a German SS battalion came marching along waving handkerchiefs of surrender on their rifles.

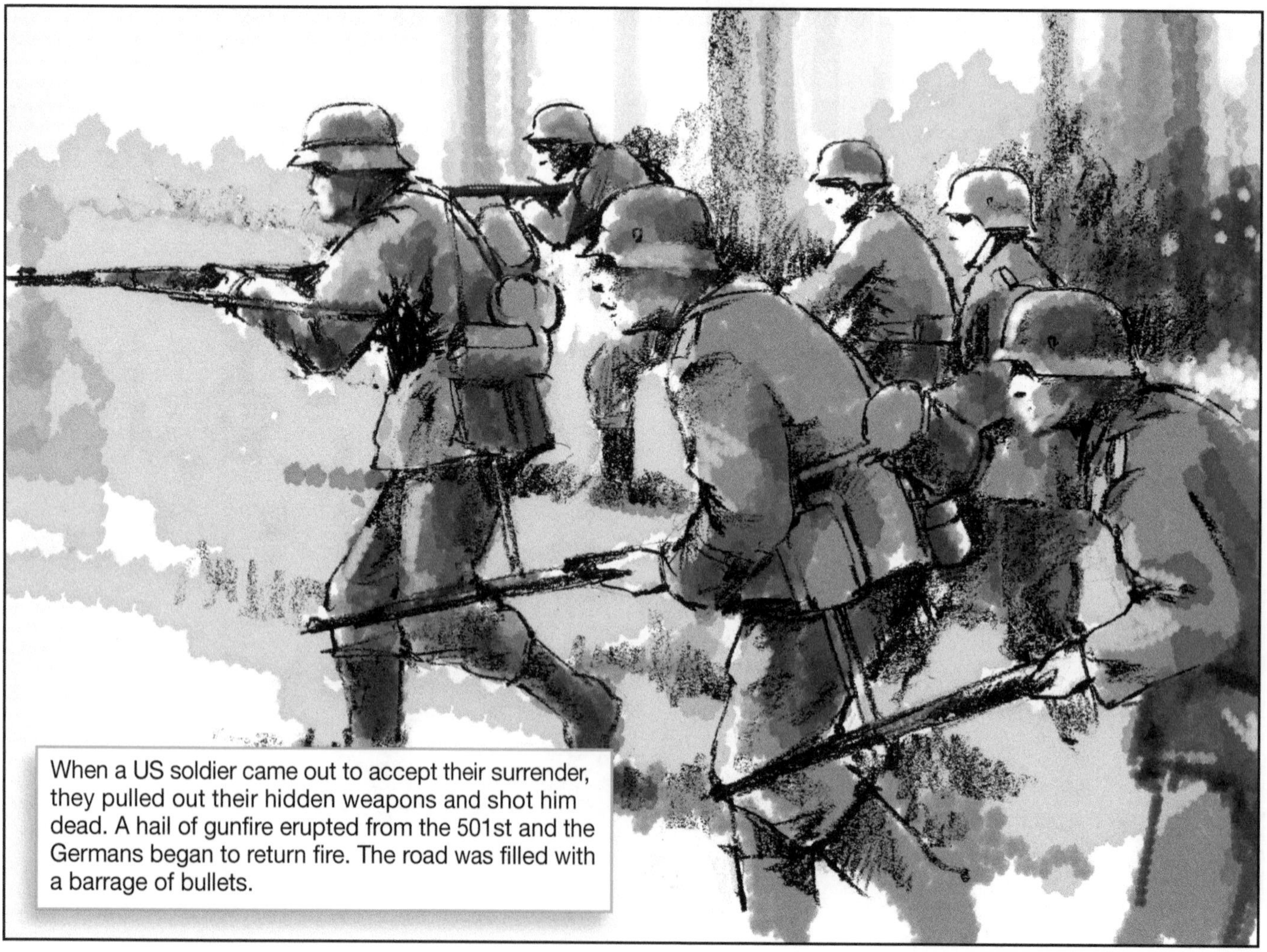
When a US soldier came out to accept their surrender, they pulled out their hidden weapons and shot him dead. A hail of gunfire erupted from the 501st and the Germans began to return fire. The road was filled with a barrage of bullets.

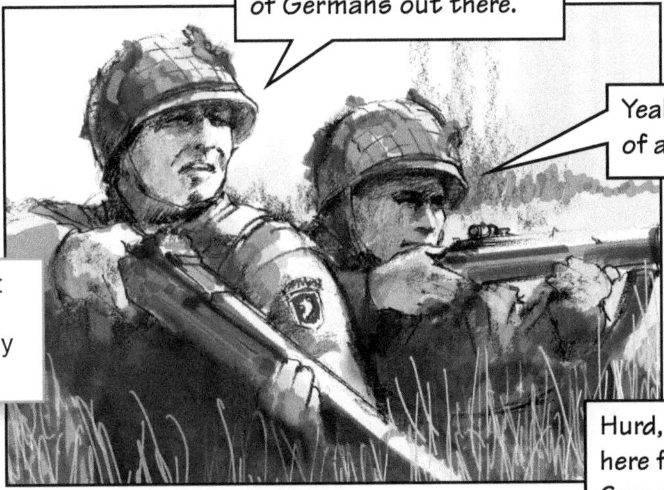
Hey, Gillis, what are we going to do? There's a lot of Germans out there.
Yeah, there's a hell of a lot of Germans.
Private Hurd decided to scout out the situation and paused to visit with Sgt. Gillis, a buddy from home.[10]

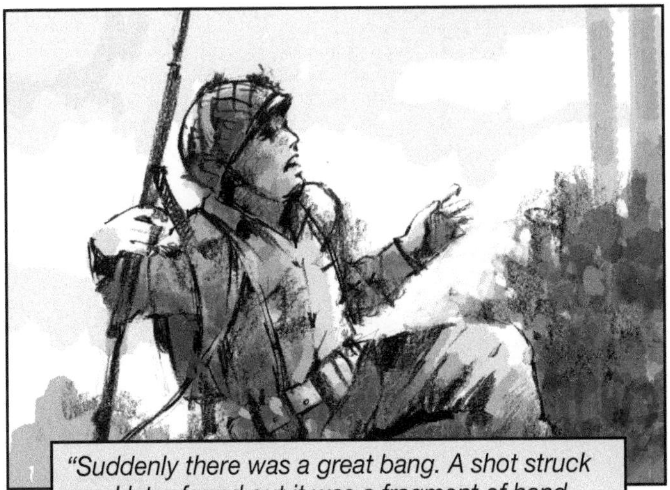
"Suddenly there was a great bang. A shot struck me. I later found out it was a fragment of hand grenade. It hit my chest with such force it knocked me off the hedgerow, completely stunned, with a pretty big size chest wound."[11]

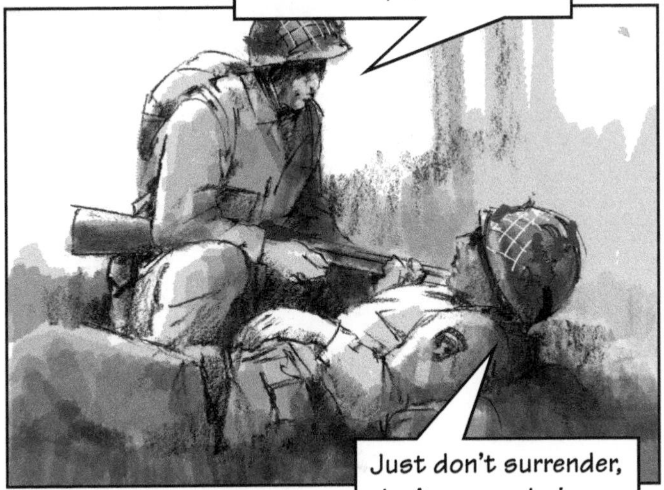
Hurd, I've got to leave you here for a minute. Father Sam will help you.
Just don't surrender, don't surrender!

JUNE 12, 1944

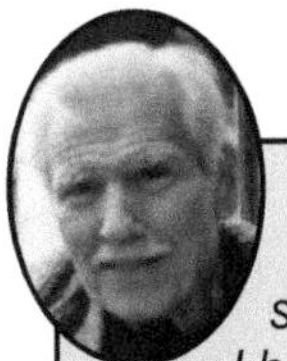

"A medic and the Father[12] were close by and came right to my support. They pulled me up and I had my arms around each of them. Louis Frey – he and I were together on campaigns – was coming along and he could see us and wished the camera man had been there, it was the classic picture of the wounded soldier."

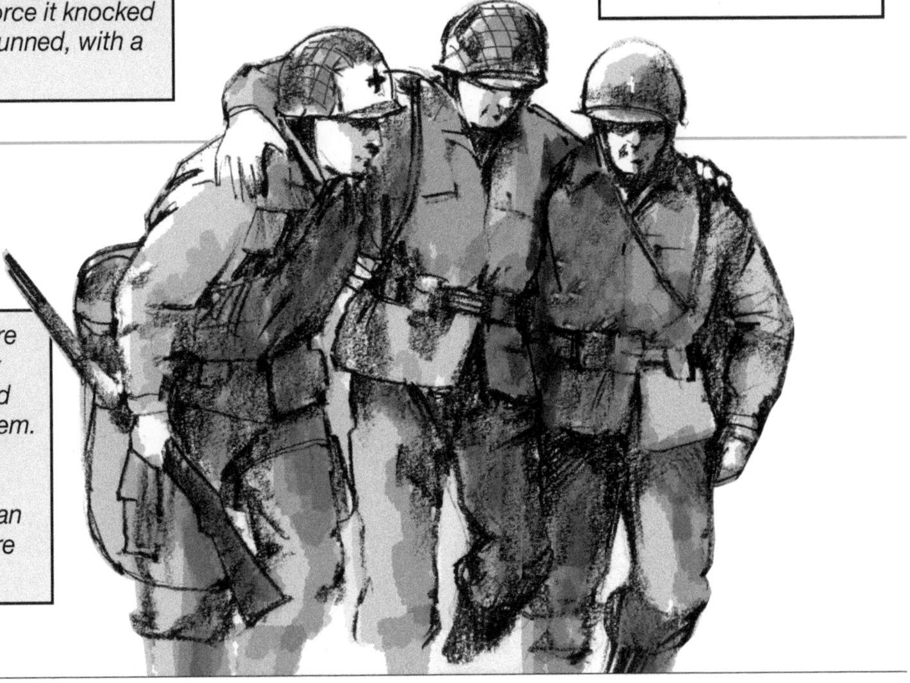

[10] As told to Mark Bando by Leo Gillis of F/501, a fellow Detroiter.

[11] As told to his daughter, 2004.

[12] Father Sampson was the beloved regimental chaplain of 501st Parachute Infantry Regiment and went on to serve in the Korean War.

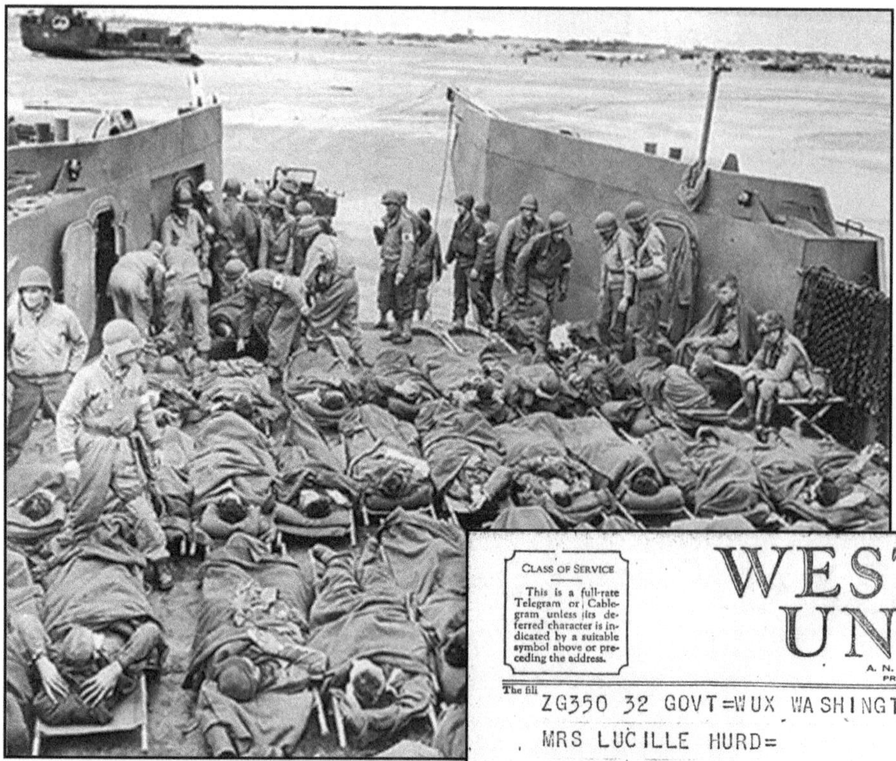

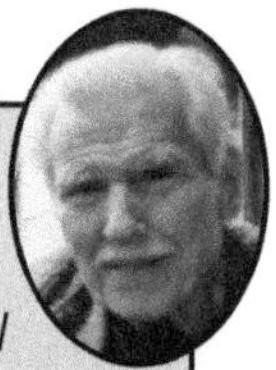

"Another memory I have is of being on this beach on the stretcher waiting for transport to the army hospital in England. Incoming GIs were coming in on landing craft. It was now about six days after D-Day and soldiers were still coming in. They looked at us wounded with quite a bit of attention. They were thinking 'this is real now.'"

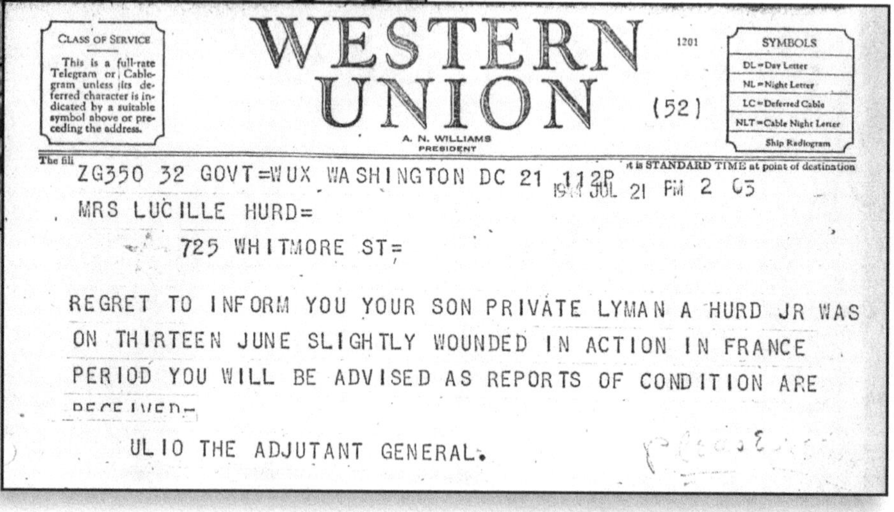

CLASS OF SERVICE
This is a full-rate Telegram or Cablegram unless its deferred character is indicated by a suitable symbol above or preceding the address.

WESTERN UNION

A. N. WILLIAMS
PRESIDENT

1201

SYMBOLS
DL=Day Letter
NL=Night Letter
LC=Deferred Cable
NLT=Cable Night Letter
Ship Radiogram

(52)

ZG350 32 GOVT=WUX WASHINGTON DC 21 112P 1944 JUL 21 PM 2 03

MRS LUCILLE HURD=

725 WHITMORE ST=

REGRET TO INFORM YOU YOUR SON PRIVATE LYMAN A HURD JR WAS ON THIRTEEN JUNE SLIGHTLY WOUNDED IN ACTION IN FRANCE PERIOD YOU WILL BE ADVISED AS REPORTS OF CONDITION ARE RECEIVED=

ULIO THE ADJUTANT GENERAL.

MID-JUNE 1944 - LT. SEFTON VISITS HURD IN THE HOSPITAL[13]

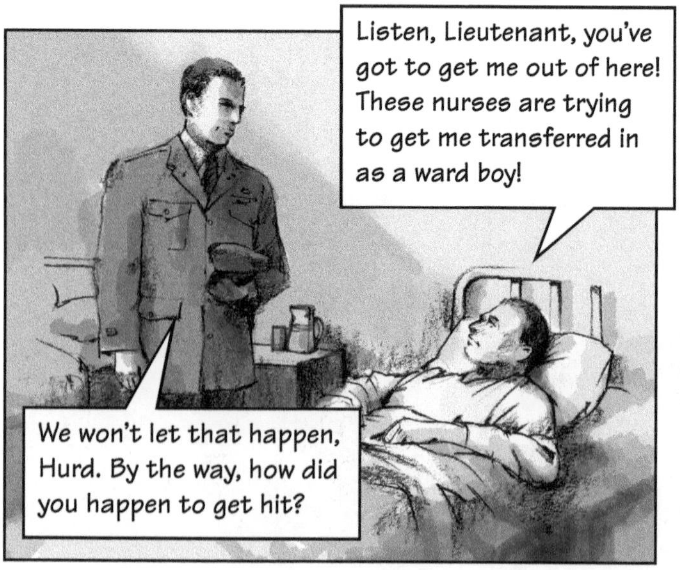

Listen, Lieutenant, you've got to get me out of here! These nurses are trying to get me transferred in as a ward boy!
We won't let that happen, Hurd. By the way, how did you happen to get hit?

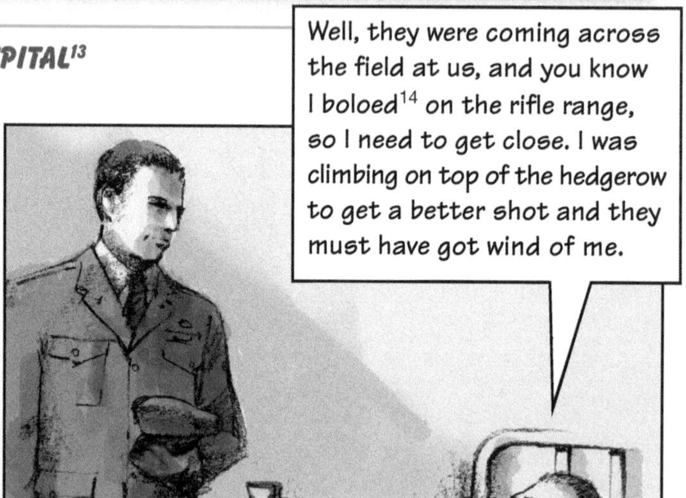

Well, they were coming across the field at us, and you know I boloed[14] on the rifle range, so I need to get close. I was climbing on top of the hedgerow to get a better shot and they must have got wind of me.
There's no way I'm surrendering this soldier for hospital duty!

[13] G. William Sefton, *It Was My War*, (Sunflower University Press 1994), p. 42-43. Also as told to Mark Bando.

[14] *Boloed* means to fail a test or exam.

Bonjour, Bonjour,

I'm greeting you from an army hospital. Don't worry thanks to all your prayers I am still in pretty good shape. No doubt you have read of our adventures in France. I wish I could forget the tragic experience all of us underwent. The French people did seem glad to see us. Entering Carentan, some old Frenchmen had dressed themselves in the uniforms of the last war. They sang "It's a Long Way to Tipperary" as we went through the streets, patting us on the back. One old Grandpa ran up to me and gave me a nice little bouquet of flowers. It wasn't long before they started to kiss us on the cheeks. That was TOO much. We left them hurriedly in favor of the Germans.

Love, Allen

HAVE YOU FILLED IN COMPLETE ADDRESS AT TOP?

REPLY BY
V ··· –MAIL

HAVE YOU FILLED IN COMPLETE ADDRESS AT TOP?

Members of the 501st waiting to take a landing ship back to England.

Bando, *Vanguard of the Crusade* (Heimdal 2012)

In the little more than a month since D-Day, the 101st had suffered severe losses: 868 men were killed in action. Thousands were wounded. And hundreds were missing in action and assumed to be POWs.

During July 1944, the 101st survivors regrouped at Newbury, England, and continued training for whatever mission would be next.

AUGUST 1944

Two jumps were scheduled in August to support General Patton's forces, but his ground troops advanced so quickly, the jumps weren't necessary. This is Corporal Harold Bice and Pfc Hurd (right) preparing to board a plane at an airfield in England, but, at the last minute, the jump was canceled.

SEPTEMBER 1944 - THE HOLLAND CAMPAIGN: *OPERATION MARKET GARDEN*[15]

World War II: 1944
Soviet Union
Finland
Germany
U.K.
France
Sept.
Jan.
Oct.
June
July
Mar.
May
Aug.
Jan.

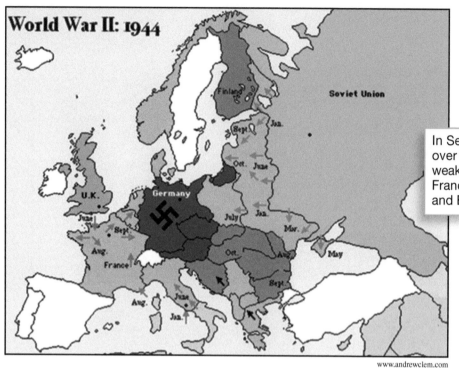

www.andrewclem.com

In September of 1944, Germany's grasp over Western Europe was beginning to weaken. The Allies had broken through into France and Belgium and liberated Paris and Brussels. Victory seemed close.

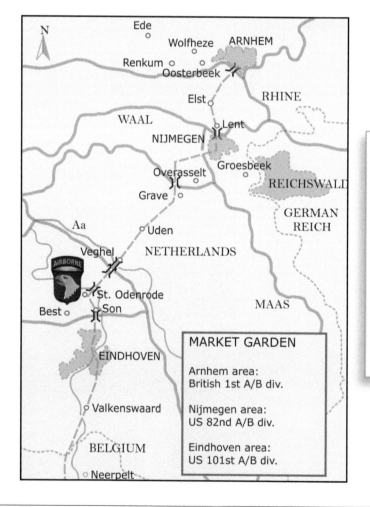

N
Ede
Wolfheze
ARNHEM
Renkum
Oosterbeek
Elst
RHINE
WAAL
Lent
NIJMEGEN
Groesbeek
Overasselt
REICHSWALD
Grave
GERMAN REICH
Aa
Uden
Veghel
NETHERLANDS
AIRBORNE
St. Odenrode
Best
Son
MAAS
EINDHOVEN
Valkenswaard
BELGIUM
Neerpelt
MARKET GARDEN
Arnhem area:
British 1st A/B div.
Nijmegen area:
US 82nd A/B div.
Eindhoven area:
US 101st A/B div.

Operation Market Garden[15] was an unsuccessful attempt to end the war more quickly by securing a passageway for British troops to cross Holland, the Rhine River, and enter the industrial heart of Germany in the Ruhr Valley.

It depended on the initial deployment of the Allied Airborne Army, a multinational force, which included the 101st Airborne, to capture and secure bridges across canals and rivers in Holland and hold open the one main highway for the British troops to follow.[16]

[15] *Market* refers to the initial airborne assault and *Garden* was the code name for the ground attack that followed.

[16] This road became known as Hell's Highway. Repeated German counterattacks cost the 101st 2,100 casualties over the nine days of the campaign.

On September 17, 1944, Operation Market Garden began with the largest airborne assault in history.

The 501st 2nd battalion was dropped into Holland as part of the overall effort to capture and secure bridges across the Willemsvaart canal and keep the highway open for British troops.

Unlike Normandy, they dropped in daylight and they landed in their intended drop zones. Surprise was complete and there was little resistance from German troops.

archives.gov/public domain

Krochka, Divisional Photographer

Men of the 2nd Battalion of the 501st Parachute Infantry Regiment assemble to enter Veghel.

Within hours, the 101st was largely successful in fulfilling their mission. Veghel was captured, along with the highway bridges between Eindhoven and Veghel. The 501st was responsible for securing four bridges over the river Aa near Veghel.

Nov. 1, 1944   [17]

Dear Family,

Sometimes war can be most enjoyable. I will never forget the great joy of the people of a certain town we liberated. Orange is the national color of the Dutch. So these people, dressed in orange, hung out their orange flags, paraded through the streets and sang their national anthem. At the end of the parade a few of the boys happened to be free; among them Frey and myself. The people grabbed us and carried us down to the streets with them. We danced in the streets with them and tried our best to sing their national anthem. They even lifted us up on their shoulders for a bit, nothing was too good for us. The whole town seemed to be in a frenzy of joy. I cashed in on the joy with a few <u>solid</u> kisses.

                                                                                    Allen

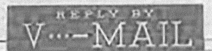

HAVE YOU FILLED IN COMPLETE ADDRESS AT TOP?   REPLY BY V····—MAIL   HAVE YOU FILLED IN COMPLETE ADDRESS AT TOP?

---

[17]Letter home reminiscing about the Operation Market Garden liberation of Veghel.

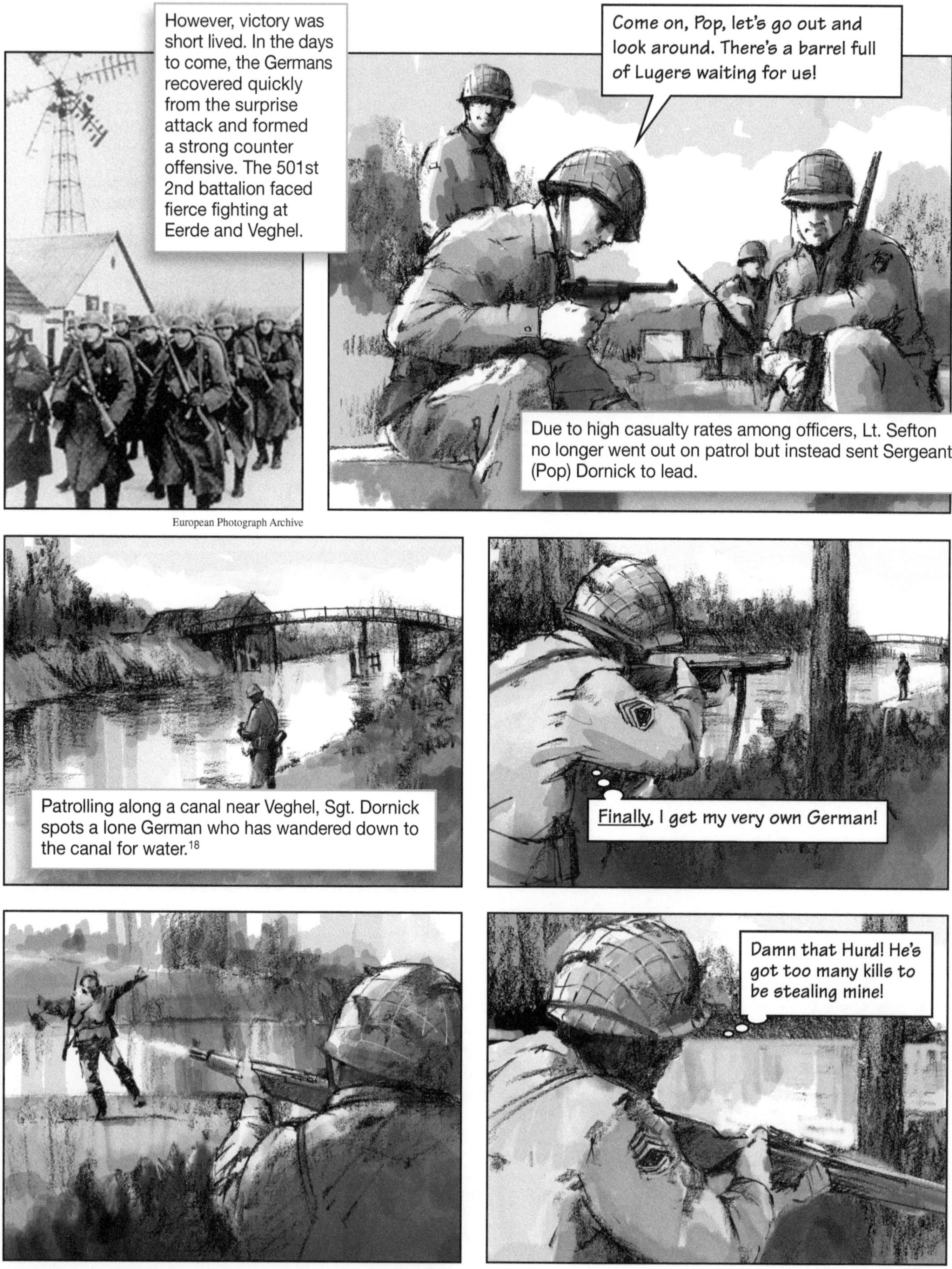
However, victory was short lived. In the days to come, the Germans recovered quickly from the surprise attack and formed a strong counter offensive. The 501st 2nd battalion faced fierce fighting at Eerde and Veghel.
Come on, Pop, let's go out and look around. There's a barrel full of Lugers waiting for us!
Due to high casualty rates among officers, Lt. Sefton no longer went out on patrol but instead sent Sergeant (Pop) Dornick to lead.
Patrolling along a canal near Veghel, Sgt. Dornick spots a lone German who has wandered down to the canal for water.[18]
Finally, I get my very own German!
Damn that Hurd! He's got too many kills to be stealing mine!

European Photograph Archive

[18] As told by Lt. G. William Sefton to Mark Bando.

501st on the Island.

Krochka Divisional Photographer

The 501st was spread thin and an influx of German troops resulted in fierce fighting in Veghel. In early October, the regiment, along with the 101st, moved north to the Island, a narrow strip of land between two rivers. Here they dug foxholes and fought the enemy close at hand across dikes and rivers.[19]

October 25, 1944

Dear Family:

I wish someone in Washington would keep Morgenthau[20] from sounding off. That joker's statement about breaking Germany into small farms is going to make Germany fight a whole lot harder. They're going to be so damn united that even their dogs will come out on the street and bite us.

"Jerry" clipped me with a bit of shrapnel a couple of weeks ago. Hit me on the right side and came out under my arm pit. It wasn't bad enough to take me from duty. And best of all I get an oak leaf cluster for my Purple Heart ribbon. If I get wounded 3 more times I get a free trip to Washington and a date with Mrs. Roosevelt.

Bye, Allen

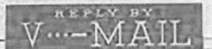

HAVE YOU FILLED IN COMPLETE ADDRESS AT TOP?

REPLY BY V····-MAIL

HAVE YOU FILLED IN COMPLETE ADDRESS AT TOP?

Finally, in November, the 501st was pulled back to join the 101st for rest and recuperation at Camp Mourmelon in the French town of Mourmelon le Grand.

Barracks at Camp Mourmelon, France.

Bando

"Nothing much did happen in Holland, so we were taken back to France just outside of Paris. One memory I have is, as I was walking along in the tiny town I could hear piano music – Chopin – coming from a residence. So I knocked on the door and an older woman answered. I told her I heard the music and enjoyed it; do you mind if I come in and listen to it? She was very happy to receive me and the next day or two I took a buddy and we enjoyed her company a great deal."[21]

---

[19] Colonel "Jumpy" Johnson, the inspirational leader of the 501st, was killed in action on a dike, October 8, 1944.

[20] Morgenthau was US Secretary of the Treasury, 1934-1945.

[21] As told to his daughter, Denise Hurd, in 2004.

DECEMBER 1944 - ON TO BASTOGNE

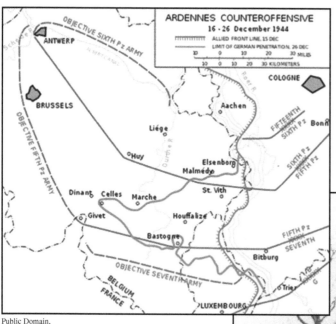

ARDENNES COUNTEROFFENSIVE
16 - 26 December 1944
ALLIED FRONT LINE, 15 DEC
LIMIT OF GERMAN PENETRATION, 26 DEC
MILES
KILOMETERS
OBJECTIVE SIXTH Pz ARMY
ANTWERP
BRUSSELS
COLOGNE
Aachen
Bonn
Liège
Huy
Elsenborn
Malmédy
St. Vith
Dinant
Celles
Marche
Givet
Houffalize
Bastogne
Bitburg
Trier
LUXEMBOURG
BELGIUM
FRANCE
OBJECTIVE FIFTH Pz ARMY
OBJECTIVE SEVENTH ARMY
FIFTEENTH
SIXTH Pz
FIFTH Pz
SEVENTH

Public Domain,
https://commons.wikimedia.org/w/index.php?curid=5384528

On December 14, 1944, the Germans launched their last major offensive in the Ardennes Forest, which came to be known as the Battle of the Bulge. The surprise attack was an attempt to push the Allies out of the Belgium port of Antwerp and force the armies on the Western Front to surrender. It was Germany's last chance to win the war.

The attack caught Allied troops unprepared and many infantry units were overrun. Barely beginning to recuperate after Operation Market Garden, the 101st was hurriedly called by General Eisenhower to defend important crossroads in the Belgium town of Bastogne.

German troops passing abandoned American equipment. Wikimedia/Wikipedia/common

December 1944 was the coldest winter in German history. The unit had to leave so quickly, they were short of food, ammunition, and winter clothing.

Members of 101st heading for Bastogne.

DECEMBER 16, 1944

"Dramatically, we were told to get into these trailers; we weren't told why, but we could tell it was urgent, a big rush, rush, rush. So that was our introduction to the Bastogne campaign. Here it wasn't a parachute drop, but a truck trailer. The drama built up because in Europe, it's crisscrossed with roads that lead to little villages. At these critical junctions, we would never stop. I can feel such emotion now because we didn't know what was happening, but we knew it had to be something important."[22]

[22]As told to his daughter, 2004.

DECEMBER 19, 1944

Bertogne
Noville
Foy
Bizory
Bastogne
Longchamps
Champs
Hemroulle
Savy
Marvie
Wardin
Senonchamps
Villeroux
Sibret
N-34 Highway
N-12 Highway
E-40 Highway
N-15 Highway

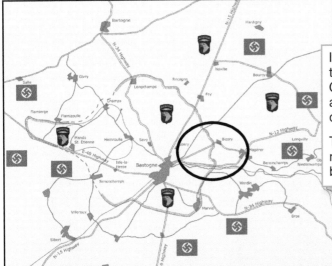

It was a 200-mile trip to Bastogne. The 501st, along with the rest of the 101st Airborne, were quickly encircled by German troops. The American soldiers were outnumbered approximately 5-1 and could not get supplies or air support due to the winter weather.

The 501st 2nd Battalion moved east from Bastogne into the most direct line of attack and met the Germans in defensive battle near the town of Bizory.

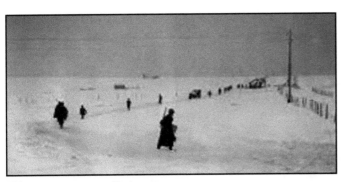

101st paratroopers near Bastogne.

THE ARDENNES OFFENSIVE
(BATTLE OF THE BULGE), 1944
BELGIUM
FRANCE
LUXEMBOURG

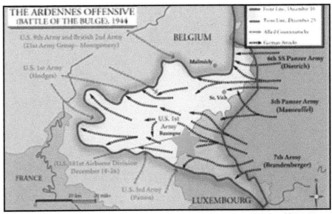

historynet.com

"So we got into a snow area and we were getting closer and closer; we still didn't know the particulars and were just sent marching along the road. I was by myself briefly and there was a dead American soldier. He had galoshes and it was heavy snow, so I pulled them off and put them on my feet. When I got back to some of the fellows, they looked at my galoshes and said, 'oh boy, we're going to start following you around because we want those galoshes.' I got a lot of attention (laughs)."

"We were then pressured by the German offensive. They pushed into our unit from different directions. Finally, as everybody knows what followed in the campaign, they did surround us but they didn't push in far enough. And we would rebuff them and they'd try another place to push in. If they'd kept on concentrating [on one spot], they might have broken through."

DECEMBER 22, 1944

Ignoring the urging of his men to take cover, Sgt. "Pop" Dornick was killed by German mortar fire while walking along a road in Bizory.

"WHY WASN'T IT ME?"

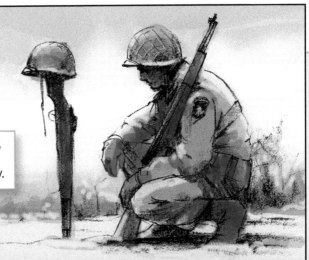

DECEMBER 24, 1944

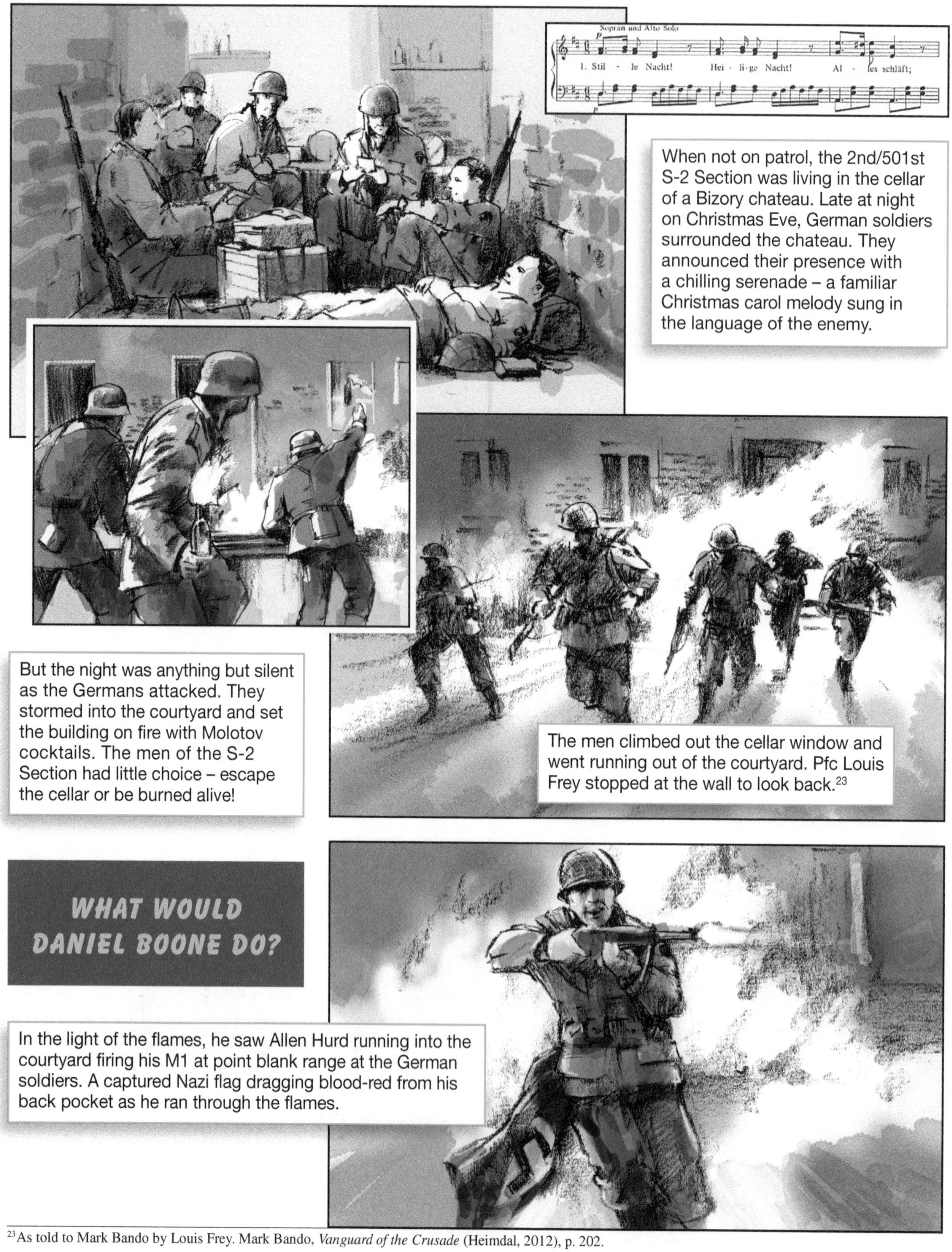
Sopran und Alto Solo
1. Stil - le Nacht! Hei - li-ge Nacht! Al - les schläft;
When not on patrol, the 2nd/501st S-2 Section was living in the cellar of a Bizory chateau. Late at night on Christmas Eve, German soldiers surrounded the chateau. They announced their presence with a chilling serenade – a familiar Christmas carol melody sung in the language of the enemy.
But the night was anything but silent as the Germans attacked. They stormed into the courtyard and set the building on fire with Molotov cocktails. The men of the S-2 Section had little choice – escape the cellar or be burned alive!
The men climbed out the cellar window and went running out of the courtyard. Pfc Louis Frey stopped at the wall to look back.[23]
WHAT WOULD DANIEL BOONE DO?
In the light of the flames, he saw Allen Hurd running into the courtyard firing his M1 at point blank range at the German soldiers. A captured Nazi flag dragging blood-red from his back pocket as he ran through the flames.

[23] As told to Mark Bando by Louis Frey. Mark Bando, *Vanguard of the Crusade* (Heimdal, 2012), p. 202.

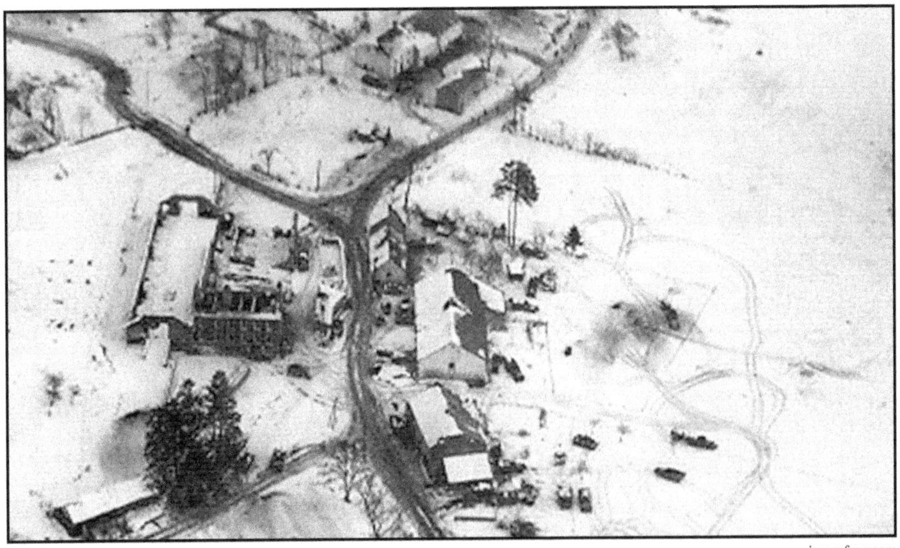

The Bizory chateau 501st HQ after the Germans retreated.

jamesfrey.com

JANUARY 3, 1945

The Second Battalion continued fighting deep in the Bois Jacques woods.

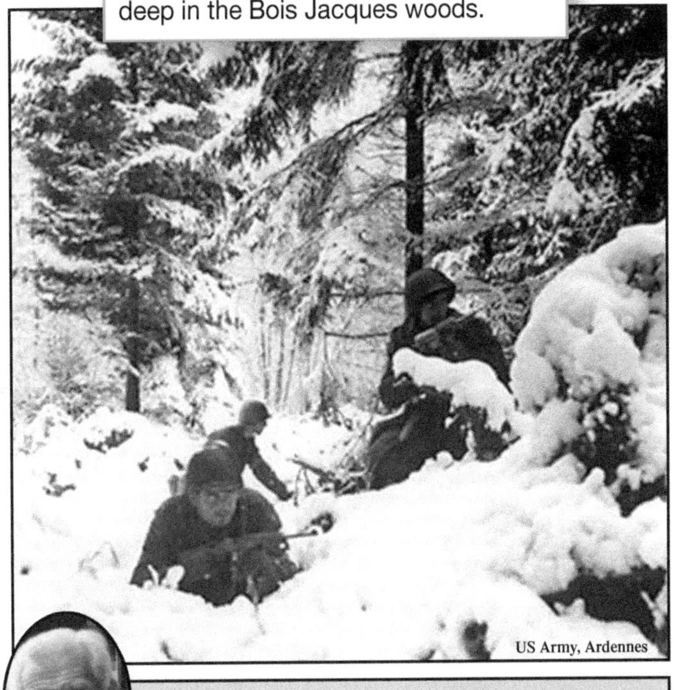

US Army, Ardennes

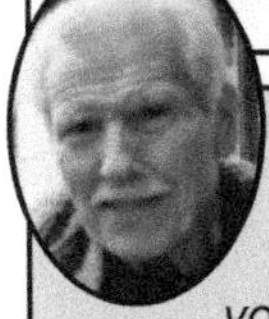

"At one juncture, there was enemy coming into this heavily wooded area. We were putting fire into that area and I heard the scream of a young man. A terrible scream. That scream just brought to me in focus how wrong [war is] – how much needs to be done."[24]

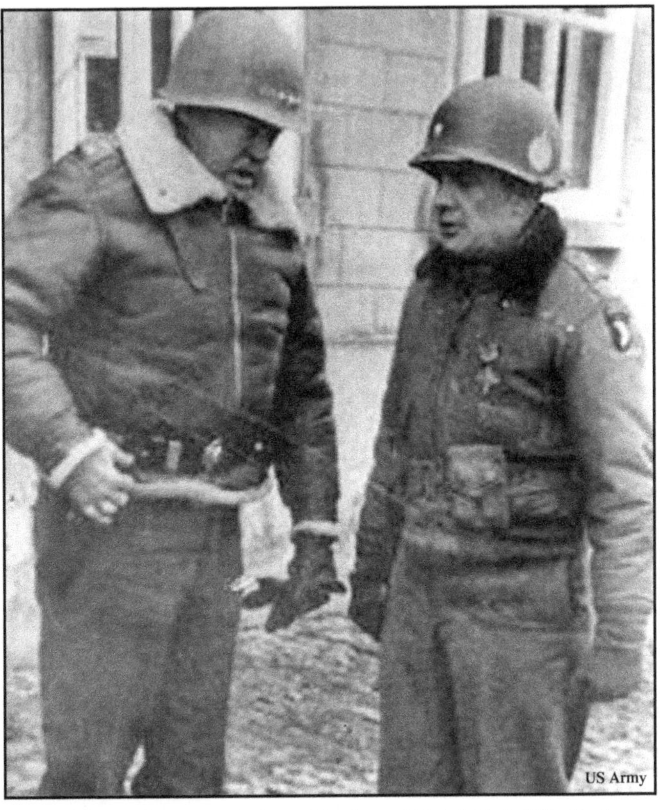

US Army

General George Patton and General Anthony "Nuts" McAuliffe, Bastogne.

"Finally, we were relieved by other units and General Patton. He [Hitler] didn't have enough fuels. He thought he could get it from the enemy, but he overstretched – it was his final play. But it's more dramatic to think of the aging general,[25] who, when asked to surrender, says, 'Nuts!' It caught the attention of the press and media, which played it up a great deal. We were probably a little bit more concerned ourselves (laughs)."

[24] As told to his daughter, 2004.

[25] General McAuliffe.

JANUARY 21, 1945

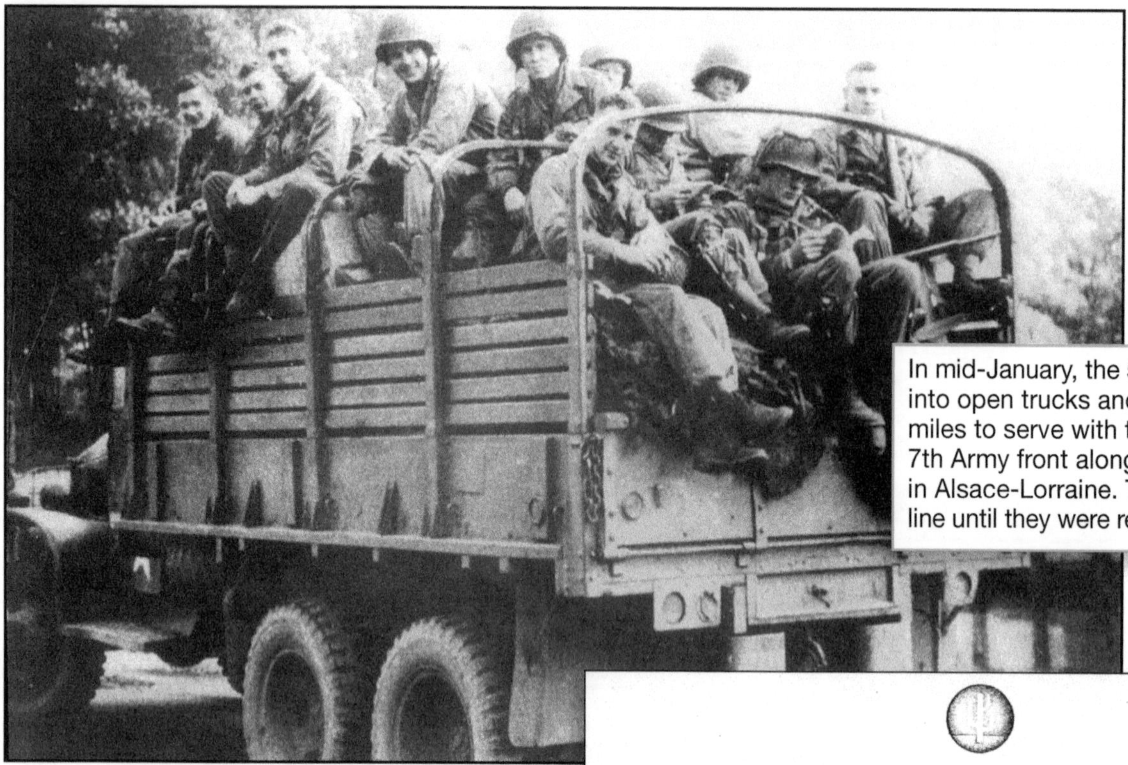

Members of the 101st leaving Bastogne for Alsace. Bando, Theaker

In mid-January, the 501st was loaded into open trucks and transported 200 miles to serve with the 101st on the 7th Army front along the Moder River in Alsace-Lorraine. The 101st held the line until they were relieved in February.

"I had gone to Bastogne with 40 men in the platoon and there were only 14 of us left… and those who were left were feeling pretty much that the war was a lousy business and we had been ill used. We were hardly cheering about going down and trying to pull chestnuts out of the fire in another area."

- Lt. Sefton, 2nd/501st[26]

27

103D INFANTRY DIVISION

OFFICE OF THE
COMMANDING GENERAL

APO 470, U. S. Army
20 February 1945

Mr. Lyman A. Hurd
725 Whitmore Road
Detroit 3, Mich.

Dear Mr. and Mrs. Hurd:

I received yesterday your request for information concerning your son, Pfc Lyman A. Hurd, Jr., of Headquarters Company, 2d Battalion, 501st Parachute Infantry. As you see, I am no longer with the 101st Airborne Division. However, I was able to learn from an officer in Lyman's unit that he is in good health and is doing full duty. I asked that he be requested to write to you at once.

Since the German offensive of December, mail delivery has been very uncertain. It is just now returning to normal. I hope that by this time you have heard from your son.

Sincerely,

A. C. McAuliffe

A. C. McAULIFFE
Major General, United States Army
Commanding

After weeks with no letters, desperate with worry, Mom takes matters into her own hands and writes to General McAuliffe!

[26] Lieutenant Sefton of 2nd/501st as told to Mark Bando, *Vanguard of the Crusade* (Heimdal, 2012), p. 233.
[27] Actual letter. McAuliffe was the Division Commander during the Bastogne Campaign.

February 20, 1945

Mother dear,

Listen to your son. The army, unlike the boy scouts, is a highly impersonal organization. If you don't hear from me for quite some time, don't get excited and start writing to generals, they have enough on their minds besides having to worry about every mother's son in the outfit. McAuliffe called personally causing me no end of embarrassment. You just stay away from Generals and confine your letters to just 1 poor, small Pfc.

Allen

HAVE YOU FILLED IN COMPLETE ADDRESS AT TOP? REPLY BY V---MAIL HAVE YOU FILLED IN COMPLETE ADDRESS AT TOP?

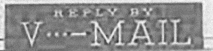

February 23, 1945

Dear Family,

Hope you haven't written to any generals lately. I can't stand having so much brass worrying about me. I don't see why a two star General should worry about me when my 1st Sgt. doesn't give a damn. Try and curb your worrying. Death now means very little. I've seen men die all around me. I lost my best friend in Bastogne. The damage is done. The blood has been spilled – all over the world. It's too late to worry and cry now. The important thing isn't if we come back. No, the all important issue is will the future generation of men have to leave like we did to fight and die.

Allen

HAVE YOU FILLED IN COMPLETE ADDRESS AT TOP? REPLY BY V---MAIL HAVE YOU FILLED IN COMPLETE ADDRESS AT TOP?

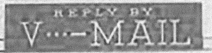

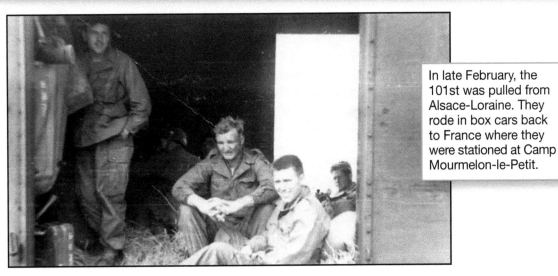

In late February, the 101st was pulled from Alsace-Loraine. They rode in box cars back to France where they were stationed at Camp Mourmelon-le-Petit.

Allen Hurd, second from right, and Pfc. Louis Frey, center.

Dear Family,

We came back into France to base camp on freight cars. We rode first class. First class in France means 40x8 box cars with hay on the floors. Plenty of fresh air and good opportunity to give the countryside a once over when you ride these broken down relics.

We passed bridge after bridge demolished by our air force. Railroad cars, tank cars litter the side of the track. I know now what it means when they say "our air force bombed the railroad marshalling yards at such-and-such a place." Believe me, they do a DEVASTATING job of it.

In the fields of France you can read the history of the war. Foxholes, thousands of them, forests split and torn by artillery shells, burned out vehicles of all descriptions, bomb craters, ration cans, ammunition boxes, all this and so much more shout their gruesome history at you as you pass by.

Allen

HAVE YOU FILLED IN COMPLETE ADDRESS AT TOP?

REPLY BY V---MAIL

HAVE YOU FILLED IN COMPLETE ADDRESS AT TOP?

The trains carried the soldiers to a tent city at Mourmelon-le-Petit, very near the camp at Mourmelon-le-Grand, where they had been stationed in December. Although some soldiers got furloughs and passes to see the sights of Paris, most of the 101st remained on alert for the final jump of the war, possibly into Berlin.

Allen Hurd returning from chow, Mourmelon-le-Petit.

MARCH 1945 - VICTORY & HOMECOMING

On March 15, the entire 101st Airborne Division was assembled and presented with a Distinguished Unit Citation by General Eisenhower for extraordinary heroism in action in the defense of Bastogne. It was the first time in history the award was presented to an entire division.

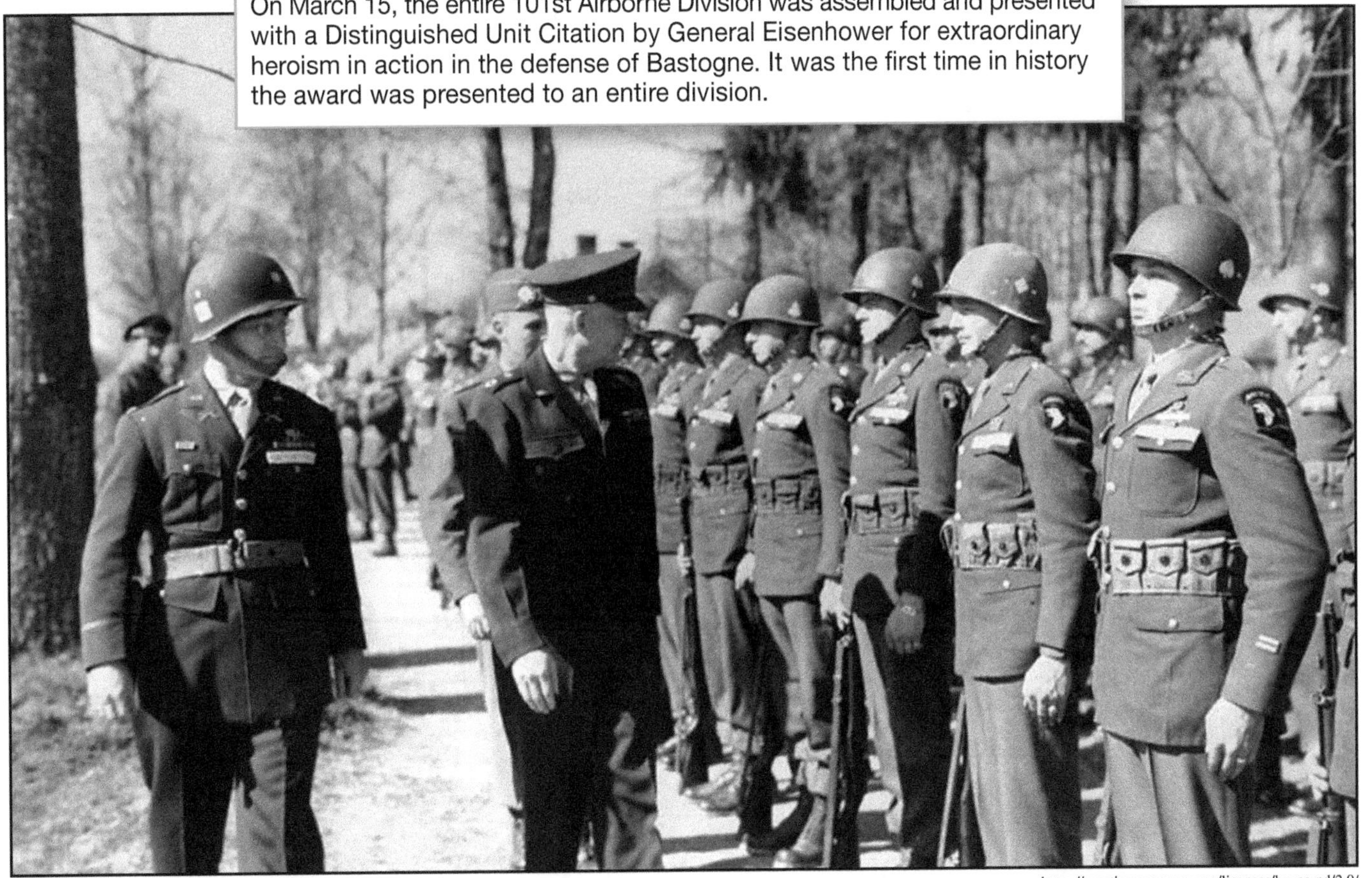

General Eisenhower inspects the troops at Mourmelon-le-Petit.

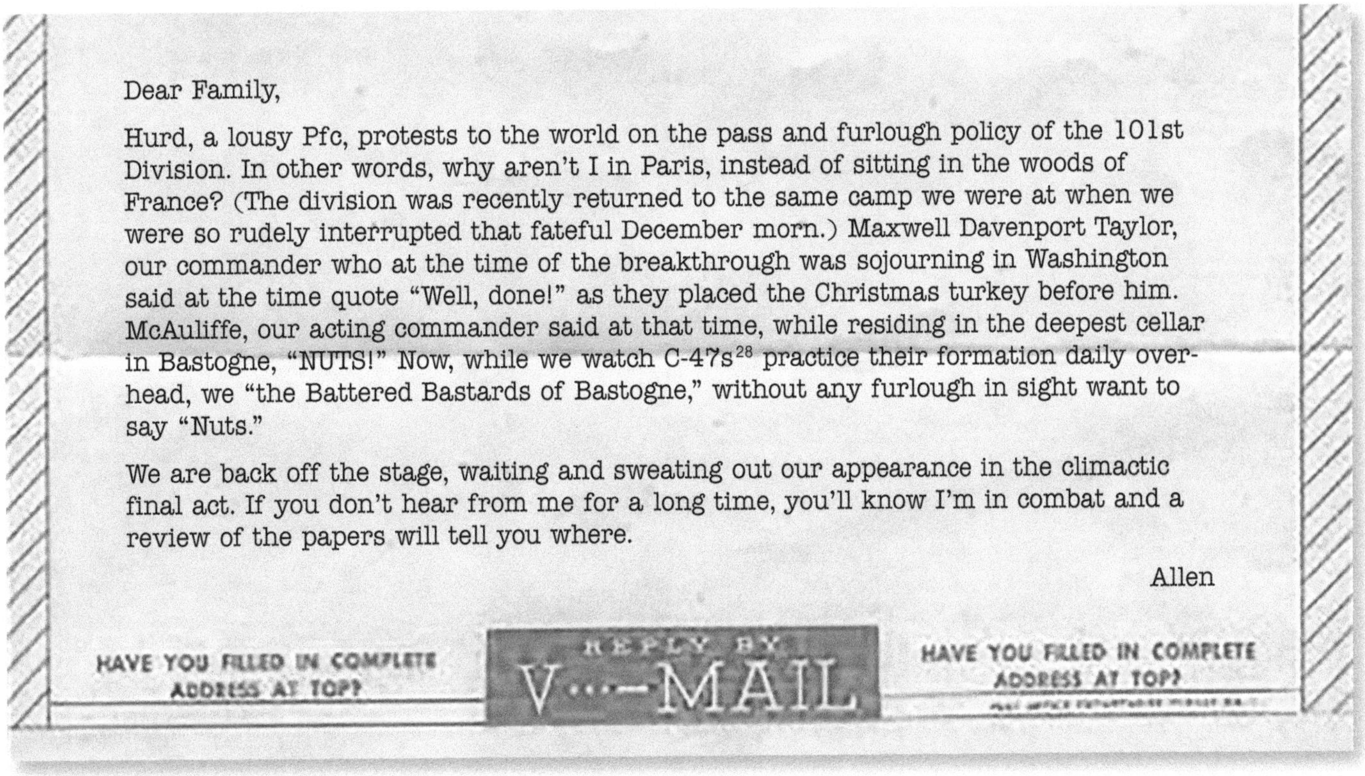

Dear Family,

Hurd, a lousy Pfc, protests to the world on the pass and furlough policy of the 101st Division. In other words, why aren't I in Paris, instead of sitting in the woods of France? (The division was recently returned to the same camp we were at when we were so rudely interrupted that fateful December morn.) Maxwell Davenport Taylor, our commander who at the time of the breakthrough was sojourning in Washington said at the time quote "Well, done!" as they placed the Christmas turkey before him. McAuliffe, our acting commander said at that time, while residing in the deepest cellar in Bastogne, "NUTS!" Now, while we watch C-47s[28] practice their formation daily overhead, we "the Battered Bastards of Bastogne," without any furlough in sight want to say "Nuts."

We are back off the stage, waiting and sweating out our appearance in the climactic final act. If you don't hear from me for a long time, you'll know I'm in combat and a review of the papers will tell you where.

Allen

HAVE YOU FILLED IN COMPLETE ADDRESS AT TOP?

REPLY BY V---MAIL

HAVE YOU FILLED IN COMPLETE ADDRESS AT TOP?

[28]C-47s were the planes used to carry paratroopers to their drop zones.

FINALLY, FURLOUGH!

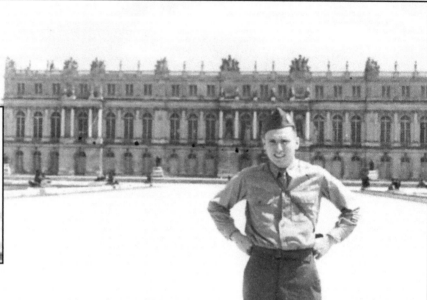

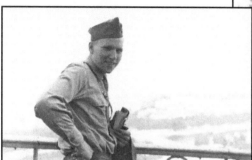

Taking in the view from the Eiffel Tower.

At the Palace of Versailles.

APRIL 1945

81
LUX
GERMANY, 1944

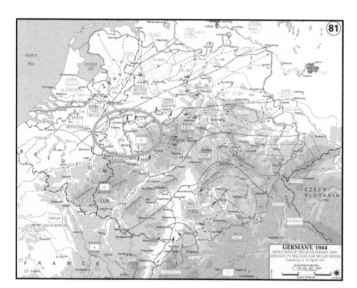

In early April, the 101st moved to the west edge of the Ruhr pocket near Dusseldorf, where they conducted combat patrols. After the Germans began to surrender, 101st joined the race to Berchtesgaden. The 501st Regiment was held back in France in case the Nazis tried to massacre civilians and POWs as they retreated.

These massacres never occurred, and the 501st eventually rejoined the 101st at the abandoned Nazi headquarters at Berchtesgaden.[29]

U.S. National Archives

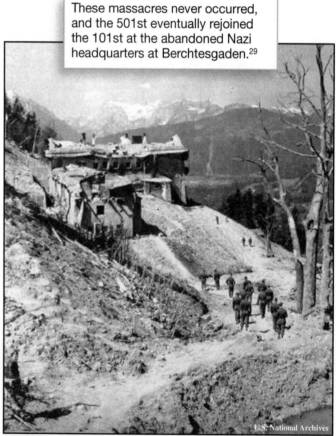

Hitler's home, The Berghof, destroyed by bombing raids before the 101st arrived.

[29] The location of Hitler's headquarters in southeast Germany near the Austrian border. Hitler and other Nazi leaders had luxury homes in the Berchtesgaden area, known for its beautiful mountain scenery.

This was known as the Golden Age for the division as they celebrated victory with Nazi luxuries, including horses liberated from the SS horse farm.

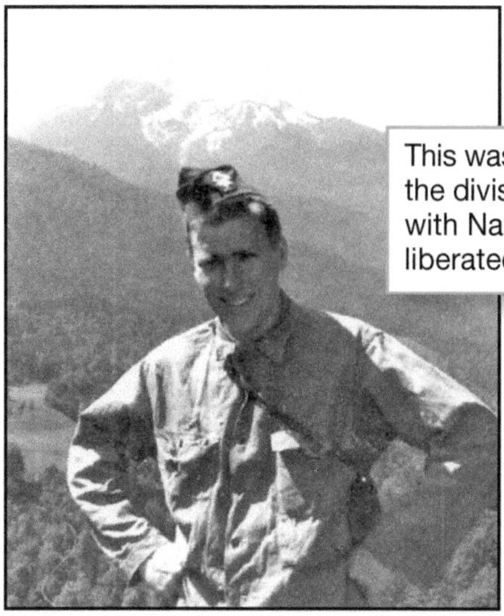

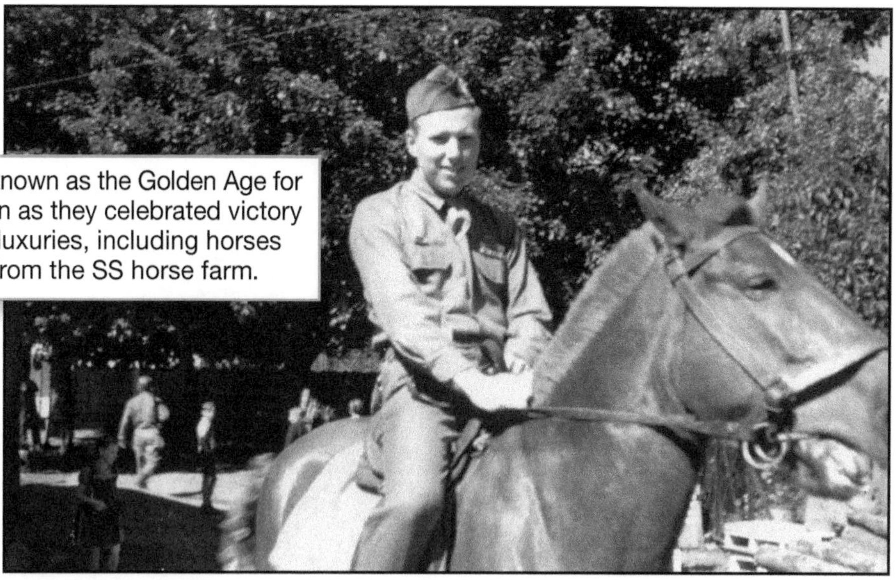

Allen Hurd enjoying the moment in Berchtesgaden.

MAY 8, 1945

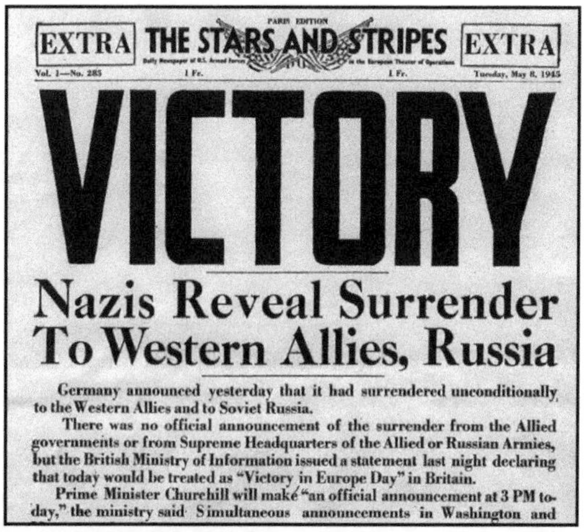

PARIS EDITION

EXTRA **THE STARS AND STRIPES** EXTRA

Daily Newspaper of U.S. Armed Forces in the European Theater of Operations

Vol. 1—No. 285 | 1 Fr. | 1 Fr. | Tuesday, May 8, 1945

VICTORY

Nazis Reveal Surrender To Western Allies, Russia

Germany announced yesterday that it had surrendered unconditionally to the Western Allies and to Soviet Russia.

There was no official announcement of the surrender from the Allied governments or from Supreme Headquarters of the Allied or Russian Armies, but the British Ministry of Information issued a statement last night declaring that today would be treated as "Victory in Europe Day" in Britain.

Prime Minister Churchill will make "an official announcement at 3 PM today," the ministry said. Simultaneous announcements in Washington and

The Germans officially surrendered on May 8, 1945. Entire units of German soldiers dropped their weapons and were allowed to walk home.

On June 26, 1945, the 501st was inactivated. Some soldiers went home. Others were sent to different units. Pfc L. Allen Hurd went to the 327th Glider Infantry.

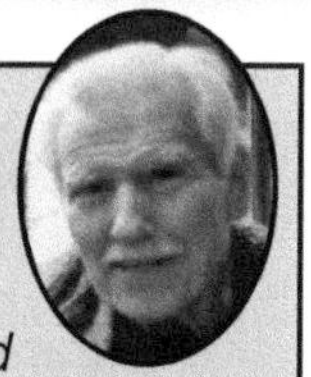

"We were stationed in Austria when news was released about the surrender and that was the end of it all. They asked where we wanted to go and based on that we were placed on different boats. I think we were also given 100 dollars. We had our choice of different boats. I decided I wanted to go to Washington, D.C. I wanted to see President Truman because I had read a book about war and peace and I felt I could help prevent this (laughs)."[30]

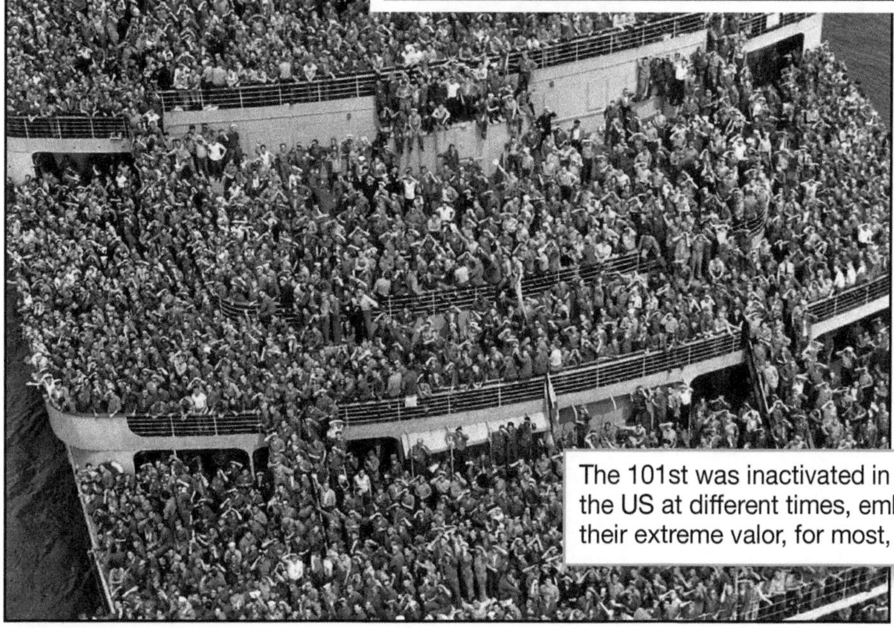

The 101st was inactivated in November 1945. The PIRs returned to the US at different times, embedded in different units. So, despite their extreme valor, for most, there was no triumphant victory parade.

New York Historical Society

Crowded ship bringing American troops back to New York harbor after V-Day, 1945.

[30]As told to his daughter, 2004.

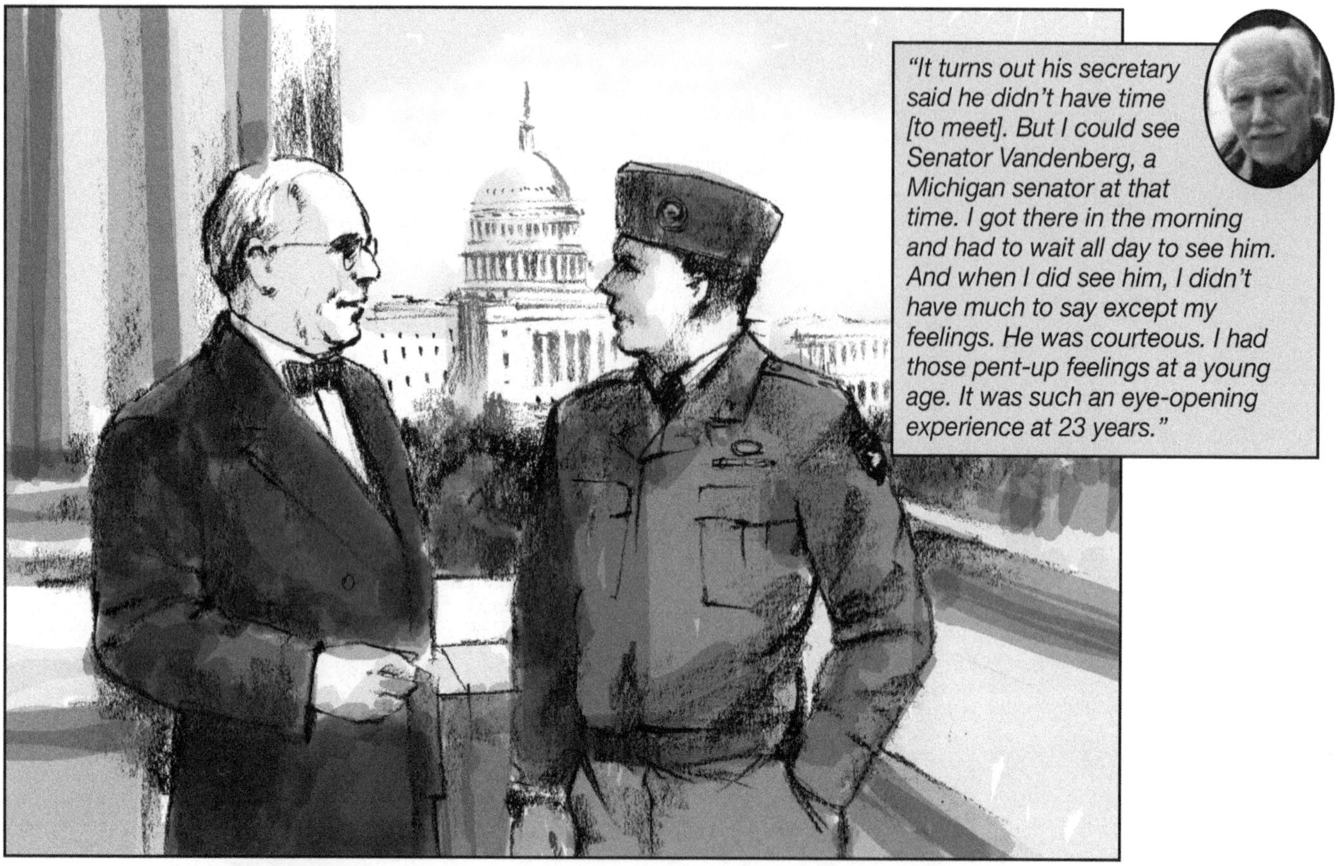
"It turns out his secretary said he didn't have time [to meet]. But I could see Senator Vandenberg, a Michigan senator at that time. I got there in the morning and had to wait all day to see him. And when I did see him, I didn't have much to say except my feelings. He was courteous. I had those pent-up feelings at a young age. It was such an eye-opening experience at 23 years."

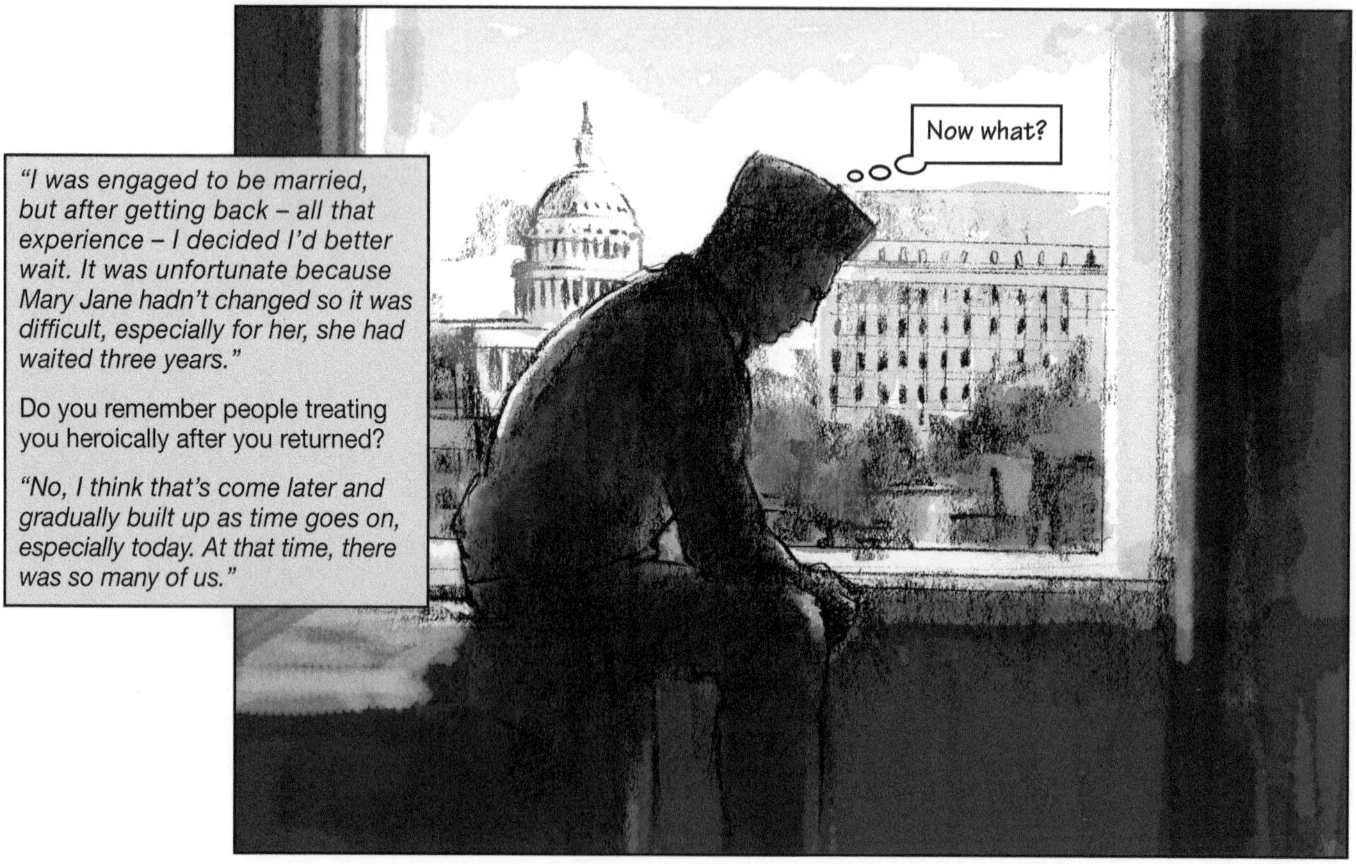
"I was engaged to be married, but after getting back – all that experience – I decided I'd better wait. It was unfortunate because Mary Jane hadn't changed so it was difficult, especially for her, she had waited three years."
Do you remember people treating you heroically after you returned?
"No, I think that's come later and gradually built up as time goes on, especially today. At that time, there was so many of us."
Now what?

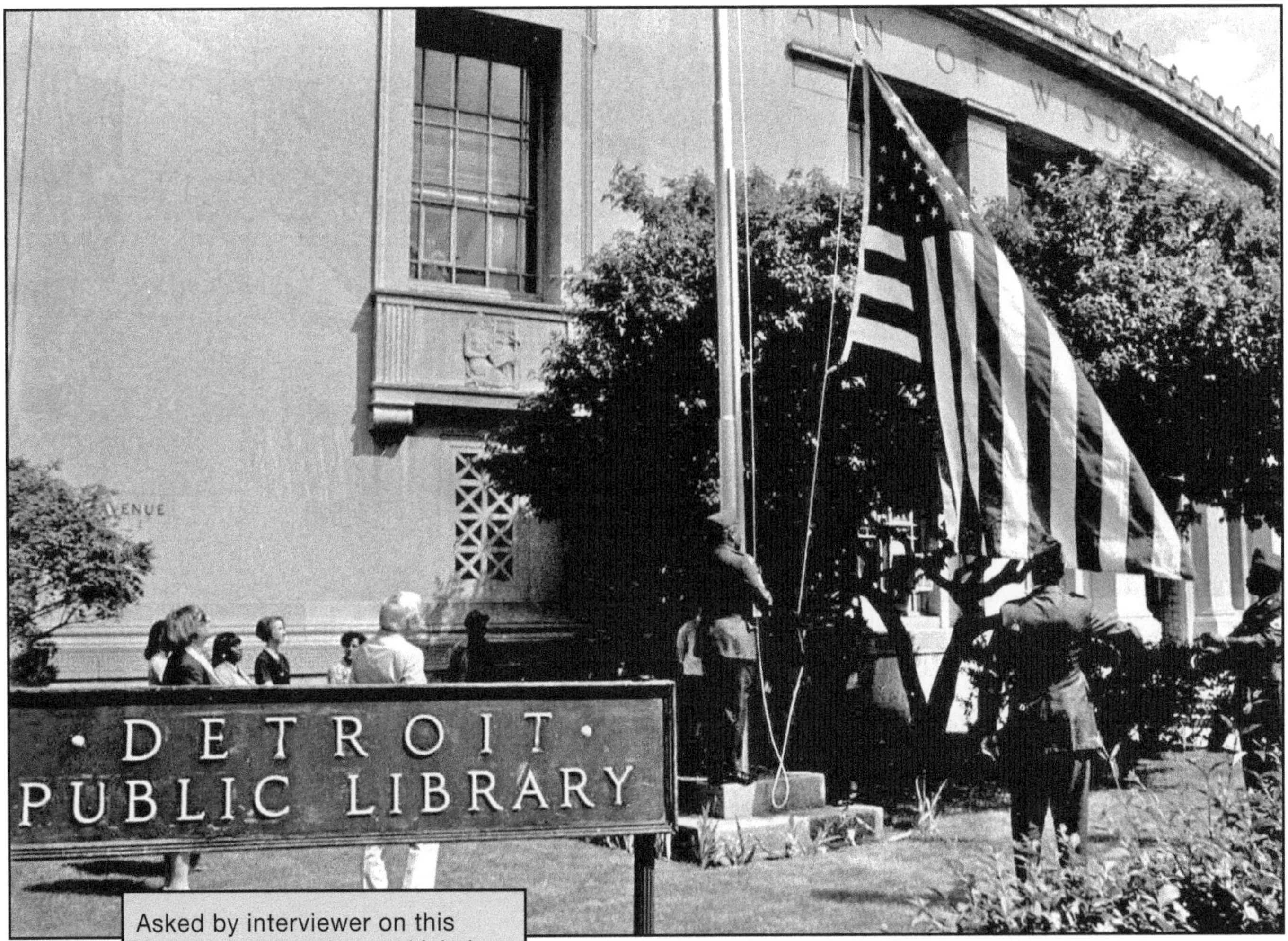
· DETROIT ·
PUBLIC LIBRARY

Lyman Allen Hurd Jr. (center) donates a flag to the Detroit Library in honor of those who died at Normandy.

Asked by interviewer on this occasion, "What do you think the young soldiers who died on the beach at Normandy would say to you today if they could talk?"

"I think what comes to mind is their bravery. I'm locked in on those who lost their lives and trying to think about how we can make sure their lives count for something and that this tragedy will not happen again." [31]

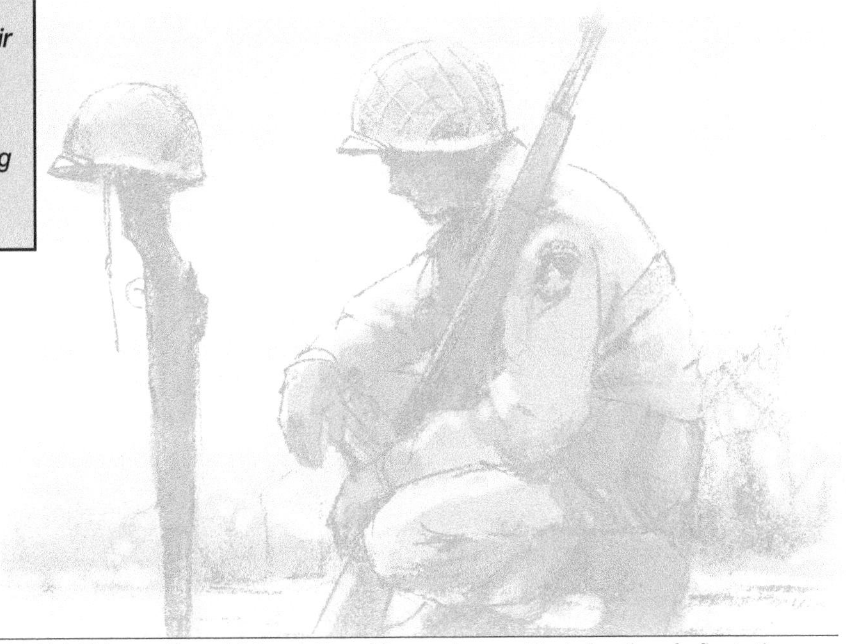

[31] From June 6, 1994 program called Face-to-Face interview with Rich Fisher on Channel 2 Detroit News. The occasion was Allen's donation of a flag to the Detroit Library in honor of those who died at Normandy.

AUTHOR DENISE HURD

Denise is a retired technical writer who for many years developed training videos and manuals for technicians in paper mills, power plants, and manufacturing. Compelled by an unexpected visit from a stranger, she applies her storytelling talents to this true story of her father to honor his memory and to share with those who may be touched and changed by his experiences. To learn more about this story and the author, visit https://hollowchest.com.

HISTORIAN MARK BANDO

Mark Bando was a patrol officer on the Detroit Police force for 25 years. He has written six books documenting the WW II experiences of the 101st including *Vanguard of the Crusade* and *The 101st Airborne Division in World War II*, along with two other WW II titles. He was made an honorary member of several current 101st regiments and has been embedded (2008, 2010) with the 101st in Afghanistan. Mark conducts WW II battlefield tours and has had the privilege of visiting sites with veterans and their children. He is a frequent lecturer and will commemorate the 75th anniversary of D-Day with a parachute jump from a C-47 into the original D-Day Drop Zone C near St. Marie du Mont, France. To learn more about Mark's books, visit his Trigger Time website at www.101airborneww2.com.

ARTIST KIM FUJIWARA

Kim Frank Fujiwara is an award-winning artist specializing in fine art, commissioned art and portraits. After graduating from Center for Creative Studies in 1979, he worked at Detroit studios as an illustrator and in 1992 he started his own studio, Fujiwara Art, Inc. Since 2012, he has concentrated on two fine art series, "The American West" and "La Belle Femme." In 2018, Kim was awarded First Place in MI Great Artist Competition. Many portraits may be seen at the Oakland Hills Country Club and Ford World Headquarters. He continues his lifetime commitment and passion at his studio in Rochester Hills, Michigan. To learn more about Kim's art, visit www.kfgallery.com.

DESIGNERS C.O. & COMPANY

Long-time friends Candy Orow and Al Akers save the neck of a self-publishing newbie by applying their talents to ensuring this layout lives up to Kim's art. In addition, Candy has helped guide our web marketing efforts to keep those Likes and Clicks coming. As partners at C.O. & Company in Farmington Hills, Michigan, Candy and Al love helping clients achieve their marketing goals. They've had the privilege of supporting companies like Volkswagen, Audi, Solvay Engineering, and Domino's Pizza. And their design skills benefit nonprofits such as The Daughters of Charity Health System, Guest House, and Seasons Hospice. To learn more about C.O. & Company, visit them at www.coandcompany.com.

Lightning Source UK Ltd.
Milton Keynes UK
UKHW050301210622
404696UK00005BA/45